Contemporary Terrorism

Contemporary Terrorism

Edited by William Gutteridge

for The Institute for the Study of Conflict

Facts On File Publications
New York, New York ● Oxford, England

First Published in the United States by
Facts On File, Inc.
460 Park Avenue South
New York, NY 10016

Library of Congress Cataloging-in-Publication Data
Main entry under title:

Contemporary terrorism.

    Includes index.
    1. Terrorism—Addresses, essays, lectures.
2. Terrorism—Europe—Addresses, essays, lectures.
I. Gutteridge, William Frank, 1919– . II. Institute
for the Study of Conflict.
HV6431.N48   1986   364.1'3   85–21505
ISBN 0-8160-1468-X (hc)
ISBN 0-8160-1787-5 (pb)

Printed in the United States of America

10 9 8 7 6 5 4 3 2

Contents

Contributors

Clive C. Aston is the Director of the Political Risk Division of Citicorp Insurance Brokers Ltd. He received his doctorate from the University of London and he has written widely on political hostage-taking and terrorism and is the author of several papers for the United Nations.

Frank Brenchley is Chairman of the Council of the Institute for the Study of Conflict. A former diplomat who was Ambassador to Norway 1968–72 and to Poland 1972–74, he was Head of the Defence and Oversea Secretariat in the Cabinet Office from 1975 to 1976.

Hans Josef Horchem is a Doctor of Law and a graduate of the Universities of Mainz and Cologne. He has made a continuing study of political extremism in the Federal Republic of Germany and is a well-known analyst of international terrorism.

Dr Peter Janke is Head of Research at Control Risks Information Division, London. He has published *Guerrilla and Terrorist Organisations: A World Directory and Bibliography* (1983), and lectures at the Royal College of Defence Studies, London.

Edward Moxon-Browne is a Senior Lecturer in Political Science at the Queen's University of Belfast. He is the author of *Nation, Class and Creed in Northern Ireland* (1983) and a contributor to *Terrorism: A Challenge to the State*, edited by J. Lodge (1981).

Dr Vittorfranco S. Pisano, formerly a Senior Legal Specialist in the European Law Division of the Library of Congress, is a consultant in international security affairs. He is the author of *Terrorism and Security: The Italian Experience* (1984) and *Euroterrorism and NATO* (1985.)

Paul Wilkinson is Professor of International Relations at the University of Aberdeen. His books include *Political Terrorism* (1974) and *Terrorism and the Liberal State* (1977).

Introduction

William Gutteridge

In open societies, such as the United States, Britain and the other Western European countries, arms are relatively readily accessible and movement is more or less free; these factors facilitate the organisation of political violence or terrorism. The Communist countries, and some of the Third World, have so far been largely immune partly because rigorous repression of dissent there anticipates trouble and also because censorship and tight control of the media prevent publicity. Since the bomb explosion at Plovdiv railway station in August 1984, Bulgaria has experienced a series of terrorist bombings which have, surprisingly in a Communist country, been officially admitted. But, while counterterrorist collaboration between Western countries has been developing on a regular basis, East–West co-operation on this issue is still rare.

A major obstacle in the way of a global strategy to stem terrorist violence is summed up in the now familiar saying 'One man's terrorist is another man's freedom fighter'. Movements for national liberation attract sympathy from a variety of sources (some admittedly self-interested, some simply humanitarian and idealistic), even though they usually seem to find it necessary to resort to terrorist tactics at some stage in their campaigns. In this context ideological differences obscure the moral and security issues and tend to prevent the formation of a united front against the perpetrators of terrorist atrocities. The new wave of political violence in the Middle East and South Asia in the mid-1980s, in which religious sectarianism is a potent factor, has added other dangerous dimensions to the problem, and at the same time focussed attention sharply on the real danger to civilisation and international order which epidemic terrorism could pose.

Since its foundation in June 1970, the Institute for the Study of Conflict has been engaged in the study of the causes and manifestations of political instability world-wide. Under its Director, Michael Goodwin, it has maintained a special watch on international terrorism and on movements based on small minorities attempting either to create anarchy by the destruction of democratic institutions, or to impose their will on an established majority. While terrorist activity overall has greatly increased both in scale and sophistication over the last two decades, some individual movements have declined and even disintegrated, while others have emerged from the shadows.

The purpose of this volume is to bring together a number of the more significant studies of terrorist activity published by the Institute in recent years. Discussion of the principles involved is of obvious importance in coping with and reacting to fresh incidents as they occur, while the series of case studies not only assists understanding but provides a basis for comparison. The terrorists of the late 1970s were by no means less sophisticated or psychologically tough than those now at work. The fanatical determination of the Baader-Meinhof group in West Germany, though different in motivation, can be compared to the suicidal martyrdom of Shi'ite bombers in Lebanon today.

In the first part of the book Paul Wilkinson discusses the problems terrorism poses for democratic governments and contributes an authoritative analysis of its international dimensions. Clive C. Aston has specialised in the study of political hostage-taking, incidences of which still frequently occur. Frank Brenchley writes on the question of diplomatic immunity, which was an important aspect of Libyan activities at their embassy in St. James's Square, London.

In Part Two Edward Moxon-Browne, Peter Janke, Vittorfranco S. Pisano and Hans Josef Horchem provide case histories relating to major countries in Western Europe. France has been the stage for a remarkably high level of international terrorism in recent years, with violent activities by a wide range of foreign groups against exiles from their own communities or seeking publicity. Spain, Italy and West Germany have all suffered from indigenous terrorism, with a variety of objectives including separatism or secession.

This collection of studies concentrating on terrorist manifestations in Western Europe should help to meet the need for greater knowledge and understanding at a critical time when Western governments are having to confront unpredictable and dangerous threats to security.

Part One

Democracy and the Terrorist Threat

Terrorism versus Liberal Democracy: The Problems of Response

Paul Wilkinson

Major conflict has been avoided since the Second World War but small wars have persisted and political violence has grown in non-totalitarian States. Sometimes these have been manipulated or even stimulated by outside interests—often major powers. But rebellion against the State can take many forms and arise from many causes, which should be distinguished if the response is to reinforce just rule rather than simply to crush revolution.

Four major categories of conflict spring to mind immediately: struggles following withdrawal from colonies, as in Portuguese Africa (though in many cases political negotiation has sufficed); separatist or autonomous movements arising from ethnic, religious or linguistic differences, which continue to fight for minority rights in all five continents; ideological struggles, usually waged by small groups, to subvert a society from within; and exiled groups who work to promote revolution at home in authoritarian régimes. Political violence rarely falls neatly into one category; it is more likely to involve several elements, but for political response to be effective these elements must be recognised. Terrorism as a tactic may be employed in any of these conflicts, and this paper considers the problems of response which confront a liberal democracy, with some suggested counter-measures.

Nature of terrorist challenge

Political terrorism may be briefly defined as a special form of clandestine, undeclared and unconventional warfare waged without any humanitarian restraints or rules. It is well known that both governments and revolutionary groups employ terror, but this study is concerned primarily with the terrorism of revolutionary movements directed against governments and societies of liberal democracies, meaning those States which enjoy the benefits of constitutionalist government, democratically elected and sovereign legislatures, established rights of peaceful political opposition and dissent, and effective protection of civil liberties.

I include among others in this category the member States of the EEC, the USA, Canada, Sweden, Norway, Austria, Switzerland, Turkey, Israel, Japan, Australia and New Zealand.

Terrorism has characteristics which distinguish it from other forms of violence. It is indiscriminate in its effects in that nobody is sacrosanct, and this helps to create an atmosphere of fear and helplessness. Terrorists

3

frequently claim to "select" the victims of their macabre lust for punishment and revenge: no one is innocent, all are potentially guilty, if only by alleged association with "class enemies", "imperialists" and "enemies of the revolution".

Terrorists do not recognise any rules of conventions of war for combatants, non-combatants or the treatment of prisoners. They use particularly ruthless weapons and methods to attack civilians, including foreigners who are not remotely involved. Their typical weapons are bombings, assassinations, massacres, and bargaining with lives of hostages. Political terrorism is therefore unpredictable and arbitrary, and can be seen as an attempt to exercise a peculiar kind of tyranny over its victims.

It is quite wrong to assume that all terrorists are psychopaths. Many are motivated by passionate idealism. The pure idealism of the kind portrayed by Camus in the character of Kaliaev, or by Conrad in the portrait of Victor Halden in *Under Western Eyes*, is probably rare in the real world of terrorism, yet it is important to recognise the powerful ideological convictions that sustain many political terrorists.

Most would claim with Leila Khaled that their movements are "fighting for humanity—all those who are oppressed and tortured".[1] Nevertheless, many terrorist movements have attracted and exploited common criminals and there are "hit men", couriers and arms suppliers who are primarily out to make quick profits from such activities. Most hard-core terrorists, however, are fanatically sincere and fully prepared to sacrifice their own lives. The typical terrorist tends to be of above average intelligence and education, is highly resourceful, and is trained in weaponry and explosives. It is a serious error to underrate the terrorists' will to succeed and their destructive capabilities.

There is often much confusion, both among analysts and terrorists themselves, concerning the rationale, strategic aims and tactical objectives of revolutionary terrorists. They cease to be political when they lose the will and interest to realise their longer-term political objectives: the obsessive pursuit of death and destruction for its own sake is purely psychopathic. (This is not to deny that such movements often contain psychopathic elements.) They are ready to justify the use of any means, including the shedding of innocent blood, to bring about the elimination of their most hated "oppression" or social or political "injustice".

Hence their propaganda of word and deed constitutes a peculiarly distorted reverse image of government: revolutionary terrorists frequently claim to be "executioners" administering "revolutionary justice", and their decision to resort to these methods is often rationalised as being the only effective means of struggle open to them. They claim that their methods are the only sure way to break the will of the government, and that terror is bound to win in the end. Yet in fact such tactics are by no means "dictated" by the needs of a revolutionary situation. Terrorists may share the same revolutionary-strategic aims as non-terrorist revolutionaries; the destruction of the existing political system, seizing power and carrying through the revolutionary programme.

4

Effectiveness challenged

Almost invariably, however, there are bitter tactical internal controversies. Sometimes, as with the "Rejectionist" groups in the Palestine Liberation Organisation (PLO) coalition, certain extremist factions develop rival maximalist programmes in conflict with the political leadership of the movement. It is important to recognise that many revolutionary theorists, from Marx and Lenin to Guevara, have argued that terrorism is at best ineffectual and at worst damaging to the revolutionary movement.

Critics can point to an impressive weight of historical evidence showing that terrorism *alone* has never sufficed to bring about a political or social revolution. Practically the only clearcut instances of political terrorism *per se* succeeding in realising strategic or long-term aims are: the 1945–47 campaign to force Britain to relinquish the Palestine Mandate; the terrorism used by Egyptians against British occupation forces in the Suez Canal zone in the early 1950s; and the EOKA campaign against the British between 1955 and 1959 leading not to *Enosis* but to the establishment of an independent republic of Cyprus.

It is important to note that these campaigns were all independence struggles against a hated British presence. The conflicts were asymmetrical in the sense that all the independence movements concerned were militarily weak compared to the British security forces, but they had the considerable psychological advantages that accrued from widespread popular support. (This made the intelligence and counter-insurgency work of the security forces infinitely harder.)

Moreover, the terrorists knew that British political leadership and public opinion were weary of expensive colonial conflicts and lacked the will to maintain a presence by force. In such conditions terrorism became, as Brian Crozier pointed out, the chosen "weapon of the weak".[2] Yet it is worth bearing in mind that the track record of terrorism as a weapon for overthrowing indigenous autocracy, liberal democracy and totalitarianism is abysmal. Even in the case of colonial independence campaigns most were solved through political measures rather than through resorting to terrorism.

It is a common but elementary mistake to equate terrorism with guerrilla warfare in general. Political terrorism proper through the use of bombings, assassinations, massacres, kidnaps and hijacks can and does occur without benefit of guerrilla war. This has been so throughout history. Historically rural guerrilla war was largely waged without resort to terrorist tactics, although today urban and rural guerrilla movements in Africa and Latin America do employ terrorism.

Guevara believed terrorism to be "a measure that is generally indiscriminate and ineffective in its results, since it often makes victims of innocent people and destroys a large number of lives that would be valuable to the revolution".[3] He also claimed it could turn a people against a revolutionary movement and may provoke police repression, hindering the revolutionary movement and its communication with the masses. On the other hand, Debray has argued that city terrorism has a strategic value, provided it is

5

properly subordinated to the needs of the struggle in the countryside: "it immobilises thousands of enemy soldiers in unrewarding tasks of protection".[4]

Terrorism for publicity

The urban guerrilla theorist, Marighela, defined terrorism as "an action usually involving the placement of a bomb or explosion of great destructive power. . . . It is an action the urban guerrilla must execute with the greatest cold-bloodedness . . .".[5] He sees it as a necessary adjunct to the urban guerrilla's repertoire, but he offers even less guidance than other revolutionary theorists as to the appropriate tactical objectives for terrorism. Debray, as we have noted, emphasises its usefulness as a diversionary device in the context of a wider guerrilla war. What are the major characteristic tactical objectives of terrorism *per se*?

- Perhaps their commonest objective is to publicise a cause by means of the massive and immediate publicity which will follow a terrorist atrocity.
- It may win concessions or short-term objectives such as the release of terrorists from gaol, payment of ransoms or alterations in government policy.
- A considerable number of assassinations stem from the lust to avenge the deaths of fellow-terrorists.
- Terrorism can be used as a catalyst to arouse fierce repression by the authorities, to "militarise" the political situation, to alienate the masses from the government, and to drive large numbers of them into alliance with the terrorists.
- A frequent objective is to sow inter-communal hatred and conflict.
- Terrorism can be used to destroy the declared enemies or scapegoats of the revolutionaries.
- A frequent objective is the "punishment" of members of the movement for infringements of discipline or alleged acts of betrayal.

Terrorism is employed as a weapon of psychological warfare to help create a climate of panic, or collapse, to destroy public confidence in government and security agencies, and to coerce communities and movement activists into obeying the terrorist leadership. As "propaganda of the deed" it is widely used to advertise a movement and its cause, to inspire followers and sympathisers to further acts of terrorism or insurrection, and as a signal or catalyst for revolution.

In these roles as in others, however, "terrorism is a faulty weapon that often misfires".[6] Wanton murder and destruction may have the effects of uniting and hardening a community against the terrorists, of triggering a violent backlash by rival groups or of stinging the authorities into more effective security measures in the ensuing period of public revulsion.

Partly to compensate for their military weakness, their political minority status, and the crudeness and unreliability of violence as a psychological weapon, terrorists engage in phrenetic politico-ideological struggle, aided by their political wings and front organisations. In liberal democracies they are able to take full advantage of democratic freedoms to orchestrate propaganda defaming and subverting the values, institutions and leaders of parliamentary democracy.

They find ready collaborators among the extremists of left or right to aid them on the political and propaganda fronts. Such persons are always willing to cheer on enemies of the parliamentary system and, despite occasional forays into electoral contests, it is clear that they do not care a fig for the survival of democracy. More insidious, because less clearly recognisable, is the assistance rendered to terrorists by woolly-minded liberals who succumb easily to terrorist propaganda. These fellow-travellers of terrorism fancy that it is always "progressive" to be on the side of a rebel, and are more ready to retail a terrorist atrocity story than to find out what really happened. They make set speeches about the evils of war, yet are prepared to justify murder and massacre by terrorists.

Underlying causes

The underlying causes of the continuing international proliferation of terrorism are a matter for further research and debate, but there is wide agreement among students of the subject that the following conditions have been conducive to terrorism:

1. Success in gaining short-term objectives has encouraged emulation.
2. Emulation has been facilitated by diffusion of information about techniques, tactics, and weaponry, both through the mass media and terrorist literature (such as the works of Begin, Grivas, Fanon, Marighela).
3. The overall strategic situation is conducive to terrorism as to all other forms of unconventional warfare. The major nuclear powers attempt to avoid involvement even in limited international war lest the conflict should escalate and disrupt nuclear balance and *détente*. And both major and minor powers increasingly resort to cheaper and less hazardous indirect methods of coercion such as the fostering of internal subversion and proxy terrorism within allegedly hostile States.
4. Domestic and internationally-based terrorism as methods of unconventional war by proxy have been energetically promoted by a wide variety of States such as the Soviet Union, Libya, Iraq, Syria, Vietnam, and Iran. The backing of foreign governments has enormously increased the cash, weaponry, and training facilities available to terrorist movements. Ironically, the West has unwittingly financed much recent Arab terrorism through providing some of the oil revenues of Arab States which are then tapped for large contributions to Palestinian terrorist movements.
5. The scale, complexity and vulnerability of international communications have made the terrorist more mobile and potentially more dangerous.
6. The worldwide development of mass media with international news coverage has vastly increased the terrorists' opportunity and appetite for publicity. There is almost a Gresham's Law of terrorism: "those who spill the most blood will make the biggest headlines".

Many profound theories have attempted to explain the proliferation of civil violence in general by reference to socio-economic and cultural developments such as responses to feelings of intensifying deprivation and oppression or stresses engendered in States undergoing rapid modernisation. However, none of these theories can explain why, or under what precise conditions, people resort to terrorism rather than to other forms of violence.

Whatever its underlying causes, terrorist violence confronts liberal democracies and the international system with special dangers. Most obviously it poses a threat to the life and limb of citizens. It is true that the number of casualties from terrorism is extremely small compared to the number of victims of international and civil wars. But that surely does not mean that killing and maiming by terrorists is tolerable, or that it can be safely ignored. Moreover, terrorism poisons communal relations and, if carried out extensively over a long period, it can also disrupt and destroy normal government and political and economic life. Widespread and sanguinary terrorism can sow the seeds of civil war and exacerbate international relations.

In contrast to totalitarian régimes, which ruthlessly suppress even the first flickers of dissent, liberal democracies are extremely vulnerable to harassment and disruption by terrorists. This is due to the relative ease with which the terrorist can exploit liberal democratic freedoms of international and national travel, communication and association. Yet liberal democratic States are extraordinarily resilient in withstanding terrorist attempts at a revolutionary seizure of power.

In this respect they have an overwhelming source of strength compared to dictatorships and colonial régimes: they have the unqualified support of the overwhelming majority of the population behind them and against the terrorists. The only clear case of terrorism, combined with urban guerrilla war, bringing about the collapse of a liberal-democratic government is Uruguay in 1972. Yet even in Uruguay what the Tupamaros actually achieved was not the left-wing revolution they desired but an overwhelming repressive reaction from the authoritarian right which effectively extinguished democracy.

The gravest internal dangers posed by terrorism to liberal democracy are the weakening of national security, the erosion of the rule of law and the undermining of government authority. Mere handfuls of terrorists can cause serious local disruptions and threats to life, and often cause expensive diversions of security forces, sometimes on such a large scale that they disturb delicate military balances. More prolonged or widespread terrorist campaigns (for example those affecting a whole region or major city, or involving threats to national security) may succeed in blackmailing governments into making major concessions to terrorist demands.

Dangerous trends

Moreover, it should be remembered that international terrorism also consti-

8

tutes a serious challenge to international stability and normal diplomatic and economic relations. The idea of terrorists operating from foreign bases is hardly new (it was used by the Assassins in the 11th century); neither is the attempt at an internationally concerted terrorism, or what Crozier terms transnational terrorism. An early example was Bakunin's ill-fated anarchist International.

However, during the past decade there have been some increasingly dangerous trends. There has been a dramatic increase in the number of terrorist organisations operating internationally, based mainly in Middle Eastern and European capitals, and employing a network of highly professional hit men, kidnappers and plane hijackers. Increasingly there is evidence of international co-operation, on a bilateral and regional basis, between terrorist organisations. This co-operation certainly extends to the joint use of terrorist training facilities and arms procurement.

The growing trend towards proxy terrorism by sponsor States has already been noted. Other growing trends are embassy attacks, diplomatic kidnappings ("diplonappings") and the use of business personnel and other hostages to secure release of prisoners, ransoms, or policy concessions. It must be stressed that diplonapping is not merely a violation of traditional diplomatic immunities and privileges: it is an attack on the foundations of diplomatic reciprocity and a potential threat to normal diplomatic and economic relations.

The clearest danger posed by terrorism to the international system, however, stems from the fact that certain terrorist movements are no longer restricting themselves to challenging the domestic authority and laws of States. Some are apparently ready to make undeclared war against foreign countries and citizens. Yet terrorist movements do not share the same responsibilities or constraints imposed on governments. They have no treaties, obligations, citizens or territories to consider.

The worst danger is that, acting entirely irresponsibly and blinded by desperate fanaticism, a terrorist movement may attempt to detonate an international conflict. Nor should the possibility of terrorists acquiring a nuclear weapon be discounted in view of the lax security concerning nuclear materials.

It is clear, therefore, that the international and national problems of response to terrorist threats are interwoven. To be effective, action against terrorists must be synchronized at both levels. By tolerating the terrorists' capacity to provoke international war the international community is playing with fire. And we have seen that terrorists confront liberal democracies internally with a ruthless challenge against the safety of their citizens, the security of the State, and the rule of law. Liberal democratic governments have to decide how to react to terrorist violence, and they have to carry their citizens with them behind their policy. Which policy should they adopt?

9

POSSIBLE RESPONSES

1. Submission: lessons of Lebanon

In an operative liberal democracy ordinary citizens do not expect to have to arm themselves for their own daily protection: they look to their government, armed forces and police to defend them against internal or external threats to their security. But what happens when a government, faced with intensifying terrorist attacks, fails to take the necessary measures for internal defence?

People begin to take the law into their own hands and form para-military organisations to defend their perceived ethnic, religious, political or economic interests. Rival movements set about forming virtual enclaves within the State, taking over both law and order and defence functions. Acts of terrorism trigger a vicious cycle of terror and counter-terror which can soon develop into bloody and debilitating civil war. Moreover, where a country has experienced a prolonged period of political freedom and has developed strong traditions of pluralism and participation it is extremely unlikely that a single powerfully armed movement with nation-wide popular support will emerge, unopposed, to impose itself as a one-party dictatorship.

Lebanon is not an isolated case of fratricidal self-destruction. The consequences of the communal conflict in Cyprus—before the Turkish invasion—for example, would have been much more serious if it had not been checked by UN peacekeeping intervention. And, to deal with a British domestic problem, those who shout for the immediate and unconditional withdrawal of British security forces from Northern Ireland may care to consider the probability that by conceding to this key terrorist aim the British government would unleash a bloody and weakening civil war that would spill over into all Ireland, and quite probably into British mainland cities?

2. Counter-terror and ruthless repression

Liberal democracy, by definition, precludes rule by State terror. For Western liberals it is a matter for rejoicing that our societies do not have to suffer totalitarian governmental terror of the Soviet kind. For the Soviet system has snuffed out internal revolt only at the price of stifling freedom, dignity and creativity. (There is evidence, however, that even totalitarian methods are incapable of totally eliminating violence by national liberation groups.)

The normal methods of control and terror in the totalitarian State are well known: ubiquitous use of Party and secret police agents and informers; constant checks on identity documents and occupancy of residential accommodation and movements; rigid controls on travel, communication and publication; Party screening for all applicants for professional and scientific employment, and so on. The range of possible sanctions includes imprisonment, labour camps, "psychiatric" detention, economic pressure (*e.g.* threats of dismissal from employment), and constant harassment.

Stalin and Hitler did not hesitate to make extensive use of genocide, massacre, torture and deportation. Totalitarian régimes can also use their controls to deny the would-be terrorist the necessary arms or explosive materials. If an act of political violence occurs in spite of these controls the Party dictatorship can deny it any publicity because of their control of the media, and in dealing with the insurgent they are uninhibited by any judicial restraints.

The repression used by authoritarian régimes and military dictatorships (such as Salazar's Portugal, Franco's Spain, or Greece under the Junta) against political opponents is typically brutal but tends to be far less effective than totalitarian terror in stamping out political violence. For example, the Franco régime dealt ruthlessly with Euzkadi ta Azkatasuna (ETA), the terrorist movement of the Basque separatists and allied groups, but with little effect.

Liberal democratic arguments against such barbarous repression cannot, however, merely be based on considerations of expediency and efficiency. Liberal democratic States cannot resort to terror and repression to answer revolutionary terrorism because to do so would be a violation of the fundamental dignities and rights of man. Such countries must not seek to eliminate the injustice of terrorists' violence by means of an even greater injustice, for this would be to fall into the same error as terrorists themselves.

3. Counter-terror against foreign-based terrorists, plus democracy

Since its inception Israel has striven to secure its borders and territory against both guerrilla and terrorist attacks and against the armed forces of the Arab States. This has not led, however, to any paralysis of will, nor, to Israel's great credit, has it led to the replacement of a liberal democratic system by some kind of garrison State dictatorship. Nevertheless, its situation is unique among liberal democracies.

Israelis are in constant danger of terrorist attacks. It is impracticable to seal off the land frontiers with Lebanon, Syria and Jordan. There is a large Arab population settled not only in the West Bank but also in the pre-1967 territory of Israel, many of whom are actual or potential collaborators with terrorists. Israel's response to this exceptional vulnerability has been to wage undeclared border warfare based on the principle of counter terror, "an eye for an eye and a tooth for a tooth".

It has adopted a number of special measures: air attacks and shellings of Arab border settlements and refugee camps believed to be used as Palestinian terrorist bases; commando-type raids to avenge Israeli deaths (an example is the April 1973 raid by the *Mivtah Elohim* ("God's Wrath") terror squad which killed three Palestinian guerrilla leaders in Beirut); the use of assassination squads to hunt down and kill Palestinian operators working in foreign countries.

Fighting on so many fronts and against such fanatical opponents, Israel could not expect to inflict any conclusive defeat on its terrorist opponents.

11

Clearly, its major objectives have been to contain such attacks, and to hope that the Palestinians would gradually tire of the war of attrition, and ultimately resign themselves to a longer-term political settlement between Israel and its Arab neighbours. However, there are several grounds for arguing that the policy of counter-terror offensives has been politically costly and that it has been counter-productive in terms of foreign and diplomatic support.

Terror attacks against Israel continue unabated and it could be argued that counter-terror has helped to harden terrorists' militancy and strengthen Arab popular support for the Palestinian and Shi'ite causes. Moreover, the air attacks on refugee settlements, some of which resulted in deaths of women and children, have, in the eyes of much foreign opinion, forfeited Israel's right to sympathy for its own losses in terrorist attacks. While it is understandable that Israelis have wanted to avenge the many lives they have lost, the policy can be questioned on grounds of both morality and political prudence.

Israel's use of special assassination squads has, of course, been emulated by many other States, though not generally by liberal democracies. Presumably those who justify counter-terrorism implicitly condone terrorism. Moreover, there are significant objections on prudential and political grounds. How can a liberal democracy adequately *control* such clandestine "dirty tricks" departments? How can one ensure that they are not directed against *internal* dissenters or critics of the government, and that they do not corrupt the entire political system? Who is to decide, and on what basis are they to decide, who is to be assassinated as an "enemy of the State?"

4. "Soft-line" approach

Because many governments have modified their policies on terrorism over recent years it is difficult to classify liberal States neatly into soft- and hard-liners. Nevertheless, there are many recent examples of liberal democratic governments conducting ill-judged negotiations with terrorists and conceding to most or all of the terrorists' demands. According to a recent Rand Corporation study, on average, world-wide, terrorists have a 79 per cent chance of evading death or imprisonment for their crimes. In large part this is a result of many governments opting for the soft-line response, a readiness to make a deal with terrorists to gain the release of hostages and a rapid end to each terrorist attack.

Inevitably terrorists will react to repeated acts of weakness, abrogation and vacillation by launching attacks of increasing boldness and making ever more arrogant demands. Moreover, new extremist groups will be attracted into emulating actions which are seen as a way of guaranteeing success in publicising a cause or wringing concessions from the authorities.

The costs of pusillanimity are vividly demonstrated by the long-term pattern of successes gained over governments by a specific terrorist movement: it is misleading to look at specific "deals" in isolation. Table 1 (see Appendix) charts the "success-rate" of the Japanese United Red Army

(URA) after 1970 in winning demands and evading capture. It is true that it has proved an extremely resourceful, tough and determined enemy for governments and security forces to tackle. It was one of a myriad of tiny sects on the Japanese revolutionary left. Estimates of its total number of activists varied between 30 and 300.

What is known is that most of them were university educated and sprang from affluent middle class Japanese families. They possessed the necessary language and professional skills to operate effectively as international terrorists from a variety of Western and Middle Eastern capitals. Red Army ideology professed the vague aim of fomenting a world revolution in collaboration with other internationally-based terror groups such as the PFLP (Popular Front for the Liberation of Palestine), but the group's declarations evince sheer nihilistic will to destroy rather than any positive programme.

Japanese psychiatrist Inada Nada believes they were "just cogs in a wheel seeking mechanical pleasures. They simply distinguish the ally from the enemy and proceed with that logic in mind".[7] The gang's ruthlessness in dealing with its own members was demonstrated in its massacre of 14 members in 1972 for alleged deviation. It must be admitted that, despite their small numbers, the Red Army represents a particularly difficult challenge to their own and to other governments. This is largely because of their ruthlessness, their terroristic internal discipline, and their skilful use of international bases and links with other terrorist groups.

Yet even the dangerous qualities just described do not adequately explain the URA's success rate. They reaped maximum advantage from the ineptness and weakness of governments' responses to their attacks. The weaknesses of the soft-line approach are well illustrated by the handling of the URA attack on the French embassy in The Hague in September 1974.

On 26 July 1974 a Japanese claiming to be Yutaka Furaya, with three false passports and $10,000 in forged $100 bills in his possession, was arrested in Paris when he arrived by air from Beirut. The French police discovered that Furaya was a Red Army member who claimed to have taken part in the Lod Airport attack of May 1972. It seems that the French authorities acted rapidly on information gained from interrogating Furaya. They discovered that he was carrying a coded letter outlining a planned terror offensive, involving the capture of foreign ambassadors and Japanese officials based in Europe to obtain the release of Red Army men from Japanese gaols.

Following the interrogation the French arrested over a dozen suspected Red Army members. They also expelled four Japanese who, it is believed, then moved their base of operations to Amsterdam. It is generally believed that the originator of the letter containing the plan for an offensive was Fusako Shigenobu, one so-called Queen of the Red Army, and widow of a Red Army man who committed suicide at Lod Airport.

Three Red Army terrorists attacked the French embassy in The Hague on 13 September 1974. A Dutch policeman and policewoman were injured in the initial assault, and the gunmen captured 12 hostages in the embassy. The gang's first demand was that Yutaka Furaya be released from prison in

France and handed over to them. (It is likely that they aimed not at his liberation but at retribution.) An emergency office based in the neighbouring American embassy was set up to deal with the attack. The Dutch deployed a special counter-terrorist squad and a platoon of marines around the French embassy.

Initially the terrorists set a deadline for the release of Furaya and threatened to kill their hostages one by one unless their demand was met. On the third day of the siege, however, they agreed to release three women, retaining the French ambassador, Count Senard, and eight other hostages. Two problems complicated the situation. First, although Furaya had been flown to Schiphol Airport, he at first refused point-blank to join his colleagues, thus lending support to the theory that he feared reprisals.

The other far more serious problem was that the Dutch government was not in a position to act decisively and independently; they had to consult with Paris because it was the French ambassador and his staff who were involved and because Furaya was in French custody. The Dutch also consulted periodically with Japanese embassy officials. At the outset a basic difference arose between the French and the Dutch governments. This was eventually resolved by the Dutch acceding to French pressure, and the terrorists won ultimately because the Dutch allowed the French to insist on a soft-line approach.

Initially the Dutch had their marine commando ready to storm the embassy: they had already gained access to the building and had reached the fourth floor. The French, on the other hand, were determined to prevent an attack which they feared might lead to a massacre of the hostages. After intercession by the French Minister of the Interior (M. Poniatowski) the Dutch stood down the marines. The French were clearly prepared to trade Furaya for the release of the nine remaining hostages and to provide an aircraft (though the Dutch provided a crew).

It is unnecessary to detail all the negotiations. The significant point is that due to French insistence a policy of capitulation to the terrorists' demands was adopted even though several other tough-line options were open to the authorities. The security forces were not allowed to storm the embassy. No attempt was made to pressure the terrorists into submission.

The outcome for the Red Army was that they were successful in gaining nearly all their demands: they secured Furaya's release and the four were able to get away scot free to Syria. They were even given the coded letter and papers which had been taken from Furaya by the French security service. (The only part of their scheme which misfired was the ransom attempt. They were given only $300,000 instead of the $1m. demanded, and this sum was returned to Amsterdam, probably at the insistence of the Syrian authorities who gave sanctuary to the terrorists.)

The price of the soft-line response to terrorism by governments is inevitably further humiliating defeats. In this case the French government, in common with previous governments that had followed a policy of capitulation, justified their action as a way of saving the lives of the hostages. But this is only to beg a number of critical questions: Was this the only way of saving the hostages' lives? Why were other responses not attempted? How many further lives have been placed at risk by allowing the terrorists to notch up another success? In terrorism nothing succeeds like success.

5. "Tough-line" approach

The liberal State tough-line approach means combining harsh and effective temporary measures to isolate and eliminate terrorist cells, their leaders and their logistic support, with the maintenance of liberal democracy, a vigorous political life of participation, debate and reform within the framework of the law. The keynote of this approach is not panic, repression and over-reaction, which in any case plays into the hands of terrorists, but a consistent policy of maximising the risk of punishment run by the terrorists and minimising their potential rewards. There are some historical examples of the effectiveness of this approach.

After France had suffered what is dubbed the Dynamite Decade of bomb outrages in the 1890s the government used the weapon of *les lois scélérates*. These laws were deliberately aimed at suppressing anarchist movements and journals and even made it an offence to apologise for anarchist acts of violence. Despite the predictable outcry these measures caused in anarchist circles there can be no doubt that they effectively snuffed out the anarchist terrorism that had mushroomed in the 'Nineties. And, though the punishments meted out to convicted anarchists were harsh, it is also clear that the democratic institutions and processes of the French Third Republic managed to survive intact.

Again, there is the, case of the newly independent Irish Free State confronted by the rebellion of the Irregulars who opposed the Treaty with Britain. The Free State government adopted emergency powers to deal with the terrorist and guerrilla campaign of the Irregulars between November 1922 and May 1923, setting up special military courts with the power to inflict the death penalty. In six months of the civil war almost twice as many Irregular prisoners were executed as the number of prisoners the British had executed between 1916 and 1921. These draconian measures certainly assisted the Free State government to restore order: by 24 May 1923 the leaders of the Irregulars had conceded military defeat.

Trudeau crackdown

More recently Pierre Trudeau and his Canadian Cabinet used draconian powers to suppress the terrorist acts of the Quebecois separatist organisation Front de Libération du Québec (FLQ) in October 1970.[8] A series of FLQ bombings beginning in the early 1960s killed six people in seven years. The terrorists claimed that they were trying to sensitise the Quebec population to their colonial condition but that they were not attempting to seize power. But when the terrorism entered a new phase in October with the kidnapping of James Cross, senior British Trade Commissioner in Montreal, and Pierre Laporte, Quebec's Minister of Labour and Immigration, Trudeau decided that it was time for a massive crackdown.

15

The kidnappers were certainly making more far-reaching demands as a condition for releasing Cross (who was freed on 5 December) and Laporte, including the release of what they termed "political prisoners" and the publication of the FLQ manifesto by the government. Trudeau moved in army units to protect ministers and diplomats in Ottawa on 13 October. When taxed by a reporter critical of this use of the military Trudeau rejoined: "There are a lot of bleeding hearts around. . . . All I can say is let them bleed". He declared his belief that society must use all means to defeat a parallel power challenging the power of the people. On 15 October, after a provocative demonstration by Quebec separatists, Prime Minister Bourassa of Quebec requested army intervention. He claimed that there was a conspiracy to overthrow the government.

Trudeau invoked the War Measures Act and put in the army. The Act enabled the authorities to hold suspects up to 90 days without trial and to search without warrant, and made the FLQ a proscribed organisation. Trudeau argued that the temporary suspension of certain civil rights was essential to save the democratic system, and that the ordinary criminal law was not adequate for dealing with systematic terrorism. Certainly the massive intervention of the army enabled the police to get on with the job of tracking down the kidnap victims, although at the time there was no co-ordination between the forces involved.

It is possible that the murder of Laporte was a defiant response to Trudeau's War Measures. Some remain critical of the use of the War Measures Act on the grounds that there was not a state of apprehended insurrection. Nevertheless, it cannot be denied that Trudeau and his Cabinet, by acting forcefully, rapidly and decisively, stopped the FLQ bombing and kidnapping campaign. Thus Trudeau's measures provide an illustration of the efficacy of a tough-line response to terrorism, although in the long term government investment policy and compulsory French courses for English language speakers provided the perfect political response.

However, even when the tough-line approach has eliminated a specific threat to the security of the State or to law and order by destroying *active* terrorist cells there will generally be passive sympathisers who remain. Indeed, part of the price we pay for the survival of democracy is the freedom of ideas. Hence in a working liberal democracy it is both dangerous and naïve to hope "to destroy a subversive movement utterly".[9]

To counter terrorism effectively the tough-line approach involves waging two kinds of war: a military-security war to contain and reduce terrorist violence, and a political and psychological war to secure the popular consent and support which must be the basis of any effective modern democratic government. It is fallacious to assume that terrorists need mass support before they can perpetrate murder and destruction; as we have already observed, many contemporary terrorist groups are numerically tiny. Yet it is important for the success of anti-terrorist operations that popular support for the terrorists should remain limited to a minority — indeed that they be as isolated as possible from the general population.

To be successful this strategy demands a unified control of all counter-insurgency operations, an intelligence service of the highest quality, adequate security forces possessing the full range of counter-insurgency skills and complete loyalty to the government, and last but not least enormous reserves of patience and determination.[10]

There are rarely any easy victories over terrorism. The characteristic features of political terrorism, its undeclared and clandestine nature and its employment by desperate fanatics already *hors la loi*, imply a struggle of attrition constantly erupting into murder and disruption. Moreover, the terrorists know that security forces in a liberal State are forced to operate at dangerous mid-levels of coerciveness. Judicial restraints and civil control prevent the security forces from deploying their full strength and firepower. No doubt this is inevitable and desirable in a liberal democracy, but it does mean that the tasks of countering terrorism and urban guerrilla war in a democracy are enormously complex and demanding. We must now consider them in more detail.

ANTI-TERRORIST MEASURES
Some ground rules

It is possible to draw from the recent experience of low-intensity and counter-insurgency operations certain basic ground rules which should be followed by liberal democracies taking a tough line against terrorism.

1. The democratically elected government must proclaim a determination to uphold the Rule of Law and constitutional authority, and must demonstrate this political will in its actions.

2. There must be no resort to general indiscriminate repression. The government must show that its measures against terrorism are solely directed at quelling the terrorists and their active collaborators and at defending society against the terrorists. A slide into general repression would destroy individual liberties and political democracy and may indeed bring about a ruthless dictatorship even more implacable than the terrorism the repression was supposed to destroy. Moreover, repressive over-reaction plays into the hands of terrorists by giving credence to the revolutionaries' claim that liberal democracy is a sham or a chimera, and it enables them to pose as defenders of the people.

3. The government must be seen to be doing all in its power to defend the life and limb of citizens. This is a vital prerequisite for public confidence and co-operation. If it is lacking, private armies and vigilante groups will tend to proliferate and will exacerbate civil violence.

4. There must be a clear-cut and consistent policy of refusing to make any concessions to terrorist blackmail. If the terrorist weapon can be shown to pay off against a particular government then that government and its political moderates will find their power and authority undermined. There is abundant evidence that weakness and concession provoke a rapid emulation of terrorism by other groups and a dramatic escalation in the price of blackmail demands.

5. All aspects of the anti-terrorist policy and operations should be under the overall control of the civil authorities and, hence, democratically accountable.

6. Special Powers, which may become necessary to deal with a terrorist emergency, should be approved by the legislature only for a fixed and limited period. The maximum should be six months, subject to the legislature's right to revoke or renew the Special Powers should circumstances require. Emergency measures should be clearly and simply drafted, published as widely as possible, and administered impartially.

7. Sudden vacillations in security policy should be avoided: they tend to undermine public confidence and encourage the terrorists to exploit rifts in the government and its security forces.

8. Loyal community leaders, officials, and personnel at all levels of government and security forces must be accorded full backing by the civil authorities.

9. No deals should be made with terrorist organisations behind the backs of the elected politicians.

10. The government should not engage in dialogue and negotiation with groups which are actively engaged in promoting, committing or supporting terrorism. To do so only lends the terrorists publicity, status, and, worst of all, a spurious respectability.

11. Terrorist propaganda and defamation should be countered by full and clear official statements of the government's objectives, policies and problems.

12. The government and security forces must conduct all anti-terrorist operations within the law. They should do all in their power to ensure that the normal legal processes are maintained, and that those charged with terrorist offences are brought to trial before the courts of law.

13. Terrorists imprisoned for crimes committed for professedly political motives should be treated in the same manner as ordinary criminals. Concessions of special status and other privileges tend to erode respect for the impartiality of the law, arouse false hopes of an amnesty and impose extra strains on the penal system

14. It is a vital principle that liberal democratic governments should not allow their concern with countering terrorism, even in a serious emergency, to deflect them from their responsibilities for the social and economic welfare of the community. Liberal democratic governments must, by definition, be grounded upon the broad consent of the governed. They are inherently reformist and ameliorative: it is their citizens' natural and legitimate expectation that their representatives and ministers will respond constructively to the expressed needs and grievances of the people. The business of attending to the public welfare must go on. It is, of course, true that this is one of the greater inner strengths of liberal democracy and, incidentally, one reason why its citizens constitute such a hostile "sea" for the terrorist to swim in.

It would be the height of folly for a liberal democracy faced with a terrorist emergency to halt its work of amelioration and reform. On the contrary, everything possible should be done to prevent the serious disruption and paralysis of social and economic life so ardently sought by the terrorists. Yet, the liberal democratic government should not, on any account, concede a reform or change of policy under terrorist duress. Such grave acts of weakness would only breed contempt for the normal political processes and for the law.

I must emphasise that the above general principles are not meant to be comprehensive. Much qualification and elaboration is needed to relate these ground rules to the actual problems of conducting anti-terrorist operations. Nevertheless, I do believe that these broad principles embody some of the major lessons that have been learned from anti-terrorist campaigns of the past. It is now necessary to survey the strategy, tactics, measures, and resources of anti-terrorist operations, and to identify some of the more valuable forms of international response.

The "two wars" strategy

The so-called "two-war" or "two-front" strategy was developed primarily by counter-insurgency specialists engaged in countering the "people's wars" of South-East Asia in the 1950s and '60s. It is true that these conflicts involved a mixture of high and low intensity, and conventional and unconventional warfare. Terrorism, both rural and urban, was only part of the tactics of revolutionary warfare experienced in Malaya and Indo-China. Nevertheless, while recognising the enormous differences between these conflicts and contemporary terrorism within liberal democracies, the "two-war" strategic doctrine is still broadly applicable to low-intensity operations in heavily industrialised and urbanised societies.

The doctrine prescribes the harmonisation of two distinctive kinds of campaign by the counter-insurgency forces: (1) the military and security war to identify, isolate and destroy the revolutionary forces, their leaders, logistic support, and lines of communication; (2) the political, ideological and psychological war to sustain and strengthen the base of popular support behind the government and hence to render the terrorists politically isolated and vulnerable.

Terrorists are always ready to exploit genuine grievances and profound social problems for their own revolutionary purposes. Naturally governments are in a much stronger position if they can show some bona fide successes in tackling these socio-economic problems. And terrorists invest considerable effort in the propaganda work of their political wings. Where the terrorist organisation proper is proscribed front organisations are used for this work. Governments must effectively counter the barrage of terrorist propaganda and defamation if the counter-insurgency campaign is to have any hope of success.

Case for and against death penalty

Terrorists in liberal democracies fondly see themselves as soldiers on active

19

service fighting brutally repressive régimes. They claim, therefore, that those members of their revolutionary armies who are captured should be accorded the normal rights of prisoners-of-war. When arraigned on charges of murder or attempted murder they characteristically refuse to recognise the legitimacy and jurisdiction of the courts. Their movements profess to be serving a superior law of the revolution in whose name they inflict their "executions" and "punishments" upon State and society. Yet when one cuts through the crude veil of self-righteous justification it is easy to discern the monstrous hypocrisy and inhumanity of the terrorists' position.

It is true that they are waging a kind of unconventional war, but it is an undeclared and clandestine war, involving sneak attacks on innocent citizens. Terrorist war recognises no conventions or restraints, no distinction between combatants and non-combatants: it is war against civilised society itself. Some of the London bombings in 1975 provide clear examples of this: attacks without warning on crowded restaurants, using bombs filled with coach-bolts and ball-bearings to wreak maximum death and injury.

These acts of barbarism are no ordinary crimes; they are crimes against humanity. It is widely admitted that execution was the appropriate sentence for those convicted of crimes against humanity in the Nuremberg trials. Is there not a clear *prima facie* case for invoking capital punishment for those convicted of terrorist crimes against humanity? The issue of the death penalty for terrorist murder is complex yet inescapable in any democratic society. I shall attempt to examine the arguments for and against the death penalty before briefly stating my own view.

What are the arguments of those who oppose restoring hanging for terrorist murderers? The principled abolitionists believe that what they term "judicial murder" can never be justified. Their position is quite unequivocal: no criminal is totally irredeemable or beyond the forgiveness of God or man. Abolitionists hold that it is barbarous for society to exact a life for a life: this merely adds to the violence, coarsens society, and imposes the intolerable burden of execution upon the hangmen. They also point to the danger of judicial error. In sum, it is the abolitionists' view that a humane and liberal society should not deny its own values by countenancing the execution of any criminal, however horrible his crimes.

Problem of definition

However, even those who hold this position frequently introduce additional practical arguments to support their contention that capital punishment should not be reintroduced for terrorist murderers. Some emphasise the difficulties of precisely defining the capital terrorist crimes. Acts of assassination and planting or throwing bombs would obviously have to be included. But what of those who plan and conspire to commit such offences? What of those many members of terrorist organisations who aid and abet such activities by numerous services and professional expertise?

Very often the actual bomb planter is a pathetic and politically illiterate individual at the end of a long chain set up by the "retailer" in an

20

operation directed by the terrorist organiser who keeps safely away from the action. The political leadership frequently goes scot free even when the activists are captured by the police. These features of terrorist organisations make the precise allocation of moral responsibility extremely difficult. It is of the nature of many terrorist groups that their members are ruled by terror and intimidation. Once an individual is *hors la loi* through involvement in the terrorist organisation, he or she is often coerced into committing further offences. Often threats of horrible reprisals against the individual member or his family are used to secure compliance with an order. One is reminded of Gorky's comment that a guilty man is often "like a stone thrown by an unknown hand. Is the stone therefore guilty?"

The anti-capital punishment side also argue that convictions of terrorist murderers would be much harder to secure if the courts knew that those found guilty would hang. They argue that some of the guilty would inevitably slip through the fingers of the legal system. Other practical arguments put forward repeatedly in this debate by the anti-hanging side are:

1. Hard-core fanatics will not in any case be deterred. Indeed, it is argued, some will actually court martyrdom to make a niche in "revolutionary history" and to inspire brother-terrorists to emulate them.

2. By creating martyrs out of those executed the terrorist movement can forge a powerful psychological weapon to win mass support. (The case of Dublin's Easter Rising Martyrs in 1916 is often quoted in support of this argument.)

3. It is claimed that if the death penalty is reintroduced there will be a serious escalation in the level of violence as terrorists will take further hostages to gain the release of brothers under death sentence, and will try to intimidate the government into reprieving or releasing prisoners, or to wreak revenge for executions carried out.

It is these prudential arguments that have notably dominated the statements of the Home Secretary and other anti-capital punishment spokesmen, not the case from abolitionist principle. In sum, they argue that the re-introduction of the death penalty for terrorist murder would fail to act as a deterrent and would most probably lead to an escalation of violence.

How powerful are the counter-arguments of the pro-capital punishment lobby? Firstly, they have a powerful counter to the abolitionist argument from principle. The terrorist murder, unlike the typical domestic murder or crime of passion, is cold-bloodedly planned as part of a deliberate policy of systematic murder. It can therefore be argued that while the common murderer who committed his crime on impulse or in a moment of passion may be ultimately reformed and returned safely to society, the terrorist murderer will simply kill and kill again unless the State imposes the death penalty.

Moreover, the imprisonment of captured terrorists invites daring attempts to spring them from gaol or to secure their release by terrorist blackmail. (The figures in Table 2 show that terrorists have all too frequently succeeded in evading justice by these means.) It is also clear that while large numbers of terrorists are held in gaol their colleagues will make one of their general aims the granting of an amnesty. Hence it is argued that imprisonment is neither an adequate protection for society nor an adequate deterrent to others. To leave a convicted terrorist alive in gaol is to take a high risk that the terrorist will kill again. Therefore, the only good terrorist is a dead one.

Deterrent effect

But would the hanging of convicted terrorists deter others from taking their places in the terrorist organisations? The pro-death penalty side can point to some historical evidence that would indicate that it has a deterrent effect. In the campaign of the Irish Free State government against the Irregulars in 1923 the executions of Irregulars certainly played a part in forcing the Irregular leadership to concede defeat. But, of course, it was by no means the only factor. The Irregulars had been forced to operate in remote rural areas. They had only small numbers of men and weapons against increasingly well equipped government forces.

Their crucial weaknesses were their lack of foreign military support and their failure to obtain some compensating mass political support in Ireland. There is also evidence that the death penalty was a useful deterrent in the Malayan terrorist emergency. Yet even there the fanatical hard-core continued the struggle undaunted: what happened was that the supply of new terrorist recruits and active collaborators began to dry up. It is believed that this was in part attributable to the use of the death penalty.

One of the most effective arguments for bringing in the death penalty for terrorism in a democracy must be the growing evidence that this is desired by the overwhelming majority of citizens. It is important for ensuring continuing public confidence in, and support for, any democratic system of government that the public should believe in the soundness of its laws, and widely accept that its punishments are just and reasonable. It has been argued that the State owes it to its citizens to take the lives of those who systematically set out to destroy the innocent. It is, if you wish, part of the implicit contract between ruler and ruled in a civil society. It is also a clear demonstration to the terrorists that the liberal State values the safety of its citizens before any considerations of short-term expediency.

It is the writer's view that a powerful case can be made for the reintroduction of capital punishment for convicted terrorist murderers in the United Kingdom under present conditions. But I believe it would be foolish to regard capital punishment as a panacea. What is needed to beat the terrorists is a flexible and carefully co-ordinated programme of national and international measures of the kind briefly surveyed in the concluding paragraphs of this study. There is certainly no clear-cut evidence either way concerning the deterrent value of the death penalty with regard to the hard-core terrorist.

If the death penalty for terrorist murder is to be reintroduced in Britain the government, security forces, judiciary and penal system should all be fully prepared for a sudden and severe escalation in terrorist violence, at least in the short term. There should be adequate contingency plans for dealing with large-scale terrorist attacks on prisons, police stations and law courts. The provision of larger numbers of special armed police units and counter-insurgency forces held in reserve to deal with more serious attacks should be an essential part of these arrangements. Prison security will need to be drastically improved, and prison service staff should be given full training in anti-terrorist security measures and equipment as a matter of urgent priority.

Police as intelligence agents

An intelligence service of the highest quality is clearly a vital prerequisite for any effective counter-insurgency campaign. It is absolutely crucial for combating terrorist bombings and assassinations which present difficulties of a rather different order from the problems of full-scale guerrilla war. The archetypal terrorist organisation is numerically tiny and based on a structure of cells or firing groups, each consisting of three or four individuals. These generally exercise a fair degree of operational independence and initiative, and are obsessively concerned with the security of their organisation and lines of communication. Usually only one member of each cell is fully acquainted with the group's links with other echelons and with the terrorist directorate.

Experienced terrorists develop sophisticated "cover" to protect them against detection and infiltration. They are adept at disappearing into the shadows of the urban and suburban environment. They increasingly tend to acquire the funds and resources necessary to shift their bases between cities and across frontiers. Modern internationally based terrorist organisations take full advantage of the mobility afforded by air travel, and are adroit at shifting their bases of operations when things become too hot for them.

For all these reasons the police are the most appropriate intelligence agency for combating terrorism. I do not share Brigadier Kitson's view[11] that intelligence gathering should be primarily an Army responsibility. It is true that in the special circumstances of the troubles in Ulster police effectiveness has been somewhat vitiated by the sectarian conflict. But in most Western States the police Special Branch or its equivalent has enormous advantages over the military in the investigation and prevention of terrorist crimes.

They have firm roots in the local communities and possess an invaluable "bank" of data on both extremist and criminal groups. Moreover, the Army does not possess the manpower, time or police training to duplicate the work of the police forces. Defence chiefs have to make their primary concern the meeting of external defence obligations, and they generally prefer to husband their intelligence services for use in operations in which the Army is militarily involved.

Police in Western democracies have learned many valuable lessons from their recent experience of terrorism. There have been three main trends in this development: (1) improvements in techniques of intelligence gathering, infiltration and surveillance, and in data computerisation. By these means background information can be more readily developed into contact information; (2) improvements in the machinery for co-ordination of anti-terrorist operations at national level; and (3) greater international co-operation, and exchange of data on international terrorism on a regular basis.

One obvious step towards greater rationalisation of British measures, as the writer has proposed elsewhere, is the creation of a police Anti-Terrorist Squad with a nationwide remit to deal with all terrorist crimes. It would be a pity to concentrate all the expertise of such a unit purely on combating the IRA. This long overdue development appears imminent at the time of writing, and it is to be hoped that the new squad will be generously endowed with manpower, research support, professional scientific advisers (including psychologists and psychiatrists) and specialised training facilities.

The Army's role

What should be the role of the Army in countering terrorism? Even in the initial phases of a terrorist campaign, it can provide invaluable aid to the civil power. Bomb disposal, sharpshooting, and training and testing in new techniques and weaponry are some obvious roles in which military expertise may be invaluable. But I believe that the Army should be handed the overall task of maintaining internal security and order only as a last resort; troops should be brought in when it is obvious that the civil power is unable to cope and that there is a very real risk of civil war. If they are given this task they should be given a clear remit and briefing on their role by the civil authorities, and they should be withdrawn as soon as the level of violence has dropped to a level at which the police can act effectively.

There are a number of dangers involved in deploying the Army in a major internal terrorist emergency role which need to be constantly borne in mind: (1) an unnecessarily high military profile may serve to escalate the level of violence by polarising pro- and anti-government elements in the community; (2) there is a constant risk that a repressive over-reaction or a minor error of judgment by the military may trigger further civil violence. Internal security duties inevitably impose considerable strains on the soldiers who are made well aware of the hostility of certain sections of the community towards them; (3) anti-terrorist and internal security duties absorb considerable manpower and involve diverting highly trained military technicians from their primary NATO and external defence roles; (4) there is a risk that the civil power may become over-dependent upon the Army's presence, and there may be a consequent lack of urgency in preparing the civil police for gradually re-shouldering the internal security responsibility.

Britain is fortunate in having an Army steeped in democratic ethos. They have shown enormous skill, courage and patience in carrying out a number of extraordinarily difficult counter-insurgency tasks around the world since 1945. Their loyalty in carrying out their instructions from the civil government has never been put in question. In Northern Ireland it is doubtful whether any other army could have performed the internal security role with such humanity, restraint and effectiveness.

It would be naïve to assume that all liberal democracies are as fortunate. It is notorious that many armies, particularly conscript armies, have been infiltrated and subverted by extremist organisations of left and right. Both the Italian and Spanish Armies have had to weed out left-wing and right-wing activists who were undermining military discipline. The recent history of Greece affords a vivid demonstration of the consequences of widespread disaffection and political subversion within the armed forces. It is a warning that no liberal democracy can afford to ignore, for loyal and disciplined armed forces are the last line of defence for democracies in crisis.

Mobilising the public

Yet there are many other valuable lines of defence open to liberal democracies before the Army is put to the ultimate test of preserving the State. The ordinary, loyal and decent citizens are themselves a priceless asset in combating terrorism if only they can be mobilised to help the government and security forces. One way of doing this is to enrol large numbers of able-bodied men into the police reserve. One is aware that these auxiliaries are treated with some disdain by the professionals, and that there is considerable resistance in some quarters to extending the police reserve. Nevertheless, when so many of our major city police forces are below efficient strength a large injection of police reserve manpower could considerably ease the situation.

It would have an obvious benefit for the effective conduct of anti-terrorist operations. Full-time and specialist-trained officers would be freed from more routine duties and more time and manpower could be devoted to combating terrorist crime. Moreover, there is no reason why police reserves could not adequately perform many of the extra duties of patrols, searches, and vehicle checks that may be necessitated by a terrorist emergency. The writer strongly recommends that measures to increase the police reserve be given urgent consideration.

Another valuable way of mobilising public assistance against terrorism is through a concerted programme of public information and education about how to recognise bombs and terrorist weapons, the procedure to be adopted when a suspicious object is sighted, the kind of information that might be valuable to the police, the speediest method of communication with the anti-terrorist squad, and so forth. There should also be much more use of television, radio and public advertisement to convey this essential information. There is a rich fund of experience from Ulster and elsewhere concerning the most effective methods of mobilising the public behind an anti-terrorist campaign.

The security authorities should also take care to brief special groups such as property-owners in areas under attack and businessmen concerning the particular terrorist hazards that they are most likely to confront, and to give special advice on appropriate counter-measures. It is to be hoped that the police in British cities have already held such consultations with owners of premises and places of entertainment. The police should also make a regular practice of informing regional hospital authorities of the kind of emergency situations that are likely to arise through terrorist attacks. This task of public education and mobilisation is just as vital to the task of saving lives as the formulation of contingency plans for military and police action.

One general aim of such measures should be to make the public far more security conscious. Members of the public must be constantly vigilant for suspicious objects or activities in the environs of buildings, for signs of tampering with vehicles, and for unattended bags and parcels. Gunsmiths and commercial suppliers of chemicals and explosives should, as a matter of routine, check that their customers are *bona fide*. Any irregular transactions or unaccountable losses should be immediately reported to the police. The eyes and ears of the security forces must be the citizens.

Indeed, without the fullest public co-operation special preventive measures against terrorism are bound to fail. Take, for example, the matter of storage of detonators and explosive substances for industrial purposes. It would be no earthly good the government bringing in a new Act to impose severe penalties for failing to keep explosive stores fully secure if the actual workers and managers involved in their industrial use still failed to observe the minimal rules of security. Police are generally called in only when there is an explosives or weapons theft, *i.e.* when it is probably too late. Truly preventive action against terrorism demands the fullest co-operation of every member of the public.

NOTES

[1] Interview, BBC "Man Alive" programme on terrorism 12 June 1975. Leila Khaled was overpowered, and a man accomplice killed, when they tried to hijack an Israeli airliner over Britain on 6 September 1970. She was released after being held for 23 days at Ealing police station.

[2] Brian Crozier, *The Rebels: A Study of Post-War Insurrections* (London: Chatto and Windus, 1960).

[3] Che Guevara, *Guerrilla Warfare* (Harmondsworth: Penguin Books, 1970), p. 26.

[4] Regis Debray, *Revolution in the Revolution?* (Harmondsworth: Penguin Books, 1968), p. 74.

[5] Carlos Marighela, *Manual of Urban Guerrilla Warfare,* 1969.

[6] Robert Moss, *Urban Guerrillas* (London: Temple Smith, 1972), p. 64.

[7] *Newsweek,* 18 August 1975.

[8] *Quebec: The Challenge from Within* (Conflict Studies No. 20).

[9] Frank Kitson, *Low Intensity Operations: Subversion, Insurgency and Peacekeeping* (London: Faber and Faber, 1971), p. 50.

[10] Police used these qualities with notable success at the end of 1975 in their handling of the kidnapping of Dr. Tiede Herrema, a Dutch industrialist, in Eire, and of the Balcombe Street siege in London, which ended in the surrender of four IRA suspects.

[11] Kitson, *op. cit.,* Chap. 4, "The Army's Contribution," pp. 67 *ff.*

APPENDIX

TABLE 1

MAJOR JAPANESE UNITED RED ARMY OPERATIONS
MARCH 1970–OCTOBER 1975

Date	Operation	Outcome
30 March 1970	Japanese aircraft hijacked by nine men armed with Samurai swords and daggers. They landed in North Korea.	Fate of hijackers not known.
30 May 1972	Three Red Army men attacked passengers at Lod Airport, killing 26 and wounding over 70.	One was killed; one shot himself. One serving life in Israeli gaol.
20 July 1973	One Red Army man, three Arabs and a girl hijacked a Japanese aircraft to Benghazi and destroyed it on the ground.	Girl hijacker accidentally killed. Others freed from Libyan custody only a year later.
31 January 1974	Two Red Army men and two Arabs attacked Shell refinery in Singapore and hijacked a ferry in Singapore harbour.	Terrorists captured by police.
8 February 1974	Five terrorists (including URA members) seized the Japanese embassy, Kuwait, and took hostages to force release of the Singapore terrorists.	Four Singapore prisoners flown to Kuwait, then flown with five embassy terrorists to S. Yemen and released.
13 September 1974	Three Red Army men attacked the French Embassy in The Hague, took hostages and demanded that Japanese terrorist Yutaka Furaya (imprisoned in France) be handed over, plus $1m. ransom.	Flown to Syria with Furaya plus $300,000, then released. Ransom cash returned to Amsterdam.
4 August 1975	Five Red Army terrorists seized Swedish and American consulate offices in Kuala Lumpur and demanded release of seven Red Army members from Japanese gaols as the price for release of over 50 hostages.	Flown to Libya with five colleagues released by Japan (one Red Army prisoner in Japan was too sick to travel; and one refused to rejoin his colleagues). All who escaped to Libya were released.

27

TABLE 2

ARAB TERRORISTS CAPTURED IN EUROPE, JANUARY 1972–JANUARY 1974

	Number captured	Release secured by threat	Released for other reasons	Convicted and sentenced	Awaiting or on trial
Italy	12	—	7	2	3
France	2	—	—	2	—
Britain	5	—	4	1	—
Austria	8	2	6	—	—
West Germany	7	3	—	—	4
Greece	3	1	—	2	—
Turkey	2	—	2	—	—
Cyprus	10	7	3	—	—
Holland	1	—	1	—	—
	50	13	23	7	7

First published 1976. Minor amendments 1985.

Terrorism: International Dimensions

Paul Wilkinson

I. AN ASSESSMENT OF THE THREAT

Terrorism is a weapon of coercive intimidation, typically involving the taking of hostages and the threat of the gun and the bomb, designed to make governments submit to demands. Although terror tactics are often employed by factions in guerrilla war, their recent escalation, both internationally and within liberal democratic states, has mainly been the work of groups specialising in terrorism without any accompaniment of guerrilla war.

It is well known that throughout history tyrannical régimes have used terror as an instrument of repression and control and that thousands more lives have been lost through state terror than by factional terrorism, but the present study is concerned exclusively with the systematic use of terrorism by factions as an offensive or disruptive weapon against states and communities and against rival factions.

However, the central fact of state terror in contemporary international relations cannot fail to be relevant. First, and most important, much factional terrorism is justified by its perpetrators on the ground that they are struggling against cruel and oppressive régimes, and that any means are justified—even the shedding of innocent blood—in pursuance of this.

Another key factor is the difficulty of drawing a clear distinction between state and factional terror: many terrorist movements, as we shall observe in detail later, are directly encouraged, sponsored and aided by régimes in order to weaken or subvert rival states. And it follows from the intimacy of these connections that the pro-terrorist states are hardly likely to become enthusiastic or reliable partners in international cooperation against terrorism. On the contrary they have taken every opportunity to thwart any firm international action and to "legalise" their protégé terrorist movements by pressing their cause at the United Nations, and by attempts to redraw the framework of international law to accommodate them.

The growth of terrorism

The use of terrorism by factions against régimes is probably as old as the repressive terror of rulers. As early as the First Century the Jewish Sicarii and Zealot movements employed it as one of their tactics in a protracted guerrilla war against the Romans. Perhaps the first clear example of a movement employing terrorism as a major weapon and as propaganda of the deed internationally is the Assassin Sect of the Eleventh and Twelfth centuries which sent its agents on their missions of murder throughout the Moslem world. Interestingly it was also from the Middle East that the

29

major impetus to the contemporary wave of international terrorism arose in the late 1960s.

In the 1950s and early 1960s there were, on average, less than a dozen terrorist attacks each year involving foreign citizens or targets, though there was a flurry of terrorist activity in Latin America in the wake of the Cuban revolution. But it was the fanatical Palestinian movements, frustrated and desperate to avenge the Arab defeat in the Six-Day War of June 1967, who made the fateful decision to use international terrorism as their major weapon against Israel and its Western allies. This campaign ushered in a new age of terrorism as one movement after another emulated the publicity-catching tactics of hijackings, bombings and shootings.

Steady rise in incidents

What is remarkable about the overall level of incidents is the sharp and almost continuous increase from just over 100 incidents to well over 400 a year in 1974–76 and to almost 1,000 a year in 1978. This tenfold increase over the decade is far greater than the rise in normal crime in Britain and most other European countries. For example, the percentage increase over the preceding year for crimes of violence against the person in England and Wales was 11 per cent in 1975, 10 per cent in 1976 and 6 per cent in 1977. The increases in crimes of robbery were higher (for instance 31 per cent increase in 1975, and an 18 per cent increase in 1977),[1] but these in no way match the world-wide rate of increase in terrorist incidents. By any reckoning it represents a considerable growth in attacks on life, limb and property and a real challenge to the concept of an international rule of law.

The most considerable growth in the last few years has been in explosive bombings, incendiary attacks, and assassination attempts. As a group these have increased at the rate of over 30 per cent annually.

The only forms of terrorism to show an overall decline internationally are aircraft hijackings and letter bombings. In the former case the main reasons can be clearly established; the introduction of thorough passenger body and baggage searches, pioneered in American airports and now being adopted by major airlines and airports elsewhere; the closing of hijacker sanctuaries both by bilateral agreements (as in the US–Cuba pact of 1973) and by the threat of sanctions from the international community and the aviation unions; and the tough military actions by governments in the rescue operations exemplified at Entebbe and Mogadishu have compelled the terrorist movements to consider alternative tactics involving less risk to their own lives.[2] Despite this governments and aviation authorities cannot afford to relax their vigilance or dismantle their security systems. There are still terrorist groups, criminals, and "crazies" who exploit such opportunities, and find loopholes in security all too frequently for comfort.[3] Moreover the increasingly effective measures against traditional aircraft hijacking can never, for obvious reasons, suffice to prevent attacks on airport ground facilities or missile attacks on aircraft in flight or on runways. Nor should we overlook the possibility of terrorists blackmailing a government into letting them have a "getaway aircraft" to take them, with their hostages, abroad. This is precisely what happened after the attack by Carlos and his gang on the OPEC oil ministers' conference at Vienna in December 1975.

The other potentially dangerous effect of the more effective anti-hijack measures is that the alternative tactics developed by terrorist movements to attract equivalent international publicity will involve a greater threat to innocent life, possibly a shift from micro- to macro-violence, involving perhaps a threat to detonate a crude nuclear device or to release radioactivity to contaminate a whole area.

The overall decline in the incidence of letter bombing is also largely due to improvements in counter-terrorist technology. Governments and industrial concerns rapidly acquired the machines to check all incoming mail. (It is true that small firms could be reluctant to meet the cost of the equipment, but these are not generally the terrorists' target—they are after the prestige targets, symbols of great power or wealth.)

Seriousness of the problem

It is sometimes claimed that the figures show that the costs of terrorism in terms of human life are low. Obviously they do not match the level of casualties in major civil or international wars, but it is hardly sensible to compare them, for terrorism is quite obviously a form of low-intensity violence. Yet it would be a grave mistake to underestimate the deadly destructiveness of its effects, particularly on those communities that have been the victims of protracted terrorist campaigns. For example, assuming deaths in proportion to the US population, 138 times that of Northern Ireland, an equivalent total in American terms to 2,000 deaths in Northern Ireland would be 276,000. The fact is that any large modern industrial society would regard such a level of political violence as intolerable; but in areas of major terrorist campaigns such as Ulster, the Basque country in Spain and parts of Lebanon, death stalks the streets every day and hardly a family remains unscathed.

It is also clear that certain nationalities are particularly at risk as targets of international terrorism. The USA is regarded in the terrorist ideology of most of the neo-Marxist revolutionary groups as the arch-enemy, the embodiment of "capitalist imperialism", and hence its representatives, businessmen and citizens are seen to be appropriate targets. Between 1968 and 1977 more than 200 US diplomats and more than 500 US private citizens and businessmen were victims of terrorist incidents abroad. Fifty Americans were assassinated.

Terrorism clearly threatens and violates the fundamental human right "to life, liberty and the security of person" proclaimed in Article 3 of the Universal Declaration of Human Rights. The preamble to that declaration (proclaimed by UN General Assembly resolution 217A (III) of 10 December 1948) condemns "disregard and contempt for human rights" which "have resulted in barbarous acts which have outraged the conscience of mankind", and the achievement of a world in which all human beings shall enjoy freedom from fear is one of its explicit aims. Yet terrorists, by attempting to exploit the weapon of fear and intimidation, are systematically destroying human rights by bomb and bullet.

Naïve and confused liberals sometimes assume that a just cause justifies whatever means its supporters resort to in order to win their objectives. Who can deny that there are both majority and minority groups in the world today who suffer from injustice and oppression at the hands of dominant groups and régimes? The savage brutality of many of these régimes may explain much of the savagery of acts committed against them, but can surely never morally justify the use of terror. By adopting the weapon of the Nazis and the Soviet terror apparatus, albeit on a smaller scale, the terrorist is just as guilty of degrading and trampling on humanity as the monsters of Auschwitz, Buchenwald and the Gulag.

For the man or woman who is willing, for example, to massacre the innocent by bombing public places is clearly also willing to treat fellow-human beings as though they were expendable sub-humans. By deliberately perpetrating such atrocities, for whatever alleged tactical advantage, such people are committing crimes against humanity. I have argued elsewhere[4] that just as we describe as war criminals those who commit atrocities in time of war, so we should recognise the fact that there are revolution-criminals who commit atrocities in the name of "revolution" or "liberation". And it is the duty of States and the international community to deal with them accordingly.

It is a particular irony that a high proportion of terrorist incidents has occurred within the liberal democratic states of Western Europe where both formal recognition and implementation of human rights are most advanced. In these, the most open and free of the world's states, terrorist crimes understandably appear especially heinous. In any parliamentary democracy, which by definition enjoys freedoms of speech, association and opposition, there are always peaceful means available for publicising a cause, or campaigning for political change.

One encouraging sign of the health and strength of democratic values and institutions is the fact that the overwhelming majority of our citizens identify with the victims of terrorism—the hostage, the planeload of hijacked passengers, the victims of terror bombing—and feel a deep sense of outrage and revulsion against the terrorist. The problem this creates for the democratic government is the demand for effective counter-action. The cry goes up "something must be done" but democratic governments know that it is in fact a difficult and delicate task to defeat a terrorist campaign while ensuring that human rights and democratic government remain undamaged. The task is made infinitely more difficult by the fact that modern terrorism has become highly internationalised in its *modus operandi*. Hence, as we shall discuss in detail later, there are major problems involved in securing the most appropriate and effective means of international co-operation to prevent terrorists slipping across frontiers and exporting murder and fear.

Threat to legal systems

First and foremost then, terrorism is a serious world problem not because of the sheer amount of violence involved but because it constitutes a threat to innocent life and rights. Not only does it challenge the concept of an international rule of law, it also directly attacks the national legal systems. Acts of terrorism constitute crimes under the codes of practically every State. Moreover, many of the more nihilistic terrorist gangs active in democracies, such as the Red Brigades in Italy, set out to make war on the whole concept of legality, and on the legal system itself: they murder lawyers, jurors, policemen and witnesses, they intimidate courts. In many countries (such as Turkey, Italy, and Northern Ireland) the activities of terrorist gangs present a serious obstacle to the rule of law and judicial process.

It is relatively rare for terrorists to use their acts of blackmail to make substantive changes in foreign or domestic policy although in September 1973 the Austrian government was blackmailed into closing the Schonau transit camp for Soviet Jews en route to Israel. An almost invariable terrorist demand, however, is for the release of terrorist prisoners from jail. This demand is a challenge to the authority not only of the legal system but of the democratic government itself. If governments were to give way to such blackmail not only would they invite similar actions by other groups, and the inevitable escalation in price in terms of terrorists whose release is demanded, they would also destroy their own credibility by raising the question "who is in control, the democratically elected government or the terrorists?"

There are very few historical examples of governments toppled through the use of terrorism as the primary weapon. Dictatorships and totalitarian governments have proved particularly intractable opponents. The main reason for the negligible incidence of terrorism in the Soviet Union and communist States generally is the ubiquity and ruthlessness of their systems of secret police surveillance and control. Under conditions of such severe repression it is highly unlikely that a terrorist movement could find support.

Liberal democracies have so far managed well in preserving their systems against terrorist attempts to destroy them from within. Furthermore—and this is a measure of the inner strength of liberal democratic values and institutions—they have done so without destroying or even seriously damaging their own democratic processes and legal systems. The only clear example of the collapse of a working liberal democracy under assault from terrorism is Uruguay in the period 1969–72. By the early 1960s the country was the most liberal and welfare-minded of all Latin American States. But under increasing pressure from a skilful urban terrorist campaign by the Tupamaros in Montevideo the government over-reacted in 1972, and a paramilitary "emergency" government took control on the grounds that it would deal with the crisis. In effect it suspended basic rights and instituted a system of repression, including torture, becoming for a time one of the harshest régimes in the region. But the population did not rise in favour of the neo-Marxist Tupamaros movement as the guerrillas expected, instead liberal democracy was replaced by authoritarian government.

The clearest examples of terrorism succeeding in its strategic aims of removing a government and taking power are from the period of colonial independence struggles, forcing British withdrawal from Palestine, Cyprus and Aden, and playing a major role in compelling France to withdraw from Algeria. These "successes" can, however, be explained by the special historical circumstances obtaining in all three cases. The British colonial authorities had no desire to remain permanently in control, yet found themselves unable to find a clear-cut bargaining agent to whom they could hand over power and who they could be confident would enjoy support from the major ethnic groups in the population. In Palestine they were in a three-cornered conflict with Arabs and Jews, in Cyprus with Greek and Turkish Cypriots, and in Aden with Adeni nationalists and those who favoured union with Yemen.

Another important factor was the already straitened economic circumstances of the colonial powers. Neither France nor Britain were prepared to bear the cost of long wars in distant territories. Nor was there sufficient political or public support for such involvements. Metropolitan publics were war-weary and could not see why more of their soldiers' lives should be lost defending positions in which, it was believed, the country had no long-term vital interests at stake. These conditions clearly do not apply to contemporary terrorist campaigns within Western European democratic states. Yet it is obvious that the "colonial model" of the terrorist war of attrition, ultimately making it appear too costly for the authorities to maintain control, has given some encouragement to extremist minorities in Europe who fondly believe that they are living in a "colonial situation". This is one of the myths assiduously nourished in Provisional IRA propaganda.

Challenge to democracy

The abysmal track record of terrorism in bringing about the collapse of democratic régimes does not mean that the Western democracies can afford to be complacent. As we have noted, terrorist campaigns may cost hundreds of lives. They directly challenge the authority of democratically elected governments.

Nor should the severe socio-economic costs of prolonged terrorism be overlooked. A climate of bitterness and hatred is created, poisoning the relations between different ethnic and religious groups, and destroying the basis of normal democratic politics. This is achieved by killing or terrorising moderates and conciliatory elements. By destroying the middle ground for compromise and by polarising factions and communities terrorists will try to make democratic politics impossible. Intimidation and violence are invariably combined with a frenetic terrorist propaganda campaign defaming leading parliamentarians, judges, the security forces and all those associated with the continuance of constitutional government and the administration of the law. Whole generations are inducted into the ethos of violence and patterns of suspicion and hatred, rendering the long-term task of conciliation and a return to "normal" democratic politics all the more difficult.

The economic costs can be colossal. Damage to industrial plant and business premises and the disruption of communications tends to scare away investment and cause the loss of job opportunities. Tourism may suffer from a serious drop in demand. And the costs of compensation for damage to houses and business property become an enormous burden on the finances of government already overstretched to meet the increasing costs of security. Hence, although it is fair to conclude that terrorism is rarely in itself sufficient to threaten the survival of democratic political systems it does constitute a grave threat to human rights, a challenge to law and order and a damaging blow to the welfare and economic advance of society.

Furthermore, as I have shown in detail elsewhere,[5] once terrorist violence becomes firmly rooted it has an inherent tendency to escalate. Each successive incident tends to induce an act of counter-violence by the régime or by opposing factions in a mounting spiral of violence which no one can control or stop. The experience of Lebanon in 1975–77 shows the warfare of private armies spilling over ineluctably into general civil war.

Major current trends and threats

A hard look at the "track record" of terrorism also invites another question: as political terrorists so rarely win their long-term objectives, why over the past two decades has terrorism become such a widespread and fast-growing phenomenon? There are certain conditions inherent in the global strategic balance and in the current state of international relations which are clearly conducive to unconventional warfare of all kinds (and one must remember that much contemporary terrorism in Africa and Asia has been interwoven with wider conflicts and revolutionary wars). The most obvious conducive factor is the nuclear balance of terror. The superpowers and their close allies have been effectively deterred from direct military assaults on each other's territory. But this has not resulted in their conflicts being entirely confined to the diplomatic and economic levels.

On the contrary, one side has been engaged, ever since World War II, in an indirect undeclared war carried on very largely through proxy forces and client movements struggling for power in third areas, such as South-East Asia, the Middle East, and Africa.

Soviet training for guerrillas

The Soviet Union has become increasingly successful in recent years in its interventions in support of selected national liberation movements. An important part of its strategy has been to train and deploy cadres from these movements in the arts of terrorism and subversion. These can then be deployed, on an opportunistic basis, both in conflicts in the region concerned and, on occasion, as a method of sowing disruption and helping to weaken or destabilise non-communist states elsewhere. This weapon has the dual advantage that sponsorship and ideological support can always be denied or withdrawn, and it provides a continuing method of exerting ideological influence, infiltration and control, through the process of intensive training in ideology and revolutionary subversion provided at the various schools run by the KGB and the intelligence services of other communist states.[6]

It is firmly established that this task is shared among all the East European intelligence services, the Cuban DGI, and that of North Korea. Soviet aid to the movements is funnelled through client régimes such as Libya, Vietnam and South Yemen, all of which contain their own training centres for terrorism and sponsor the activities of protégé groups as weapons against rival states. Some of their aid goes in the form of cash and weapons direct to protégé groups such as Arafat's *Fatah* movement within the PLO. In some cases the recipient movement itself then acts as a channel to other terrorist movements.

Nor do communist states miss any opportunity of offering propaganda support to terrorists operating in the West, even when the group is ideologically poles apart from Soviet Marxism–Leninism. For instance, the East Germans secretly subsidised the magazine *Konkret*, run by Ulrike Meinhof's then-husband Klaus Rainer Rohl, to the extent of $250,000.[7] And in 1977 the Soviet media were given the job of making the most of the hearings before the European Court of Human Rights at Strasbourg over allegations that Britain had used torture in Northern Ireland.

Examples of more direct assistance by pro-terrorist states to protégé terrorist groups are not difficult to find: The captured hijackers of an Egyptian plane with 101 people on board on a flight from Cairo to Luxor confessed that they had been trained and financed by the government of Libya. The Libyan leader Colonel Kadafi also supported the notorious Black September group responsible for such atrocities as the massacre of the Israeli athletes in Munich in 1972. The weapons used by the terrorists were smuggled into Munich by Libyan diplomatic couriers.[8] Kadafi was also responsible for inciting and sponsoring the attack on the OPEC ministers' conference at Vienna in December 1975, for which he is believed to have paid Carlos over $2 million.

The foreign assistance rendered to the Provisional IRA is also of considerable interest. A four-ton shipment of Czech arms destined for the Provisionals was seized by the Dutch authorities at Schipol airport in October 1971. They had been purchased by David O'Connell, a prominent leader of the Provisionals, from Omnipol, an agency of the Czech intelligence service, in effect under KGB control.[9] The Provisionals were also allowed in 1972 to obtain Soviet RPG-7 rocket launchers. And in March 1973, off the Irish coast, the Irish navy seized a ship carrying five tons of arms and ammunition, including 250 Kalashnikov automatic rifles, supplied first to *Al Fatah* from the Soviet Union and by *Al Fatah* to the PIRA.[10] The Tass statement condemning the murder of Lord Mountbatten and three others in a boat explosion in August 1979 was clearly a diplomatic smokescreen; it cannot hide the facts of considerable Soviet encouragement and help funnelled through various client régimes and movements.

There is a wealth of evidence of Soviet backing for terrorist groups in many countries. Without doubt, their heaviest investment has been in the Palestinian movements, which in turn have become the leading brokers and clearinghouse for the world's terrorist groups. It is no surprise to learn that following the PLO raid near Tel Aviv, on 11 March 1978, which caused the deaths of 34 Israelis, Israeli intelligence found 3 maps of an East German training camp with one of the terrorists' names written on the back, and Soviet weaponry.[11] One inescapable conclusion to be drawn from all the evidence gathered by Western intelligence services must be that the Soviet Union and its clients and allies bear a major responsibility for supporting terrorist movements around the world on an opportunistic basis. They, together with a number of pro-terrorist Arab states, have provided the bulk of the cash, weapons and training for some of the most dangerous groups.

Causes of conflict

Allied to this is the significant shift in local power balances as a result of the establishment of pro-Soviet régimes. States such as South Yemen, Ethiopia, and Vietnam, for example, not only provide useful bases and sanctuaries and conduits for supporting subversive movements elsewhere, but also afford springboards for launching terrorist campaigns, sabotage and border incursions in neighbouring states.

It would, however, be misleading to stress the importance of the activities of pro-terrorist states to the exclusion of other factors. In many cases the international structure is inherently conducive to the development of terrorist movements. Since the end of the colonial independence era the frontiers of the new states have been set rigidly. Boundaries arbitrarily drawn in the heyday of imperialism are defended by the régimes of the new African and Asian states as if they were Holy Writ. Ethnic and religious minorities straddling these frontiers, often in conflict with their host states, come to feel that there is no longer any hope of renegotiating frontiers or achieving self-determination. Partly as a result of their desperation some of these groups have begun to emulate the methods of terrorist movements. They hanker for the publicity and world attention that acts of extreme violence may yield. It is easy to see why many of them have resorted to terror, though to explain is by no means to excuse or to justify the use of such means.

Then there are, however, a number of other important factors which also help to account for the massive rise in terrorist incidents:

• The hunger for "propaganda by the deed", the world-wide publicity which can be gained from a dramatic outrage.

• A shift in revolutionary doctrine, occurring around the early 1960s,

favouring a switch from revolutionary war in the countryside to warfare in the cities.
- The rapid process of urbanization in both the developed and the developing world, rendering the cities the most important and populous parts of the country—"he who controls the cities controls the country".
- The increasing vulnerability of the urban-industrial complex with its concentrations of high technology and vulnerable and important targets.
- The contagion effect: as other revolutionary groups saw the "successes" of terrorism in gaining tactical victories such as the release of terrorists from jail, large cash ransoms, vast publicity and so on, they eagerly emulated such actions, copying accounts of the tactics used from the media and from urban guerrilla manuals.

Last but by no means least is the highly significant growth of pro-terrorist sub-cultures and ideology in the universities and cultural centres of the developed states. Doctrines eulogising violence as "catharsis" and as the only true means of "liberation" were given a particular fillip by theorists of the 1968 New Left revolutionaries, particularly Jean-Paul Sartre, Frantz Fanon, and Che Guevara. (Interestingly there was simultaneously a reawakening of interest in that incorrigible old pro-terrorist Trotsky, and some of the currently active terrorist groups in Western Europe are affiliated to the Trotskyist Fourth International.)

The sharpening of the ideological–political struggles for control in many countries caused by the deepening economic recession has provided a climate of opportunity for the promoters of political violence. Growing industrial conflicts in Western Europe are likely to be exploited by extremists both of the extreme left and the extreme right, and those secretly working as agents of Soviet subversion. It would not be surprising if some or all of these groups were tempted to employ terrorism as part of the broader process of disruption.

There are two other broad trends in terrorism which have particularly significant implications for governments planning a counter-strategy. First is the development of much closer international co-operation between terrorist organisations. This process, in which politically violent movements in different countries, often with extremely diverse ideologies, have formed links with one another has been growing since as early as 1966, when many members of the embryonic "terrorist international" attended the conference of the Afro-Asian-Latin American Peoples' Solidarity Organisation in Havana.

These early links were cemented at the Baddawi meeting in Lebanon in May 1972, and at meetings in Algeria, Japan and Dublin in the same year. The meeting in Lebanon was hosted by representatives of the PFLP and Black September and attended by members of the Baader–Meinhof gang, the Japanese Red Army, the Turkish People's Liberation Army, the Iranian Liberation Front, the IRA and the Tupamaros. All these groups agreed to supply each other with arms and information and to carry out operations on behalf of and in the name of a brother movement, thus making it more difficult for the security forces to identify the culprits. This tactic was employed after the May 1972 meeting in Dublin, when the IRA exploded a bomb at the West German Embassy in Dublin. The Baader–Meinhof gang then claimed responsibility for the attack.

Another illustration of growing international terrorist co-operation was the establishment in 1974 of a Paris-based co-ordinating committee of Latin American terrorist organisations called the *Junta de Coordinacion Revolucionaria* (JCR). Constituent members of this body included remnants of the Uruguayan Tupamaros (now forced to operate abroad), the Argentinian People's Revolutionary Army (ERP) and Bolivia's National Liberation Army (ELN). Much of the financial support for this Europe-based organisation was provided by the ERP. The JCR formed links with European terrorist movements and with the Cubans.

Interesting evidence emerged in 1978[12] of links between the so-called "Corrective Movement of Al Fatah," led by Abu Nidal, and the Italian Red Brigades, involving the use of a Swiss courier or contact man. The Abu Nidal faction is believed to have been behind the murder of Youssef Sebai, an Egyptian newspaper editor, in Nicosia in February 1978, and the murder of Said Hammami, PLO representative in London. This group was also connected to West German terrorist groups and with Carlos. The Nidal group included Iraqis, Libyans, Palestinians and two Jordanians—a truly transnational gang.

Terrorists' advanced weaponry

A second major trend has been the terrorists' acquisition of increasingly sophisticated weaponry. As early as 1973 Italian police found two surface-to-air missiles (SAMs) of the Soviet SAM-7 type, hidden in a terrorist flat three miles along the main flightpath from Rome Airport. Other terrorist groups have acquired these weapons, and in 1976 a group of West German and Arab terrorists were foiled in their attempt to launch a missile attack on an Israeli civilian airliner on the outskirts of Nairobi.[13] (And indeed, in the context of an African nationalist campaign a SAM has been used to shoot down a Rhodesian airliner with 56 people on board, shortly after take-off from Kariba.) It is clearly possible for other terrorist movements to obtain this kind of weapon from a sympathetic régime or from one of the better equipped Palestinian terrorist organisations. They are relatively easy to transport and hide, and the hand-held heat-seeking missile can be operated by an individual terrorist.

Another worrying factor is the possibility of precision-guided munitions (PGMs) falling into terrorist hands. There is now a wide range of these extremely accurate weapons, designed for battlefield use, using a variety of guidance systems and many of them man-portable, all features making them particularly attractive for a terrorist group. For example, a PGM could be used to assassinate a head of state and his entire entourage at a ceremonial occasion from a hiding place several kilometres distant.

However, it would be a mistake to over-emphasise the significance of these more dramatic weapons. The enormous proliferation of conventional weaponry via the international arms market, particularly to Third World countries, has inevitably resulted in the diffusion of a large number of guns and grenades to terrorist movements. Many are obtained from sympathetic terrorist states, while others are stolen, or bought from international arms dealers. Among the most popular weapons are the AK 47 (or Kalashnikov) rifle, the VZ61 (or Skorpion) machine pistol, the Heckler and Koch MP5 sub-machine gun, and the Walther P38 pistol.

Terrorists have also been busy learning how to perfect more deadly bombs. So it is not surprising to find the PIRA passing on some of its specialised knowledge on the design of booby-traps and radio-controlled bombs to other terrorist groups in return for services rendered, while at the same time learning new techniques from foreign terrorists.

Much of the pooling of terrorist knowledge on techniques and tactics takes place through terrorist training bases, for instance in Lebanon and South Yemen, where promising recruits are sent for intensive training. Another source is the profusion of manuals on guerrilla war, sabotage and subversion, produced both by governments and the more highly organised terrorist movements. A Swiss Army manual has been used for this purpose recently and in 1977–78 a glossy and comprehensive handbook produced by an Argentinian terrorist group, the People's Revolutionary Army (ERP), circulated widely among Western European terrorists.

The target areas

Over half the terrorist bombings of the past few years have taken place in Western Europe, and more than half of all international terrorist incidents have occurred in NATO Europe and North America. Latin America continues to have a high incident level, while the really dramatic growth areas are the Middle East and North Africa. It is a predictable outgrowth of the wider conflicts in those areas. In the case of NATO Europe other factors apply: the relative freedom of movement and openness of the Western states creates a greater vulnerability.

Most terrorist movements operating internationally today have a crude neo-Marxist ideology and like to see themselves as champions of the "revolutionary masses" of the Third World. They consider it to be the terrorists' duty to hit at the erstwhile colonial and still, in their eyes, "capitalist–imperialist" states of Europe as well as the United States. They believe that the relative openness of "bourgeois democracies" is a confidence trick to sedate the masses and that it is their duty to punish the "guilt" of Europe. Small wonder they take such pleasure in seeking out the prestige targets of the Western world, spreading murder and destruction.

By carefully monitoring government and police assessments, terrorist pronouncements and threats, and by discerning the pattern of the latest international terrorist incidents it is possible to identify at least four terrorist "constituencies" that will continue to be a hazard to the international community in the foreseeable future.

The general outlook for Middle Eastern terrorism appears to be "more of the same". Ironically, the more the "moderate" Palestinian leaders try to bring their followers around to accepting a diplomatic compromise on a Palestinian state, ultimately involving acceptance of Israel's right to coexist with the new Palestinian entity (necessitating a change in the Palestinian Covenant), the more the maximalist and radical terrorist factions are likely to escalate the violence to frustrate the chances of such a settlement.

The Shi'ite Fundamentalist terrorists, far from automatically desisting in the moment of diplomatic opportunity, tend instead to launch even bloodier atrocities. And there are other groups of international terrorists who will be only too ready to participate. Moreover, for the first time the Arab moderate states themselves, their embassies, their politicians and diplomats, and their aircraft, are in the terrorists' sights.

Transnational attacks

Another major "growth area" is the increasing internationalisation of terror tactics by nationalist and separatist movements which had hitherto largely confined themselves to domestic struggles.

It is not, however, only West European nationalist terror groups which are "going international". There is some evidence that ethnic movements elsewhere, especially when they feel threatened or thwarted by vigorous repressive action in their home base, will turn to this method. Thus we are likely to see other groups such as the Kurds, and the Moro Liberation Front based in the Philippines, staging hijacks and embassy attacks in an effort to further the interests of the struggle "back home".

Exile terrorist groups operating almost entirely beyond the borders of their country of origin are likely to present a growing threat. They are especially drawn to the West European and North American arenas for it is only in democratic countries that they can be confident of gaining access to the media, and where they may hope to pick up some international support and sympathy. Nor should it be overlooked that many of these groups have deep and abiding grievances against particular régimes and leaders. Many of the communities these groups claim to represent have suffered grievously in the past—the Armenians and the Croats are just two examples—and hence there is a ready reservoir of sympathy and support among their respective emigré communities in many Western cities.

These terrorist groups inevitably pose a problem to the international community since repression or police action in their countries of origin forces them to operate abroad. Nor are their attacks directed exclusively against the representatives, such as diplomatic and consular officials of the régime they seek to influence or remove. These are, of course, their primary targets, but increasingly in recent years third states have themselves come under fire from these groups as a result of their attempts to curb terrorism within their own borders, to bring exile terrorists to trial or to apply extradition or deportation procedures.

This was exemplified in August 1978 when Croatian terrorists seized hostages at the West German Consulate in Chicago. The Croats, who threatened to kill the hostages unless their demands were met, were trying to force the West German authorities to free Stjepan Bilandzic, founder of a Croatian terrorist group, then serving a sentence in West Germany for his part in an attempt to assassinate the Vice-Consul of Yugoslavia stationed in Cologne.

The Yugoslavs regarded Bilandzic as one of the most important Croat extremists, and they wanted him extradited. The German authorities were reluctant to do this: they thought it questionable whether any Croat separatist could receive a fair trial in Yugoslavia and feared that amongst the Croatians living abroad in West Germany and elsewhere some could be provoked into retaliation. The Yugoslav authorities clearly expected full co-operation as the *quid pro quo* for their assistance in capturing four West German terrorist suspects in Yugoslavia. Indeed, the dilemma did not end with the eventual surrender of the terrorists to the Chicago authorities. When West Germany failed to extradite Bilandzic and several other Croatian exiles, Yugoslavia released the four West German terrorists from custody.

Exile terrorist groups have two other notable characteristics. First, they are extraordinarily persistent. This call of *patria* seems to remain undimmed even after decades of exile. This longevity of terrorist determination is well illustrated by the Armenian case. The horrifying tragedy of Turkish atrocities against the Armenians occurred over 70 years ago. Yet still there is a steady succession of Armenian exile attacks on Turkish representatives and other targets abroad. In June 1978 a group calling itself "New Armenian Resistance" (NAR) claimed responsibility for bomb attacks on the Turkish Bank in Haringey, London, and the Turkish Embassy in Brussels. An anonymous message to *Agence France Presse* in Brussels stated the attacks were to:

> Show the Turkish fascist state and Western imperialism that the Armenian people have a right to exist. The New Armenian Resistance calls on all Armenians to take up arms for a reunified, independent and Socialist Armenia.

This group and the self-styled Armenian Liberation Army may also have been responsible for the assassinations of Turkish ambassadors in several European cities a few years ago. The NAR statement is a characteristic example of the way in which national self-determination claims and a crude neo-Marxist terminology are merged in these groups.

Their second major characteristic is a form of intransigent fanaticism which makes them particularly difficult and ruthless opponents for democratic governments to deal with. A clear illustration of this was the conduct of the South Moluccan terror gangs in 1975 when they hijacked a Dutch train and dealt particularly ruthlessly with hostage passengers. The South Moluccan demands for a free South Moluccan state to which they could return clearly exceeded the powers of the Dutch people or government to deliver. And did they seriously believe that the Indonesian government would submit to this demand even though the terrorists had seized the

Indonesians' own consulate? The hopelessness of their cause may well have been closely related to their dangerous volatility and their fanatical capacity for sacrificing their own lives. South Moluccans are certainly likely to pose a continuing and dangerous terrorist threat for their host society, with all the attendant dangers of a backlash from the host population and a wider conflict.

The new Assassin sect

A by no means insubstantial threat which has become more apparent since 1977 arises from international terrorism on behalf of religious groups. In recent months this form of attack has reached a level of intensity recalling the heyday of the medieval Assassin sect. As this report goes to press Syrian Alawite and Sunni Moslem extremists are engaged in a sectarian terror war. In Iran and Iraq acts of violence by Shi'ites and votaries of the new-style fundamentalist Islam have been increasing rapidly. And a faction of the *Ananda Marg* group has been waging an international terror campaign against Indian government representatives,[14] calling for the release of their leader, Prahbat Sarkar, from jail.

The range of potential victims of international terrorism has also greatly increased. In a real sense everyone is in the front-line against this kind of sneak attack. Even when the terrorist claims to be selective and precise in his choice of target he cannot be certain that others will not be killed or injured in crossfire during an armed attack, or in a bombing attack who will be killed or injured by the blast. As noted earlier, bombing and incendiary attack remain far the most popular form of terrorist attack, resulting in a continuing steep rise in the numbers of casualties caused.

At the same time, as we have noted, there has also been a resurgence of assassination. But whereas, historically, the assassins' targets were generally confined to leading political figures and royalty, terrorists have recently tended to extend their "death lists" to include other individuals such as industrialists (like Herr Schleyer, murdered by West German terrorists), lawyers, judges, policemen, and middle-ranking diplomats and government officials.

The trend makes the problems of security and personal protection in democratic societies all the more acute. On the other hand, to the extent that it brings the threat of terrorism home to a much wider range of opinion leaders and ordinary citizens it also has the effect of closing ranks against the terrorists, enhances public support for resolute government action and creates a climate of greater co-operation and understanding between police and public. Further evidence of these helpful trends can be seen in the 1978/79 public demonstrations against terrorism called by the political parties in Bilbao, San Sebastián, Belfast and Rome.

Which are the more likely targets for attacks on property, industry, and communications? As suggested earlier one particularly vulnerable high-prestige, high-value target is the oil industry, its storage depots, pipelines, drilling platforms and tankers.[15] The PIRA attack at Canvey Island in

Britain on 17 January 1979 highlighted the potential danger of terrorist attacks on gas and oil storage facilities and all installations containing concentrations of industrial fuels and chemicals.

Further bomb attacks on civil nuclear plant and sites are another likely development. It is not likely, as often assumed, that the terrorist group will deliberately seek to perpetrate a nuclear disaster. More probable are bomb attacks by revolutionary or ecological extremist groups hoping to thwart a particular civil nuclear project, as was the case, for example, in the ETA attacks on the Lemóniz nuclear reactor in Northern Spain. But, of course, there is the very real danger that such "direct action" would trigger a disaster.

Finally, mention should be made of the danger of more hijacks and terrorist attacks on public transport on the ground. As aircraft hijacks become more hazardous to mount, so vulnerable airport terminals, and also rail and bus networks will become more attractive targets. So far only the South Moluccans and the PIRA have gone in for train hijacks on any scale. Fascist terrorists in Italy have blown up a train, and the Spanish ETA shot up a French passenger train. The fate of the South Moluccan terrorists may discourage rail hijacks but bombing and shooting attacks, or perhaps missile attacks on trains carrying important leaders or other terrorist targets, are an awesome prospect. The fact is that most rail companies and their staffs are not security-minded and there are few, if any, preventive or emergency procedures or contingency plans to deal with such attacks. (In September 1979 the "secret" detailed track route of the British royal train from Aberdeen to London for the Mountbatten funeral was lost, leaked—or stolen?—and reached the hands of a newspaper reporter.)

Rail security, even in countries with a good record of effective counter-terrorism, is generally so poor that it is an open invitation to the terrorist. As for attacks on buses, these have, on occasion, been mounted by Palestinian, PIRA and Japanese terrorists. It is difficult to see how public bus services can be adequately protected, especially in rural areas. They are wide open to hijack, bombing, and armed assaults. Attacks on passenger trains and buses may well become a growth area for terrorism in the 1980s.

II. INADEQUACY OF THE INTERNATIONAL RESPONSE

Attempts at international measures

The assassination of King Alexander of Yugoslavia and French Foreign Minister Louis Barthou at Marseilles in 1934 led to France proposing the establishment of an international criminal court to try terrorist criminals. The somewhat dilatory response of the League of Nations was to summon a conference on the subject at Geneva in 1937. This resulted in the drafting of two conventions.

The first proscribed acts of terrorism, which included attempts on the life of heads of state or their spouses and other government representatives. It also prohibited acts of international terrorism involving injury to persons or damage to property committed by citizens of one state against citizens of another state. The other convention set up an International Criminal Court and accorded it jurisdiction over terrorist crimes. But these bold and radical measures never came into effect because only 13 states had ratified the conventions before war broke out in 1939. The idea of an International Criminal Court for terrorist offences remains, however, a favourite cause among certain international lawyers, though in the absence of an agreed international criminal code, it appears not only premature but unrealistic in the foreseeable future.

It is not sufficiently recognised that the United Nations measures on human rights are directly applicable to the case of terrorism. The *Universal Declaration of Human Rights*, in addition to guaranteeing the right to life, liberty and the security of the person also states that "no one shall be subjected to torture or to cruel, inhuman or degrading treatment or punishment".[16] The right to enjoy "freedom from fear" is stressed in the preambles of both the *International Covenant on Economic, Social and Cultural Rights,* and the *International Covenant on Civil and Political Rights*.[17] Under article 6 of the latter, "no one shall be arbitrarily deprived of his life".[18]

The UN *Convention on the Prevention and Punishment of the Crime of Genocide* (1948) forbids the killing of members of a national, racial, ethnical or religious group, causing them serious bodily harm or severe mental distress to a particular group.[19] This is clearly an explicit prohibition of terror violence, whether committed by states, factions, or individuals. In addition the UN *Declaration on Principles of International Law* concerning friendly relations and co-operation among states enjoins states to refrain from "organising, assisting or participating in acts of civil strife or terrorist acts in another State . . ."[20]

UN ambiguity on "liberation"

However there is a fatal ambivalence in United Nations treatment of the whole question of politically motivated violence. In the *Declaration on Principles of International Law* the "principle of equal rights and self-determination of peoples" is put on the same level as the principle that states "shall refrain in their international relations from the threat or use of force against . . . any State, or in any manner inconsistent with the purposes of the UN". Significantly it proceeds to spell out that all States have a "duty to promote . . . realisation of the principle (of self-determination) . . . in order to bring a speedy end to colonialism . . ." and that "every state has the duty to refrain from any forcible action which deprives peoples . . . of their right to self-determination".

The Declaration continues "In their actions against, and resistance to, such forcible action in pursuit of their right to self-determination, such peoples are entitled to seek and to receive support . . .".

Naturally enough these clauses can be read as a legitimisation by the UN of any struggle undertaken in the name of the principle of national liberation, and an open invitation for international support for such struggles. Thus the UN is seen to be supporting both sides at once in such conflicts. For example Israel, as a member state, is accorded full "sovereign equality" and protection of that sovereignty. Simultaneously other member states of the UN can claim that they are fully entitled to arm and support movements dedicated to the liquidation of Israel, on the ground that they are merely supporting a legitimate national liberation struggle aimed at self-determination.

This double standard is clearly reflected in the UN's faltering attempts to deal with terrorism. Following the Munich Olympics massacre in 1972 Secretary General Kurt Waldheim requested the UN to deal with the menace of international terrorism. A study undertaken by the Secretariat was entitled "Measures to Prevent International Terrorism which Endangers or Takes Innocent Human Lives or Jeopardizes Fundamental Freedoms, and Study of the Underlying Cause of Those Forms of Terrorism and Acts of Terrorism Which Lie in Misery, Frustration, Grievance and Despair, and Which Causes Some People to Sacrifice Human Lives including Their Own, in an attempt to Effect Radical Changes."[21]

The title tells the whole story! The discussion revealed a clear split between those states wishing the UN to condemn and act against factional terrorism and those pro-terrorist states wanting to legalise terrorism by factions as a justifiable means of struggle. The latter group used the opportunity to attack Western states for "colonial and racist terror", and blamed them for "compelling" those engaged in "freedom struggles" to use violence to secure "justice". In the ensuing Ad Hoc Committee on International Terrorism, consisting of 35 states, which met in the Summer of 1973, the Third World states concentrated all their attention on attacking "state terrorism".

Justice for hijackers

The UN General Assembly did, however, agree, in December 1973, to adopt a *Convention on the Prevention and Punishment of Crimes against Internationally Protected Persons, including Diplomatic Agents*, and this Convention has now acquired sufficient ratifications by member states to come into effect. Further progress was made in the special field of international measures against aircraft hijacking. The Tokyo Convention on Offences and Certain Other Acts Committed on Board Aircraft (1963) sets out the jurisdictional guiding principles requiring contracting states to make every effort to restore control of the aircraft to its lawful commander and to ensure the prompt onward passage or return of the hijacked aircraft together with its crew, passengers, and cargo.

The 1970 Hague Convention requires contracting states either to extradite apprehended hijackers to their country of origin or to prosecute them under the judicial code of the recipient state. And the Montreal Convention of 1971 extended the scope of international law to encompass sabotage and attacks on airports and grounded aircraft. It also laid down the principle that such offences be subject to severe penalties. Unfortunately, despite the encouraging readiness of the majority of states to ratify these conventions, there is still no international convention providing for effective sanctions to ensure enforcement and the punishment of states that aid or give sanctuary to hijackers.

In December 1976 the UN established an ad hoc committee to draft a convention against the taking of hostages. This was an initiative urged by Western Germany and other Western states, but it was so weakened in the process of drafting as to become practically useless. The only other useful recent move by the UN was a General Assembly resolution condemning hijacking.

Pro-terrorist states such as South Yemen, Cuba, Iraq, Libya and Algeria, though they may join talks on counter-measures, repeatedly give aid and succour to terrorist groups. It is important to note that pro-terrorist countries go considerably beyond mere ideological and diplomatic support: they are in fact an important part of the problem. States such as Libya, South Yemen and Iraq have provided considerable sums of money and supplies of modern weapons to their protégé terrorist gangs. They also make available extensive terrorist training facilities, sanctuary for terrorists on the run, the use of embassies as hideouts and as sources of weapons and false documents, and of the diplomatic pouch to smuggle weapons and explosives— and, when necessary, their own radio communications links.

It is easy enough to understand the indifference to terrorism of countries such as India, Bangladesh and Indonesia. They are poor countries struggling to feed vast populations and preoccupied with the need for economic development. But in those regions of the world which have suffered most from terrorism there have been some tangible advances towards closer co-operation. For instance, after the spate of diplomatic kidnappings in Latin America between 1968 and 1971 the Organisation of American States (OAS) formulated a *Convention to Prevent and Punish Acts of Terrorism Taking the Form of Crimes Against Persons and Related Extortion that are of International Significance*.

In terms of Latin American legal tradition this was remarkably bold innovation, for Latin American states have always held the principle of political asylum to be sacrosanct. The OAS Convention circumvented this by defining attacks against internationally protected persons common crimes, regardless of motive, thus making it possible to apply the *aut dedere aut punire* (extradite or prosecute) formula in all such cases. Unfortunately, however, ratification and effective implementation of this formula has been thwarted by legal conservatism.

Substantial progress has been made in the field of international co-operation in Western Europe, but as already indicated this has not sufficed to prevent this region experiencing a higher proportion of terrorist attacks than any other. The EEC Ministers of the Interior, and the police forces and intelligence services of the member states have since 1976 developed regular machinery for discussion and practical multilateral co-operation.

But the most ambitious attempt at European co-operation at the judicial level is the Council of Europe *Convention on the Suppression of Terrorism*, which 17 out of 19 Council of Europe member states signed in January 1977, when the Convention was opened for signature.[22]

"Political" offences loophole

The Convention provides, in effect, that all ratifying states will exclude the whole range of major terrorist offences, such as assassination, hostage-taking, bomb attacks and hijacking, from the political offence exception clauses that had previously been used to justify refusal of extradition; in other words to ensure that all contracting states would treat such offences as common crimes. In cases where, because of some technical or constitutional difficulty, a contracting state is unable to carry out extradition the Convention obliges the authorities to bring the suspect to trial before their own courts. Mutual assistance in criminal investigation of such offences is also made mandatory.

However, the admirable intentions of this Convention have been seriously obstructed by two major shortcomings. First, a possible escape clause was inserted into the Convention permitting a contracting state to reserve the right to regard a certain offence as political, and hence to withhold extradition.

Second, the process of ratification has been disgracefully slow, despite the speedy signature of the Convention in January 1977. France and Belgium, for example, have been reluctant to ratify on the grounds that they are constitutionally committed to guarantee the right of political asylum. (It seems odd that, despite all the careful safeguards in the Convention, they are still unprepared to exclude those charged with serious crimes of terrorism from this right.) And by late 1978 only five member states had completed ratification (Sweden, Austria, West Germany, Denmark and Great Britain). In these circumstances President Giscard d'Estaing's much publicised idea, voiced in 1978, of an *espace judiciaire européenne* (a European judicial zone) seemed, to say the least, premature.

Two other recent moves to improve international co-operation against terrorism are worth mentioning. At their Bonn Summit meeting of July 1978, the Heads of Government of Canada, France, Italy, Japan, the United Kingdom, the United States and West Germany came out with a firm collective statement promising sanctions against states aiding and abetting aircraft hijacking. Their communiqué stated:

> In cases where a country refuses the extradition or prosecution of those who have hijacked an aircraft, or refuses to return it, the Heads of State or government are additionally resolved that they will take immediate action to cease all flights to that country. At the same time their governments will initiate action to halt all incoming flights from that country or from any country, by the airlines of the country concerned.

Experts met in August 1978 to discuss the practicalities of implementing this agreement. There is every reason to welcome this firm stand in favour of sanctions by the major Western states, for it may exert a continuing deterrent effect against rogue states which have, in the past, helped to encourage hijacking. However, a cynic might note that aircraft hijacking was no longer the major terrorist threat by July 1978: action had really been needed in 1969–73 when the menace was at its peak.

Finally, there was an encouragingly positive meeting of the EEC Ministers of Justice in early October 1978 which proposed a similar Convention to the Council of Europe Convention on the Suppression of Terrorism for use between all the nine EEC states, again based on the *aut dedere aut punire* principle. Under this Convention, there would still be an escape "political exception" clause, and so there is presumably some chance that Ireland might accede to the new Convention.

Intelligence and police co-operation

One of the most important aspects of Western co-operation is the strengthening of the machinery for multilateral police and intelligence co-operation, and this has generally progressed far more rapidly than political and judicial co-operation. It takes place at five different levels.

1. Interpol (the International Criminal Police Organisation) is under its constitution strictly confined to dealing with ordinary law crimes, but as this covers many terrorist acts the organisation has had some value in acting as a clearing house for information. For instance, in July 1976 Athens police were able to identify a West German terrorist, Rolf Pohle, with the aid of the Interpol photos, and detain him.

2. NATO has developed a valuable system for exchange of intelligence concerning terrorist weapons, personnel and techniques, which has been of great assistance to member states.

3. Joint training visits and exchanges of security personnel are now well established among the EEC and NATO countries.

4. Bilateral co-operation has been provided on an ad hoc basis at the request of governments. Thus, British SAS personnel, techniques and weapons have been made available to support Dutch and West German counter-terrorist operations. And the West German computer bank of data on terrorists has been used in the fight against terrorism in Italy and elsewhere.

5. There is a permanent structure of police co-operation between EEC member states of particular value in combating cross-border terrorism.

Bilateral co-operation

It is not generally realised that one of the most effective methods of co-operation against terrorism takes the form of bilateral agreements between neighbouring states. A notable instance of this occurred in the *US–Cuba Hijack Pact* of February 1973, in which both governments agreed to return hijacked aircraft, crews, passengers and hijackers. It is true that Cuba insisted on a caveat enabling her to refuse to return terrorists affiliated to a national liberation movement recognised by Cuba. But as most hijackers who sought sanctuary in Cuba from the US were criminals or psychopaths this clause did not undermine the effectiveness of the agreement. Moreover, even though Cuba refused formally to renew the agreement, following the blowing-up of a Cuban airliner by anti-Castro exiles in October 1976, the fact is that Cuba has continued to operate in the spirit of the Pact, and it has undoubtedly contributed to the defeat of the hijacking plague that afflicted the USA between 1970 and 1972.

An even more unlikely example of partnership was the co-operation between Somalia and West Germany in the GSG-9 (Grenzschutzgruppen 9—the German anti-terrorist unit) operation to rescue the Lufthansa hostages at Mogadishu. After all, Somalia was a Marxist régime which had previously been used as a base by terrorists organising the Air France hijack to Entebbe. Yet, encouraged by the prospect of economic assistance, the new state rendered valuable service by allowing in the German rescue squad.

If such diverse political systems can co-operate profitably, surely it should not be beyond the power of the Western European states to improve their own bilateral security co-operation? There is some encouraging recent evidence that this is being developed in two areas particularly hard-hit by terrorist violence over the past decade: the Basque region and Northern Ireland. In January 1979 France abolished refugee status for Spanish nationals in France, on the sensible ground that Spain, as a democracy, no longer had political refugees. Almost simultaneously 13 Spanish Basques living near the Spanish border were banished to the remote Hautes-Alpes in eastern France. This was France's very positive response to Spanish Government demands for more vigorous co-operation to stamp out terrorism.

French border country has long been regarded as a valuable sanctuary and launching-point for ETA terrorism, and the new measures will do much to assist the Spanish authorities' counter-terrorist drive. France itself has a strong interest in helping to combat ETA terrorism, for the recent assassinations in France of two Basque leaders in revenge attacks were an unpleasant warning of the way in which ETA terrorism could spill over the frontier.

In the wake of the Provisional IRA massacres at Warrenpoint and Mullaghmore on August Bank Holiday Monday 1979[23] the governments of the Irish Republic and the United Kingdom have held a series of meetings to discuss closer security co-operation. The measures agreed in the talks held in September and October are an excellent practical illustration of co-operation between two parliamentary democracies to curb a terrorist campaign of murder which threatens them both. The new measures, including improved border co-operation, are a bold and imaginative effort to curb terrorism which is now the major obstacle to a lasting peace and reconciliation in Ireland.

Extradition problems

If the international community is to minimise the rewards of terrorism and maximise its risks and costs it must be seen to be possible to bring terrorist suspects to justice even when they slip across frontiers. But extradition is a highly complex and unpredictable process. Many states do not have extradition agreements, and where these do exist they frequently exclude political offences—the term "political" is often very liberally construed. Differences in criminal codes, procedures and judicial traditions also have to be taken into account. Often the extradition procedures become highly protracted, owing to difficulties of obtaining evidence and witnesses from abroad. In the British extradition hearings in the case of Astrid Proll in 1978/79 there was a further complication—a dispute over nationality. (Despite delays and difficulties, however, Astrid Proll was eventually extradited to West Germany where she was charged with attempted murder of two policemen and other crimes.)

Extradition proceedings succeed in the cases of only a small minority of terrorist suspects. Between January 1960 and June 1976, 20 states requested extradition of 78 hijackers but this was granted in only five cases, though 42 of the offenders were prosecuted by the recipient state. Small wonder that in many cases states use deportation as a form of "disguised extradition" and as this is a civil—as opposed to criminal—proceeding it does not afford the individual the same opportunities to present his or her own case. However, deportation merely shifts the problem to another state, and does not ensure that a suspected terrorist is brought to justice. On all these grounds this method ought not to be encouraged. A far more desirable course is for states to attempt to standardise their criminal codes and procedures to facilitate the application of the "extradite or prosecute" principle.

Nor is it the case that states can always be depended upon to honour the letter or spirit of their extradition agreements. A government which fears a retaliatory attack by terrorists or which is subject to blackmail by, say, the Arab oil weapon, may well decide that "national interest" demands that they let a suspect go free. A notorious case occurred in January 1977, when Abu Daoud, suspected of involvement in the planning of the Munich massacre, was arrested in Paris on an Interpol warrant issued by the West German police. Israel immediately announced that it would request Daoud's extradition, on the ground that he was to be charged with the murder of Israeli citizens.

A Paris court rejected attempts to extradite him, and he was allowed to travel to Algeria. The West German authorities expressed surprise and regret at this decision, and the international community drew the conclusion that the French government had put its desire for remunerative new commercial agreements with Arab states before its obligations to combat international terrorism.

III. GUIDELINES FOR THE DEMOCRACIES' RESPONSE

If, as has been argued, effective action through world bodies is currently impracticable, what should the Western democracies do to counter the threat of international terrorism? As has already been made clear, this threat is largely directed towards the democratic societies of Western Europe and North America. What can we usefully do?

First and foremost, we should keep our democratic systems in good political and economic repair. In particular we should try to respond positively to the changing needs and demands of the populace, including protecting the rights of minorities. This requires balanced and effective structures of representative democracy at both local and national level, with ultimate control by the elected bodies over the bureaucracy, armed forces, police, and security services, ensuring their full accountability. A sure sign of danger is the accretion of overweening power by officials or by specific agencies of the state.

An independent judiciary is a prerequisite for the maintenance of the rule of law and the constitution and a vital ally of the elected government and legislature in ensuring democratic control and accountability. In a terrorist situation it is essential that the authorities and security forces act entirely within the law. Extra-legal actions will only tend to undermine democratic legitimacy and destroy public confidence. Any breach of legality will be exploited by terrorist propagandists to show the hypocrisy of government and security forces' claims to be acting in the name of the law, and to try to persuade waverers that the government is not worth supporting.

Operating outside the strict rule of law is thus not only morally wrong: it is likely to be counter-productive. In observing these legal constraints democratic governments must constantly make it clear that when terrorists are convicted and punished it is not because of their professed political beliefs but because they have committed serious criminal offences. So because the punishment is for criminal *deeds* and not for political motives or causes it would be totally wrong to accord jailed terrorists some "special status" as "political prisoners". Refusal to grant such status is entirely consistent with the philosophy of judicial control common to all the Western democracies, and is implicit in the terms of the European Convention on the Suppression of Terrorism which seeks to define certain terroristic offences as common crimes.[24]

It is also vital for democratic governments to strive for a sound and healthy economy, and it is in all their interests to co-operate more effectively in creating the right policies to deal with those now universal twin evils of Western economies—runaway inflation and high unemployment. In a climate of massive recession and industrial collapse it is inevitable that the fear and frustration generated among the working population will give rise to militant and violent confrontations. Economic chaos and collapse create a far greater danger of destabilisation of democracy than the actions of a handful of terrorists are likely to cause. *For it is in the conditions of major economic breakdown that the real threat of a wider escalation into internal war (in which terrorism would play merely a minor or catalysing role) really lies.*

Avoiding over-reaction

Hence, the best advice one can tender to democratic governments on international terrorism is not to over-react against this particular menace[25] and to attend to the vital strategic tasks of ensuring economic and political survival. There are, of course, some useful practical steps that can be taken, for example among the EEC members, to improve the machinery of international police and security co-operation. Some of the more cost-effective of these possible measures are suggested below, and in the writer's view they would be worth adopting because they would help to save innocent lives and would substantially increase the rate of apprehension and conviction of terrorists. It would, moreover, be a great advantage if other states less advanced than Western Europe and the USA in their measures for international co-operation in this field could be encouraged to follow the West's example and to accede to, and implement, the basic international conventions and agreements designed to curb terrorism.

What is needed is a cool appraisal of the longer-term threat posed to liberal democratic society by terrorism, and the kind of measures that will help effectively to protect innocent life without sacrificing the rights of the individual. More radical responses involving sweeping emergency legislation and modification of normal judicial procedures and processes are not normally justified in the democratic West. The only exceptions are perhaps Northern Ireland and the Basque region in Spain where emergency powers have become necessary as a result of the worst protracted terrorist campaigns experienced in Western Europe this century.

In the West such emergency or special powers would normally not only be unjustified and unnecessary; they would be totally counter-productive. For the real danger of resorting to sledge-hammer methods to cope with the relatively low intensities of political violence experienced in most Western countries is that they would extinguish democracy in the name of security. If we were to do this we would effectively be doing the terrorists' work for them and, moreover, with a speed and certainty that they themselves are incapable of achieving.

IV. SOME PRACTICAL STEPS

There are some additional general measures, both national and international, that should be taken by the Western democracies. The steps suggested below would not be expensive to implement, and none of them would court the dangers of unbalanced response or overaction that have already been emphasised.

1. The Western democracies should patiently continue their efforts to alter the climate of international opinion to improve the long-term chances of creating a more effective framework of international law to deal with terrorism. Thus, despite all the difficulties and obstacles discussed earlier, all Western states should lend their diplomatic support, votes, and influence, in international organisations and conferences:

- To persuade non-ratifying states to accede to existing useful multilateral agreements, such as the Tokyo, Hague and Montreal conventions to curb air hijacking,
- To press for strengthening existing conventions particularly in regard to enforcement provisions and sanctions, and,
- To lend their full weight to useful fresh initiatives for international conventions. Even when it seems unlikely that a new initiative will surmount all the hurdles of international opposition, or when it is clear that only a handful of states will accord such measures immediate ratification, support is still worthwhile: if nothing else, it serves to educate the international community in the danger of terrorism and the vital need for international co-operation to counter it. Moreover, by exposing the opposition and obstruction of other states, such exercises help to identify the crypto-terrorist régimes. There is, furthermore, always the chance that the sheer weight of international pressure may cause a government to reconsider its earlier support for terrorism, or to move from neutrality or ambivalence to positive support for humanitarian international measures designed to protect the innocent.

2. A second useful step would be to press for speedy ratification and implementation of the Council of Europe Convention on the Suppression of Terrorism, and the parallel European Community agreement.

A coordinating group

3. There is also a real need to create a small international commission or specialist department, preferably under the aegis of the EEC, to coordinate Western co-operation against international terrorism. There is already a framework of regular meetings of European Ministers of the Interior, and for police coordination and intelligence sharing. Bilateral co-operation between police forces, intelligence services and specialist anti-terrorist units is far more advanced than collaboration at the judicial and political levels, but is at present conducted on a piecemeal basis.

A central coordinating anti-terrorist cell of say half-a-dozen top security and intelligence experts, with adequate research and administrative support and access to all meetings of Community Ministers of the Interior and Justice, and the intelligence and police chiefs of member states, could add immeasurably to the precision and quality of the international response. The new unit should provide expert analysis of intelligence data, assessment of capabilities and threats, a continuing research and development back-up, including work on the pooling of counter-terrorist weaponry and technology, training and briefing services, and advice to Ministers, police, and security services.

One of its most urgently needed contributions would be to provide coordinated contingency plans and crisis-management machinery when two or more member states are involved in an incident. It should also help to organise joint exercises in hostage rescue and other counter-terrorist operations and supervise training of personnel of member states in hostage negotiation. This coordinating commission could also serve as a means to improve anti-terrorist intelligence links between the EEC states and other democracies such as the USA, Japan, Canada and Australia. It could promote research in improved technologies of prevention and encourage higher standards of security education in government and industry.

4. All democratic governments must hold firm to a strict policy of "no deals with terrorists", and no submission to blackmail. Consistent national policies of minimising terrorists' chances of rewards and maximising the probability of punishment are most likely to stem the flow of terrorist killings in the longer term.

Countering propaganda

5. The democracies must also learn to defeat the terrorists' sustained propaganda war. Efforts to disguise themselves as legitimate "freedom-fighters" must be exposed. The free media in particular owe a responsibility to the democratic societies which enable them to exist.[26] It is their job to expose the savage barbarism of the crimes and atrocities committed by terrorists. It is not their job to condone such acts or to lend murderers the freedom of the air to preach and promote more deaths. But, of course, in the last resort it is not a democracy's government or its security forces, or even its media that will determine the outcome of the long, long war against international terrorism: it is the degree of public support for democracy.

6. There is furthermore a real need for a voluntary and totally independent international organisation to minister to the special needs of victims of international terrorism. Some governments, such as the Dutch in the wake of the South Moluccan attacks, have shown considerable imagination and insight in ministering to the needs of the survivors of terrorist incidents, and the families of the bereaved. The United Kingdom has taken steps to provide for compensatory payments to victims of terrorist troubles, and for damage to property and business premises. By comparison with some of the awards the pensions and other benefits for members of the security forces seem pitifully inadequate, and this is a matter the British government should attend to as a matter of urgency.

However, one must remember that in most countries victims of terrorism receive no assistance whatever from the state. And even where some provision exists there is often a vital need for medical and specialist services which only a voluntary organisation could provide. Over most of the world these are forgotten people. Yet they often have the most desperate needs for specialist medical care, psychiatric help, and family and financial support. The proposed organisation might perhaps be best established under the aegis of the International Red Cross. And of course, even if it proves necessary to set up a separate body, the advice and expertise of that body of mercy should be sought.

But the most important consideration in arriving at an appropriate response to terror violence must be the strengthening of democracy and human rights. It is by these means above all that we can be sure of denying victory to those who have been corrupted by hatred and violence.

NOTES

[1] Sources: CSO *Abstract of Statistics 1977*, No. 114; and *Hansard* (written answers) 7 March 1978.

[2] For some evidence of this see interview with "Bombi" Baumann, reprinted in *Encounter* (September 1978).

[3] For instance, on 7 September 1979 an Alitalia aircraft en route from Teheran to Rome was hijacked an hour after its stopover at Beirut.

[4] *Terrorism and the Liberal State*, pp. 47–68, Macmillan, 1977.

[5] In *Political Terrorism* (1974) and *Terrorism and the Liberal State* (1977), Macmillan.

[6] See *The Surrogate Forces of the Soviet Union* by Brian Crozier, *Conflict Study* No. 92.

[7] See M. Lasky, "Ulrike Meinhof and the Baader–Meinhof Gang", *Encounter*, June 1975.

[8] See *Conflict Study* No. 41, *Libya's Foreign Adventures*.

[9] David Anable, *Christian Science Monitor*, March 15, 1977, pp. 14–16.

[10] See John Barron, *KGB*, New York, 1974, pp. 76–77.

[11] *Newsweek*, 17 April 1978, p. 33. On Soviet aid for these and other terrorist groups see also "Al Fatah; Voll in den Handen Moskaus", *Der Spiegel*, Nr. 33/1979; and "Am langen Arm des KGB: Terroristen-Bos Aarafat", *Deutschland-Magazin*, Nr. 9/1979.

[12] *Al Ahram*, 24 April 1978.

[13] On 11 September 1979 an Israeli court sentenced two West German terrorists to 10 years' imprisonment for their part in the plot.

[14] Three members of the sect were convicted at St. Alban's Crown Court in November 1978 of plotting to kill London-based officials of the Indian High Commission (*The Times*, 4 November 1978).

[15] A dramatic illustration of the potential dangers occurred on 31 August 1979, when a microwave communications station in the Iranian oil province of Khuzestan was blown up. In consequence all telephone links between the Port of Khorramshahr, the major oil refinery at Abadan and the rest of the country were severed. This attack, and the sabotage of gas and oil pipelines in Iran in July, indicate some of the dangerous effects of terrorism and widening political instability in the Gulf region, and elsewhere in the Middle East.

[16] Univ. Declar. of Human Rights, Arts. 3, 5, GA Res. 217A, UN Doc. A/810, at 71, 72–73 (1948).

[17] GA Res. 2200, 21 UN GAOR. Supp. (No. 16) 49, UN Doc. A/6316 (1966).

[18] Ibid. at 52.

[19] GA Res. 260A. UN Doc. A.810 (1948), 78 UNTS 277, 286 (1951).

[20] GA Res. 2625, artl. 25 UN GAOR Supp. (No. 28), 121, 123, UN Doc. A/8028 (1970).

[21] 27 UN GAOR Annex (Agenda Item 92) 1, UN Doc. A/C. 6/418 (1972).

[22] The only member states which refused to sign were Ireland and Malta.

[23] Eighteen British soldiers were murdered in the Warrenpoint ambush on the same day that the Mountbatten boat was blown up at Mullaghmore.

[24] This principle was strongly reiterated by the European Union of Police Federations at its conference in Cologne, 19 September 1979. The conference recommended the acceptance of a European police charter which includes the removal of political status from terrorist groups such as the IRA. It is noteworthy that this move was welcomed by the delegate from the Garda Police Association who stated "The view of my association is that people who contravene the criminal code are only criminals and no cause can justify them being other than that".

[25] One of the terrorists' major strategems is to provoke the authorities into a repressive over-reaction that will alienate the people and drive them into the arms of the terrorist movement. See Carlos Marighela, *Minimanual of the Urban Guerrilla*.

[26] See *Television and Conflict*, ISC Special Report, May 1979.

First published 1979. Minor amendments 1985.

Political Hostage-taking
in Western Europe

Clive C. Aston

Attempts by terrorist organisations to discredit liberal democratic states have constituted a main form of subversion over the last decade or so. Hostage-taking, in particular, seeks to undermine the authority of governments by threats to individuals and playing on the emotions of their families and of other sympathetic citizens. Clive Aston not only assembles in this study new and often sensational statistics, but describes in detail the moral and political dilemmas facing legal governments. He shows how important is the maintenance of the nerve and courage of those responsible for law and order and the need for popular support for firm action to preserve civilised societies, especially in Western Europe.

The taking of hostages for political gain is one of the most dramatic and potent forms of contemporary terrorism. No other tactic is more likely to cause a severe disruption to the normal flow of national and international relations. Governments are truly held to ransom and political order directly threatened. States have more than once been forced into altering their national policies according to the dictates of small armed groups able to operate with seeming impunity in hydra-like fashion. On the international level, incidents such as the 1979 occupation of the US Embassy in Tehran by militant students may indeed pose "the most serious threat to world peace since the Cuban missile crisis".[1]

Political hostage incidents are political crises requiring political solutions. Unless effectively responded to and successfully managed, incidents may have immediate as well as long-term adverse repercussions for a host government. The ultimate aim of governments in responding must be to contain and minimise the effects of the crisis. This can only be achieved by understanding how the incident itself will restrict the various possible response options available to a host government.

Geographical distribution[2]

As Table 1 illustrates (see centre pages) there have been 146 political hostage incidents within the countries of the Council of Europe between 1 January 1970 and 31 December 1982 plus a further 15 attempted incidents and a final 14 which were planned but never conducted. There does not appear to be any easy explanation why some countries became unwitting hosts to a political hostage incident and others did not. There seems little to differentiate the seven countries which escaped (Denmark, Liechtenstein, Iceland, Luxembourg,

Malta, Norway and Portugal) from the 14 which suffered. All share up to a point comparable traditions, customs, values, norms, political and economic systems and, most importantly, the same legal prohibitions against the taking of hostages. Even the 14 countries which have experienced incidents appear to differ little.

There is, however, one correlation which can be made. Countries with long-standing separatist movements or non-integrated foreign exile communities or with pronounced local cultures of violence have suffered most. Examples abound. Spain has long been faced with the separatist movement ETA (*Euskadi ta Askatasuna*) in the northern Basque region and leads the Council of Europe countries with the greatest number of incidents. The South Moluccans in the Netherlands and the Harkis in France have not generally integrated into the host society and remain cloistered in their own communities. Italy has experienced the second largest number of political hostage incidents and also leads the Council of Europe countries in criminial hostage-takings. In 1982 alone 39 people were kidnapped and held for ransom.[3]

It has also been suggested that "kidnappings are more likely in countries where the terrorists are operating on home terrain and have an underground organisation . . . (and) barricade and hostage incidents are more likely when the terrorists are operating abroad or in countries where they lack the capability for sustaining underground operations."[4] The experience of Western Europe bears this out. Of the 75 politically motivated kidnappings known to have occurred, 74 have been conducted by indigenous groups or local chapters of foreign groups. Similarly, of the 71 sieges, 66 have been conducted by groups operating abroad or with no local underground capability. Expatriate students, for example, have been involved in 23 incidents of which all but one were sieges. There is a notable exception to this putative rule. The Palestinians possess an undeniable organisational ability and an effective underground capability in Western Europe but have never engaged in kidnapping.

Nature of group involved

As Table 2 illustrates, responsibility for seizing hostages for political gain has been claimed by 35 different, though not necessarily autonomous groups and factions. However, not all incidents have been conducted by terrorists. In one, the 1978 kidnapping of Father Hugh Murphy in Ulster, the supposed terrorists were officers of the Royal Ulster Constabulary posing as members of the Ulster Freedom Fighters.

Groups which have engaged in political hostage-taking can be classified according to various criteria, such as ideology, tactical and strategic objectives, structural size and sociological composition.[5] Some groups, such as the Harkis or the Group of the Martyr, are either not overly politicised or have an unclear, even confused ideology. Other groups, such as the Japanese Red Army or Italy's *Nuclei Armati Proletari* (NAP), are avowedly anarchist or Marxist while still others, such as the *Fuerza Nueva* of Italy or the Croats' Ustachi, are right-wing. Some groups are less doctrinaire and change their political orientation according to the dictates of the moment. The Provisional Irish

Republican Army (PIRA) only adopted a left-wing stance when it became apparent their sources of arms from the US were drying up and they would have to turn to other groups for re-supply.

The tactical and strategic objectives of groups engaged in political hostage-taking also varies considerably. The Palestine Liberation Organisation (PLO) on the one extreme, see themselves as engaged in a struggle for national liberation, while at the opposite end of the spectrum, the Fighters for the Defence of Israel seem to exist only to combat their ideological rivals. The structural size of groups also varies, from the Red Brigades of Italy with an identified active membership of over 1,200[6] to Black December, whose sole membership consisted of the three hostage-takers involved in the siege of the Indian High Commission in London in 1973. Even the sociological composition of groups is dissimilar and ranges from the 2 June Movement where over 65 per cent of the membership was from the middle class[7] to the PIRA whose membership is predominantly from the working class.

Research into why some groups or individuals seize hostages is still far from complete.[8] However, it can be assumed their behaviour will be governed by the same fundamental principles and processes which apply to all social interactions.[9] Indeed, it has been noted that the terrorists's "cause . . . is the *sine qua non* of his actions; except for his belief in the cause, he would be in all respects rational."[10] Therefore, findings from the study of similar small groups under similar conditions of external danger would be equally valid.

It can be stated as axiomatic that different groups have different norms and standards of behaviour which will serve as a model for future behaviour, especially during similar operations. These will almost certainly be adhered to by the members of the group if they wish to retain their membership in it. If the group or a faction within the group has engaged in hostage-taking before, their behaviour and conduct in, for instance, releasing women and children or sick hostages, is more likely to be replicated by other members of the same faction in the future once that particular norm has been established. For this reason particularly, accurate intelligence files on past incidents and up-to-date information on any changes in leadership or apparent behaviour patterns are an operational necessity for those government agencies likely to be called upon to respond.

It can also be taken as axiomatic that claims of membership in a particular group will imply a willingness to live up to group expectations of behaviour. More significantly, it can be assumed that the need to be seen as a member of a particular group is more overpowering and primary than the fear of retaliation or punishment because of membership. As Freud has stated:

> For the moment (the group) replaces the whole of human society, which is the wielder of authority, whose punishments the individual fears, and for whose sake he has submitted to so many inhibitions. It is clearly perilous for him to put himself in opposition to it, and it will be safer to follow the example of those around him and perhaps even "hunt with the pack". In obedience to the new authority he may put his former "conscience" out of action and so surrender to the attraction of the increased pleasure that is clearly obtained from the removal of inhibitions.[11]

A graphic illustration of the intensity and potential consequences of this need to be seen as a member of a group occurred during the final selection of the members of Black September who were later to conduct the 1972 Munich Olympics siege:

> Most of them came from average families who had family members in prisons in Israel. All were ignorant of the operation they might have to undertake. However, they were all so eager to be the lucky ones chosen. The final choice created some tragedy. One of the young fedayeen was kept out because two of his brothers had already died in combat. This young man became furious and complained and started to cry. He then went on to threaten suicide if he was not chosen. So the people responsible allowed him to join the group. He was one of the first to die from West German bullets.[12]

A further Freudian theory of group behaviour which appears to be equally applicable are the group's transference reactions toward the leader who fulfils the role of a parent surrogate. It has been noted that members of a group who are exposed to external danger "become extraordinarily sensitive to (the leader's) demands, continually attempting to do and say things that will please him, reacting with bitter disappointment at any apparent slights, and becoming depressed or aggrieved whenever they are not in communication with him."[13] An example of this need to impress and gain the approval of the leader occurred during the 1975 OPEC siege when Gabriele Krocker-Tiedemann boasted to Carlos, the leader, "I've killed two."[14]

Nature of victims

Historically, hostages were chosen according to their quality or their quantity. The kidnapping of Richard the Lionheart by Duke Leopold of Austria in 1193 secured a vast ransom from England whereas Barbarossa relied on the seizure of 300 hostages to secure a favourable peace treaty with Milan in 1158.

As Table 3 illustrates, the largest proportion of the 1,066 hostages who have been seized in Western Europe were innocent bystanders who just happened to be there. There are some terrorist groups who would argue, after the nineteenth century anarchist Emile Henry, that no one is innocent. For example, the three Jewish emigrés seized in 1973 by the Eagles of the Palestinian Revolution from the Chopin Express were seen to be legitimate targets because they were Jewish and, more importantly, they were emigrating to Israel. Nonetheless, there are other victims, such as hotel guests and schoolchildren who appear to have been adjudged guilty simply by reason of their being in the wrong place at the wrong time.

It has been suggested that a hostage is a mere symbol as far as the terrorist is concerned.[15] Nowhere is this more the case than with politicians and other symbolic leaders, such as royalty or leading figures in the commercial or industrial sectors whose very occupations are seen as representative of the "bourgeois–capitalist" system the terrorist usually wants to change or destroy. An attack against one of these individuals is essentially an attack against the system itself. From the terrorists' point of view, it is also more cost-effective to attack a symbol of the system than to engage in a larger-scale revolutionary war for which they may not be structurally or logistically equipped.

Hostages have only rarely been seized specifically because of their nationality and nothing else. No particular nationality has been singled out for special attention by any terrorist group as part of a concerted or widespread campaign. When such incidents have occurred, either demands focused on the national's government or the government was seen capable of forcing an acquiescence to demands.

Ethnic bias is more pronounced, though not against usual targets of ethnic hatred. Jews, for example, have only twice been seized intentionally. Of all ethnic groups represented in Western Europe, Arabs have suffered disproportionately at the hands of political hostage-takers. No other ethnic group has been seized in such numbers or with such frequency; 193 Arabs have been taken hostage in 14 separate incidents. Arabs are also disproportionately more at risk from criminal hostage-takers. Threats and actual seizures have increased so dramatically in recent years that the Lloyd's kidnap and ransom insurance market has been prompted into developing a specific package of protection for Arab clients.

Nature of demands

Political hostage incidents can accurately be thought of as an attempt by the terrorist at a coercive value exchange. The hostage will only be exchanged for something the terrorist deems to be of equivalent value. This will be dictated by the perceived future needs of the terrorists, either immediately in the case of demands for escape or long-term in the case of demands for a ransom. The 1976 kidnapping of Rickard Oetker, for example, was used by the Red Army Faction as a means of obtaining funding for future operations against the West German Government.

The demands themselves tend to identify the ultimate arbiter of a decision to acquiesce. In political hostage incidents, the host government has a constitutional interest in the outcome but the nature of the demands may preclude its active involvement. It may not possess sole decision-making authority and may have to share decision-making with other actors. During the 1975 OPEC siege in Vienna, for example, there were 12 governments involved in the decision-making process. In other incidents, such as kidnappings for ransom, a government may not even learn of the incident until after it has ended. Indeed, it has been noted that during politically motivated kidnappings for ransom "there is often a lack of co-operation on the part of the primary target with those authorities responsible for prevention and control."[16]

Table 4 shows that the majority of kidnappings result in demands for a monetary ransom, while the second largest number result in no demands at all. Terrorism is "par excellence, a weapon of psychological warfare".[17] This is particularly true of hostage-takings. The very ability to seize a prominent official may in itself be all the propaganda victory the terrorists are seeking. Demands are thus rendered superfluous. The 1981 kidnapping of US General James Dozier by the Red Brigades is a case in point; although the ranks of the Brigades had been significantly thinned by police arrests during the months immediately preceding the kidnapping, they proved they were still capable not only of mounting a major operation but of escalating their campaign by striking for the first time at a supranational body.

Response to demands

As Table 5 illustrates, 60 per cent of all demands have been rejected regardless of content or hostage. Only kidnappings for ransom have achieved a significant success rate of 74 per cent, with a ransom having been paid 17 times out of 23.

Fate of hostages

Table 6 shows that 94 per cent of all hostages have been released regardless of whether demands have been met. Granting demands is no insurance of safe release; two people have been killed even though demands had been met and a further eight have been killed even though no demands had been made. Neither does refusing demands necessarily entail the hostage's death; only 26 out of 627 hostages or 4 per cent have been killed after demands had been rejected. However, this figure varies dramatically according to the nature of the incident. A full 31 per cent of kidnap victims have been killed once demands have been refused, whereas only three per cent of siege victims in comparable circumstances have died. Ironically, marginally more siege victims have died during police assaults to save them (14 out of 390 or 3·6 per cent) than during incidents when the terrorists have surrendered (5 out of 203 or 2·5 per cent).

AN OPERATIONAL TYPOLOGY OF RESPONSE

The experience of Western Europe confirms one fact above all else: political hostage incidents represent a new form of crisis. Governments are therefore restricted in the way they respond in much the same way as they are in their response to any form of crisis. Traditional techniques of crisis management should thus provide governmental decision-makers, likely to be faced with the necessity of having to respond, with a tool to operate more effectively and manage the crisis more successfully.

The concept of crisis, like that of political terrorism, suffers from definitional imprecision because of its widespread and indiscriminate use. Within the field of international relations, the study of crisis can be approached from numerous perspectives, each of which will employ a slightly different definition and imply a slightly different research interest. All agree, however, that any critical change in the stability of one country can potentially affect the stability of others, as well as threaten the delicate balance of world order. It is thus of fundamental importance to understand how the incident itself will restrict response and determine any likely disruption to national and international stability.

Although political hostage incidents are self-evidently dissimilar in many respects, all share identical characteristics. These in turn serve to define the operational restrictions imposed on a host government. While likely to fluctuate in individual relevance according to the specific modalities of each incident, six major clusters of operationally restrictive variables can be identified. These are the nature of the demands; the nature of the seizure; the location of the incident; the nature of the hostages; the nature of the hostage-takers; and the nature of host government policy.

A. Nature of demands

As stated above, the demands will determine the decision-making authority. In all, there have been five distinct variations of demands arising from incidents in Western Europe which impose slightly different restrictions on host government response.

The first takes into account the fact that demands are not always presented. This has been the case in 54 of the 146 incidents. No specific restrictions are thus imposed on host government response, though additional restrictive factors such as location may come into play.

The second category calls for host government action only. This has been the most common category of demands. In every case, the demands were directed against the host government by an indigenous group or local chapter of a foreign group. This category will not impose any restrictions on response either.

The third category are demands calling for foreign government action only. In Western Europe, the foreign government has always been physically involved in the incident as well. In such cases, the host government has no decision-making authority and its response options are restricted accordingly. If it does attempt to respond unilaterally, it risks disrupting relations with the targeted government, especially if the response goes awry.

The fourth category is far more complex and involves demands which call for a combination of both host and foreign government action. In every case, the host government has been called upon by the terrorists solely to provide them with safe conduct out of the country. The main political demands have always focused on the foreign government. Once again, the foreign government will also be physically involved in some way. The incident will either involve victims who are its nationals or will be conducted within its legation. Here, the host government is again restricted in its response options. It must rely on the foreign government for an indication of how to respond. If the foreign government decides not to grant the main political demands, alternative options for response will have to be considered.

The final category of demands are those directed solely against the private sector. Here, the target may be constrained in its response options by the law or at least by the host government's policy for handling such matters. However, loyalty to the hostage may outweigh loyalty to the government or its laws. As a result, not only is a host government again restricted in its response options by not possessing any decision-making authority but it may not even be told the incident has occurred until it is over.

This, then, represents the first operational restriction on a host government's response options: what are the demands and who has final authority to grant them and what is the response likely to be?

B. Nature of the seizure

Not all incidents take place for the same reason. Nonetheless, it is possible to distinguish two main variations: those the terrorists have not planned and those they have.

1. *Unplanned*

Here again it is possible to make a further distinction between the various possible types of unplanned incident.

(a) *Spontaneous*. However unlikely it may seem, incidents can occur spontaneously during the heat of the moment when emotions or passions have been raised to a fever pitch for some reason. Such incidents most closely resemble those initiated by a "frightened man on a binge".[18] The terrorists are in this case unlikely to have engaged in any preplanning or made any preparations or even given much thought to the consequences of their act. They will be trapped into unfamiliar role behaviour by the situation for which they are unlikely to be psychologically prepared. They may, therefore, act in the manner they feel they are supposed to or in the manner the media have shown others to have acted in the past. Governmental decision-makers must here remember that the terrorists are not in control of the situation and have no real goal to direct them. Given time and guidance they may well surrender peacefully and release their hostages unharmed.

(b) *Kidnap/Siege*. This will occur when the responding authorities locate the hideout where a kidnap victim is being held and physically surround it. A further variation is where a siege occurs after an attempted kidnapping when, for example, the police respond too quickly for the terrorists to escape or when the terrorists are delayed by their victim for long enough for the police to arrive. This occurred during the attempted kidnapping/siege at the Yugoslav Embassy in Stockholm by the Ustashi in 1971.

In such circumstances again, the terrorists will be forced into a situation for which they are unlikely to be psychologically prepared. A certain mental disorientation will develop once they lose the initiative they would normally possess during a kidnapping.[19] They will also lose their own freedom of movement and apparent invisibility and will no longer feel invincible. Consequently, feelings of frustration will set in and they will become angry and more aggressive toward the police on the outside whom they will see as the source of their frustration. Potentially, this frustration could be displaced on to the hostages with dire results.

Governmental decision-makers need to remember that this form of siege tends to be particularly violent. In fact, seven of the eight incidents which can be subsumed under this category have involved an exchange of gunfire between the terrorists and the police once the location has been discovered and surrounded. More significantly, only twice have the terrorists surrendered of their own accord.

(c) *Hostages taken in an escape bid.* When another form of attack is frustrated or interrupted or when suspected terrorists are about to be arrested, hostages may be seized in an escape bid. In many ways, this form of siege closely resembles those conducted by an "escaping felon".[20] The terrorists can also be described as "caught in an unplanned situation . . . confused, frightened and . . . being forced to make snap decisions in a crisis without the opportunity to assess the situation realistically."[21] Governmental decision-makers can react to this form of siege as they would to a spontaneous one.

(d) *Hostages taken to prevent hindrance to main attack.* Here, the terrorists will have planned their action in some detail, though the hostages represent an additional complication they will not have expected and will play little, if any, part in their plans. They were seized simply because they happened to be in the way and because the terrorists did not want them to hinder the main attack or raise the alarm. Governmental decision-makers are unlikely to become involved in incidents of this type. Demands are not presented and the host government will only become aware of the incident once it is over and the hostages have been released.

2. Planned

In incidents which have been planned the terrorists will have taken as much time as they will have needed to ensure the operation's success. Not much will have been left to chance. The terrorists are unlikely to implement the final plan unless they are relatively confident they will survive and their demands will be met. The leader in particular will need to ensure the plan succeeds if he is to retain his position within the group's hierarchy. A leader whose plans constantly fail is unlikely to stay leader for long. The group will want the plan to succeed to bolster their own morale. As George Habash, leader of the Popular Front for the Liberation of Palestine (PFLP) has conceded, "you should see how my people react to a successful operation—spirits shoot sky-high."[22] The group is therefore likely to be fully prepared psychologically and well equipped logistically. Such preparedness may take many forms. For example, during the 1973 Chopin Express siege, one of the terrorists told police "I've got plenty of pills . . . I can stand it forever."[23] Groups are also quite capable of basing their preparations on the often detailed and readily available academic articles and conference papers on various aspects of a host government's contingency plans, such as the psychological dynamics of hostage negotiations. This was clearly intimated as fact during the 1975 OPEC siege when Carlos told Riyadh al-Azzawi, the Iraqi Chargé d'Affaires who acted as mediator, "tell Kreisky . . . I know all the tricks."[24]

However, not all incidents have been conducted with the same degree of professionalism. During some, the terrorists have conducted themselves with almost military precision and discipline. The terrorists guarding Aldo Moro after his kidnapping in 1978 were regularly replaced to prevent fatigue and boredom setting in. During other incidents, such as the Black December siege of the Indian High Commission in 1973, there appears to have been only slightly more planning than for an incident which occurs spontaneously.

With discrepancies as great as these, it is hard to provide any guidelines on how the terrorists are likely to conduct themselves. However, in general terms, they are likely to be more organised, more professional, more calculating and, initially at least, more adamant in their demands.

This, then, represents the second restriction on a host government's response options: why did the incident occur and how much planning appears to have gone into it?

C. Location of the incident

It is an accepted principle of customary international law that executive jurisdiction, the jurisdiction within which a government has sole decision-making authority, is primarily territorial.[25] As a result, the physical location of the incident will determine jurisdiction and thereby identify the decision-making body with ultimate authority over questions of acquiescence. Although incidents can occur in a variety of locations, only three jurisdictional alternatives are possible.

1. Wholly within jurisdiction of host government

If the incident occurs within the territory and hence jurisdiction of the host government, it will possess ultimate authority for deciding how to respond. If it occurs on private property, the host government will still retain jurisdiction but may be liable for redress through the local legal system for any damage caused by its agents during the response. This exclusive authority stems from a fundamental principle of international law which lays down as a basic right that each state shall have absolute jurisdiction "over persons and things and over events occurring within its terriroty."[26]

Friction may result when the incident requires a response from more than one governmental agency. Each will possess a separate chain of command and may be unable or even refuse to respond unless the appropriate order is received from the appropriate source. Moreover, relevant information which may be on file with one agency may not be disseminated to others. There are many likely reasons for this, such as inter-agency rivalry or inertia, because the information was not thought to be important enough at the time, because it had been overlooked or even because the "need-to-know" principle precluded its dissemination to outsiders.

Governmental decision-makers must ensure that the various agencies within their control do co-operate with one another. The sole aim of all involved is to resolve the crisis brought about by the hostage incident as quickly as possible.

2. Within embassy or consulate

Incidents which occur within an embassy or consulate pose particular problems for a host government. Of paramount relevance are the restrictions laid down by Article 22 of the 1961 Vienna Convention on Diplomatic Relations and by Article 31 of the 1963 Vienna Convention on Consular Relations which both declare diplomatic premises inviolable. Under both Conventions a host government is obliged to prevent an incident from occurring in a foreign embassy or consulate. If, or rather when it does, a host government may neither mount an assault against the premises nor take any decisions affecting it without the consent of the head of the mission or the mission's foreign ministry. Moreover, any damage done to the mission must be compensated for by the host government regardless of "however diligently the local police performed their duties in trying to prevent damage."[27]

It is worth mentioning here that reciprocal agreement must also be forthcoming if the foreign government should wish to deploy its own anti-terrorist force for an assault against its own legation. It has been noted that "a direct, physical exercise of one state's power within the territory of another—such as sending officials on to foreign soil to make an arrest—is, unless permitted by the passive state, a manifest illegality of a very elementary kind."[28] This permission has not always been forthcoming in Western Europe. During the 1974 siege of the French Embassy in the Hague by the United Red Army, the Dutch authorities refused to allow the French government to even disembark its anti-terrorist squad from the aircraft after it had landed at Schipol Airport.

3. Within international intergovernmental organisation

Incidents which occur within international intergovernmental organisations present similar restrictions on a host government's response options. Most notable is, again, inviolability. Governmental decision-makers are bound by international law to protect the premises of such organisations. No decision can be taken without first consulting the Secretary-General of the organisation or his deputy.

This, then, represents the third operational restriction on a host government's response: where has the incident occurred and who has executive jurisdiction?

D. Nature of the hostages

The act of taking hostages is frequently condemned as "a violation of the person and an infringement of the freedom and basic human rights to which everyone ... (is) entitled under international law."[29] Viewed from this perspective, numerous conventions already exist which oblige a government to guarantee protection to all within its jurisdiction.

Although the Universal Declaration of Human Rights does not have the force of law, the same fundamental principles have been transformed into treaty obligations through the United Nations General Assembly adoption of the International Covenant on Civil and Political Rights. The rights thereby guaranteed and of primary relevance here are specified in Articles 6 and 9 which provide for an inherent right to life, liberty and security of person. Similarly, the Council of Europe Convention for the Protection of Human Rights and Fundamental Freedoms provides for the same rights in Articles 1, 2 and 5.

Numerous other conventions also exist which proscribe the taking of

TABLE 1

GEOGRAPHICAL DISTRIBUTION OF POLITICAL HOSTAGE INCIDENTS IN WESTERN EUROPE

	1970	1971	1972	1973	1974	1975	1976	1977	1978	1979	1980	1981	1982	Total
Austria	—	—	—	A/S;S	—	S	—	2K	—	—	S	—	—	6
Belgium	—	—	—	—	—	—	—	—	—	S	S	S	—	3
Cyprus	—	—	K	K	—	—	—	K	—	—	—	—	—	3
France	—	—	K	S	K	K/S;3K;3S	8S	K;S	2S	3S	—	—	K	26
Federal Republic of Germany	—	—	—	—	—	P/S;K	P/K;K	K	—	P/S	—	—	P/K	7
Greece	—	—	—	2S	—	—	—	—	—	—	—	—	—	2
Italy	—	—	3K	K;S	4P/K;LK	K/S;K	3K;S	2K	K;S	K/S	K	A/K;5K;S	—	26
Netherlands	S*	—	—	K;S	A/K;S	P/S;A/S;2S	P/S;2S	P/S;2S	—	—	—	—	—	9
Republic of Ireland	—	—	—	—	K	K/S	—	—	—	—	—	2K	—	5
Spain	K	A/K	K	K;S	—	2S	K/S;4K	K/S;K4	A/K;5K;S	4K;2S	2K;2S	2A/K;7K	2A/K;2K	47
Sweden	S	AK/S;S	—	—	—	—	—	A/K	—	S	—	—	—	5
Switzerland	—	—	—	—	—	—	—	—	—	S	—	—	—	1
Turkey	—	6K;S	—	—	—	—	—	—	3K	—	2S	—	—	12
United Kingdom	S	—	—	K;S	—	S	—	K	—	—	2S	—	—	9
														161

* K—Kidnapping; A/K—Attempted Kidnapping; P/K—Planned Kidnapping; S—Siege; A/S—Attempted Siege; P/S—Planned Siege;
K/S—Kidnap/Siege; AK/S—Attempted Kidnapping/Siege.

TABLE 2

NATURE OF GROUP ENGAGED IN POLITICAL HOSTAGE-TAKING

Group	1970	1971	1972	1973	1974	1975	1976	1977	1978	1979	1980	1981	1982	Total
ARC	—	—	—	—	—	S	—	—	—	—	—	—	—	1
Black December	—	—	—	S	—	—	—	—	—	—	—	—	—	1
Committee for Revolutionary Socialist Unity	—	—	—	—	—	—	—	K	—	—	—	—	—	1
EOKA-B	K*	A/K	—	—	—	—	—	—	—	—	—	—	—	2
ETA	—	—	K	K:S	—	—	4K	K	4A/K:5K	4K	2K	2A/K:7K	2A/K:2K	38
Fighters for the Defence of Israel	—	—	—	—	—	—	—	—	S	—	—	—	—	1
FLNC	—	—	—	—	—	—	—	S	—	—	S	—	—	2
FSLN	—	—	—	—	—	—	—	—	—	2S	—	—	—	2
GARI	—	—	—	—	K	—	—	—	—	—	—	—	—	1
Group of the Martyr	—	—	—	—	—	3K:S;K/S	—	—	—	—	—	—	—	2
GRAPO	—	—	—	—	—	—	K/S	K/S	—	—	S	—	—	5
Harkis	—	—	—	—	—	—	—	—	—	—	—	—	—	1
MPAIAC	—	—	—	—	4P/K	—	—	—	—	—	—	—	—	0
Mussolini Action Squads	—	—	—	—	—	—	—	—	—	—	—	—	—	1
New Force	—	—	—	—	—	—	—	—	—	S	—	—	—	1
NRP	—	—	K	—	—	—	—	—	—	—	—	—	—	1
NAP	—	—	—	—	K	K	—	K	—	—	—	—	—	3
Palestinians/Black September/PFLP	S	—	S	5S;A/S	—	P/S;3S;A/S	S	A/K:3K	2S	S	2S	—	—	15
PIRA	—	—	—	K	K	S;K/S	—	K	2K	—	—	2K	—	11
RAF/Holger Meins Commando/2 June Movement	—	—	4P/K	—	—	—	—	—	—	P/S	K	—	—	8
Red Brigades	—	—	3K	K	K	K:S	P/K:K	A/K:3K	K	K/S	—	A/K:5K:S	P/K	18
Revolutionary Brigades	S	—	—	—	—	K/S	K	—	—	—	—	—	K	7
South Moluccans	—	—	—	—	A/K	P/S;2S	—	P/S:2S	S	—	—	—	—	7
Squadre Armati Comunista	—	—	—	—	—	—	2K	—	—	—	—	—	—	2
Squadre Proletarie di Combattemento	—	—	—	—	—	—	—	—	S	—	—	—	—	1
Students	S	K	—	—	—	S	—	—	—	4S	15S	S	—	23
TPLA	—	5K:S	A/K:K/S	—	S	—	—	—	K	—	—	—	—	8
"Ulster Freedom Fighters"	—	—	—	—	S	—	—	—	—	—	—	—	—	1
United Red Army	—	—	—	—	—	—	—	—	K	—	—	—	—	1
UPC	—	—	—	—	—	—	—	—	—	—	S	—	—	1
Ustashi	—	AK/S:S	—	—	—	—	—	—	—	—	—	—	—	2
														161

* K—Kidnapping; A/K—Attempted Kidnapping; P/K—Planned Kidnapping; S—Siege; A/S—Attempted Siege; P/S—Planned Siege; K/S—Kidnap/Siege; AK/S—Attempted Kidnapping/Siege.

TABLE 3

NATURE OF KIDNAP VICTIMS

	1970	1971	1972	1973	1974	1975	1976	1977	1978	1979	1980	1981	1982	Total
Diplomats	—	1	—	1	—	1	—	—	1	—	—	3	—	7
Police/Servicemen	—	5	—	—	—	—	—	—	4	—	2	—	—	11
Capitalists	—	3	5	2	4	2	9	6	2	2	2	7	3	47
Innocents	—	1	—	1	1	9	—	2	—	—	—	—	—	14
Government Officials	—	—	—	1	1	2	—	—	2	2	1	1	—	10
														89

NATURE OF SIEGE VICTIMS

	1970	1971	1972	1973	1974	1975	1976	1977	1978	1979	1980	1981	1982	Total
Diplomats	9	5	—	21	11	123	5	—	8	20	23	5	—	230
Police/Servicemen	1	—	3	5	—	—	—	4	—	—	—	1	—	14
Capitalists	—	—	—	—	—	2	—	—	—	—	—	—	—	2
Innocents	—	3	9	200	—	137	—	185	93	—	16	—	—	643
Government Officials	—	—	—	1	—	1	1	1	73	8	3	—	—	88
														977

TABLE 4

NATURE OF DEMANDS FROM KIDNAPPINGS

	1970	1971	1972	1973	1974	1975	1976	1977	1978	1979	1980	1981	1982	Total
Specific Political Changes	—	—	—	1	—	2	—	—	—	1	1	2	1	8
Release Prisoners	—	—	—	—	—	2	—	—	—	—	—	5	—	12
Ransom	—	2	—	—	—	2	5	6	—	1	1	4	2	23
Escape	—	—	—	—	—	—	—	—	—	—	—	—	—	—
Combination of These	—	1	—	1	2	2	—	1	—	—	—	—	—	6
Specific Corporate Policy Changes	—	—	—	—	1	1	2	—	—	1	—	1	—	6
No Demands	1	2	2	2	1	—	1	1	6	1	1	2	—	20
														75

NATURE OF DEMANDS FROM SIEGES

	1970	1971	1972	1973	1974	1975	1976	1977	1978	1979	1980	1981	1982	Total
Specific Political Changes	1	—	—	—	—	3	—	—	—	3	—	—	—	7
Release Prisoners	—	1	—	—	—	—	—	—	—	2	4	—	—	7
Ransom	—	—	—	—	—	—	—	—	—	—	—	—	—	—
Escape	—	1	—	3	—	2	—	2	1	—	1	—	—	10
Combination of These	—	—	1	2	1	5	—	2	2	—	—	—	—	13
Specific Corporate Policy Changes	—	—	—	—	—	—	—	—	—	—	—	—	—	—
No Demands	1	1	1	2	—	3	1	1	3	4	15	2	—	34
														71

TABLE 5

RESPONSE TO DEMANDS FROM KIDNAPPINGS

	1970	1971	1972	1973	1974	1975	1976	1977	1978	1979	1980	1981	1982	Total
Granted	—	2	1	1	—	4	4	6	1	3	—	—	—	25
Partially Granted	—	—	—	1	—	—	—	—	—	—	—	—	1	4
Rejected	—	2	1	—	2	1	2	2	2	—	—	10	2	25
No Demands	1	2	2	2	1	—	—	1	6	1	1	2	—	20
Unknown	—	—	—	—	—	—	1	—	—	—	—	—	—	1
														75

RESPONSE TO DEMANDS FROM SIEGES

	1970	1971	1972	1973	1974	1975	1976	1977	1978	1979	1980	1981	1982	Total
Granted	—	—	—	3	1	1	—	—	—	—	—	—	—	5
Partially Granted	—	—	—	—	—	—	—	—	—	—	—	—	—	2
Rejected	1	2	1	1	—	8	1	3	3	5	5	—	—	30
No Demands	1	1	1	2	—	3	1	1	3	4	15	2	—	34
														71

TABLE 6

FATE OF KIDNAP VICTIMS

	1970	1971	1972	1973	1974	1975	1976	1977	1978	1979	1980	1981	1982	Total
No Demands														
Released	1	2	2	1	2	—	—	—	4	1	1	2	—	16
Killed	—	—	—	1	—	—	—	1	2	—	—	—	—	4
Demands Granted														
Released	—	3	2	1	1	11	6	5	1	3	1	2	1	37
Killed	—	—	—	—	—	—	—	1	—	—	—	—	—	1
Demands Refused														
Released	—	4	1	1	2	1	1	1	1	1	1	7	2	22
Killed	—	1	—	—	—	—	1	1	1	—	—	3	—	7
Fate Unknown	—	—	—	—	—	—	2	—	—	—	—	—	—	2
														89

STATE OF SIEGE VICTIMS

	1970	1971	1972	1973	1974	1975	1976	1977	1978	1979	1980	1981	1982	Total
No Demands														
Released	3	1	—	100	—	2	5	4	15	—	6	6	—	142
Killed	—	1	3	—	—	—	—	—	—	—	—	—	—	4
Demands Granted														
Released	—	—	—	63	11	136	—	—	—	—	—	—	—	210
Killed	—	—	—	1	—	—	—	—	—	—	—	—	—	1
Demands Refused; Hostage-Takers Surrendered														
Released	7	3	—	49	—	96	—	—	8	27	13	—	—	203
Killed	—	—	—	1	—	4	—	—	—	—	—	—	—	5
Demands Refused; Assault														
Released	—	3	—	8	—	8	1	177	144	1	21	—	—	363
Killed	—	—	9	—	—	—	—	2	1	—	2	—	—	14
Wounded	—	—	—	—	—	—	—	7	6	—	—	—	—	13
Escaped														
Unharmed	—	—	—	3	—	16	—	—	—	—	—	—	—	19
Injured	—	—	—	2	—	—	—	—	—	—	—	—	—	2
Died	—	—	—	—	—	1	—	—	—	—	—	—	—	1
														977

hostages under various circumstance. The seizure of passengers on board civilian aircraft is prohibited under the provisions laid down by Article 1, s.1(a) of the 1971 Montreal Convention for the Suppression of Unlawful Acts Against the Safety of Civil Aviation. The taking of hostages in time of war is proscribed by the common Article 3 of all four Geneva Conventions of 1949. Article 34 of the Geneva Convention Relative to the Protection of Civilian Persons in Time of War is more specific and categorically states "the taking of hostages is forbidden."[30]

On 8 June, 1977, the General Assembly adopted two additional protocols to the Geneva Conventions which effectively internationalise internal struggles by national liberation movements. Once ratified and entered into force, they will afford national liberation movements the same status and obligations previously accorded only to the recognised armed forces of combatant states. Here too the taking of hostages is proscribed, first by Article 75, s.2(c) of Additional Protocol I which states "the following acts are and shall remain prohibited at any time and in any place whatsoever, whether committed by civilian or by military agents: . . . (c) the taking of hostages."[31] Article 4, s.2(c) of Additional Protocol II carries the same prohibition.

To date, the UN has not been successful in establishing a general convention against terrorism.[32] Neither, for that matter, was the League of Nations before it.[33] However, the Council of Europe and the Organization of American States have.[34] The Council of Europe's Convention on the Suppression of Terrorism does not expressly prohibit the taking of hostages, but, Article I establishes the act as a non-political offence and thereby provides for the extradition of the terrorists and their trial in accordance with criminal law.

On 17 December, 1979, the General Assembly adopted the Convention Against the Taking of Hostages.[35] But, for numerous reasons, it is unlikely the Convention will ever be entered into force and, even if it were, it would require a fundamental revision before it could be termed an effective legislative instrument.[36]

Despite this, various principles of international law can already be seen as applicable. It is tempting to suggest that hostages can be likened to the characters in George Orwell's *Animal Farm* and that specifically "all animals are equal but some are more equal than others."[37] Indeed, some hostages are more equal than others in terms of the protective obligations imposed on a host government. For our purposes here, hostages have been divided into citizens of the host government and foreign nationals and then further divided into civilians, politicians/symbolic leaders and, finally, diplomats.

1. Civilian citizens of host government

An incident involving hostages whose only crime was to be in the wrong place at the wrong time will most acutely focus attention on whether the government is willing or able to protect its citizens. Failure may lead at least to a loss of confidence in the government by its civilians and may result in the withdrawal of their support and precipitate an early election. Indeed, it has been noted that "if the terrorist weapon can be shown to pay off against a particular government then that government and its political moderates will find their power and authority undermined."[38]

2. Politicians/symbolic leaders of host government

A government's obligations to protect its civilians naturally extends to include its politicians and various symbolic leaders. In fact, this obligation can be assumed to be of a greater importance solely because of the symbolism involved. Special protection may therefore be warranted. In the United Kingdom, for example, royalty and some senior Cabinet Ministers, such as Defence and Northern Ireland, are routinely guarded by specially assigned armed police regardless of any specific threat against them. Other politicians and, for that matter, any civilian must be accorded the same level of protection should the need arise, such as if their names are found on a terrorist's list of potential targets.

If protection is not provided after a specific threat, the conduct of the government is likely to be brought into question. Furthermore, should the protection fail in thwarting an attack, this may be interpreted as a sign of weakness. This could lead to a propaganda victory for the terrorists at the very least.

3. Civilians of foreign government

International attempts at codifying a host government's obligations toward foreign nationals have so far generally met with failure.[39] The most that can be said is that under customary international law, a government is obliged to provide a "modicum of respect for the life, liberty, dignity and property of foreign nationals, such as may be expected in a civilised community."[40] More importantly, reprisals may be taken against that country's citizens in the other country.

If, for any reason, a foreign national is injured as a result of any activity beyond the control of the host government, the "state's duty is discharged if the alien is permitted redress through the municipal law system."[41] Otherwise, "a state is amenable to a claim when it is directly inculpated, either because its officials failed in their duty to prevent the act from occurring or because the actor was a state agent."[42]

4. Foreign dignitaries

The protection a host government is obliged to provide for foreign dignitaries is more codified under international law.[43] However, again the degree of protection is dependent on the nature of the dignitary in question.

(a) *Diplomatic personnel.* The first category, diplomatic personnel, have been regarded as worthy of special protection at least since 423 BC[44] However, it was not until the Treaty of Westphalia in 1648 that an attempt was made to systematise "the special duties of protection which the receiving state owed the representative of the sending state."[45] In more recent times, this practice has found expression as Article 29 of the Vienna Convention on Diplomatic

Relations which holds the person of a diplomatic agent to be inviolable. A host government is obliged to treat consuls in the same fashion according to Article 40 of the Vienna Convention on Consular Relations.

By 1971, the increase in the number of terrorist attacks against diplomatic personnel led the UN to adopt the Convention on the Prevention and Punishment of Crimes Against Internationally Protected Persons, including Diplomatic Agents. Specifically, Article 1, s.1(b) calls for special protection for all diplomatic representatives and members of his family and household.

(b) *Foreign head of state or government.* It has been noted "if a state agrees to a private or official visit by a head of state or government, international law obliges the host state to protect his personal safety and dignity."[46] This was also codified under the Convention on the Prevention and Punishment of Crimes Against Internationally Protected Persons, Including Diplomatic Agents as Article 1, s.1(a).

(c) *Personnel of international intergovernmental organisations.* The final category includes the Secretary-General and the secretariat of the various international intergovernmental organisations. The permanent representatives of the member countries of the UN are naturally accorded the same privileges and immunities enjoyed by other diplomatic agents and are therefore inviolable.[47] However, only the Secretary-General and all Assistant Secretaries-General of the UN are similarly inviolable.[48]

A host government, then, is under a very special obligation to protect these individuals. Failure to do so could, at the very least, lead to international condemnation and censure. However, holding a government "strictly accountable . . . usually plays right into the terrorists' hands, particularly when one of the kidnappers' major purposes is to harm the relations between the countries in the hope of discrediting the Government they are trying to overthrow."[49]

A further operationally restrictive variable which must be recognised here comes from the emerging field of hostage victimisation.[50] Once the incident occurs, the hostage will initially be scared, psychologically disoriented and probably in shock, all exacerbated by the presence of violence in one form or another. If the hostage survives his initial capture, and in all probability he will, his natural psychological and physiological processes will take over and he will start trying to cope with the stress of the situation. It has been observed "that the physiological stress response is an adaptive mechanism that helps the body avoid breakdowns in function, while at the same time the stress response itself can lead to breakdowns and disease."[51] An example of this was the 105 schoolchildren taken hostage at the Bovensmilde Elementary School in the Netherlands by the South Moluccans in 1977 who all developed gastroenteritis during the first week of captivity.

Undoubtedly the most important though still the least understood reaction is the bond of identification which develops between the hostages and the terrorists. It occurred most graphically during a criminally motivated siege at the Kreditbanken at Norrmalmstorg in central Stockholm on 23 August, 1973

76

when one of the female hostages apparently had intimate relations with the would-be bank robber and later refused to testify against him. It was this incident which gave the process of transference of loyalties its name of the Stockholm syndrome. It does not develop immediately but appears to be well entrenched by the third day of captivity. Most, if not all hostages have later admitted having some positive feelings toward their captors.[52] The syndrome has been defined as "that unholy alliance between captor and captive, involving fear, distrust or anger toward the authorities on the outside."[53] The degree of identification which develops is dependent on:

> (1) the length of time the hostage and the captors are confined; (2) the quality of the interaction—were the hostages well treated?; (3) the existence of predetermined racial or ethnic hostilities between the hostage and the captor; (4) the predisposition on the part of some hostages to seek and relate to their captors.[54]

The Stockholm syndrome has led to the formulation of a fundamental axiom of response for governmental decision-makers to bear in mind: "the longer the hostage situation lasts, the less likely the victims will be killed."[55] However, another product of the Stockholm syndrome is that "law enforcement must know that it can never rely upon the victim for help or even to help himself."[56]

This, then, represents the fourth operational restriction on a host government's response options: who are the hostages and how symbolically important are they?

E. Nature of the hostage-takers

As already indicated, not all terrorist groups aspire to the same goals. Neither are they driven by the same primary motives. They cannot, therefore, be assumed to have engaged in hostage-taking for the same reason nor, for that matter, can they be expected to respond in the same way. It has been suggested that such differences "may be due to the group's ideology, the availability of targets, regional cultures of violence, societal norms, group strength in terms of firepower, logistics and personnel, public support for the group (real and perceived), security systems of the potential targets and the preferences of the group's leaders."[57] Some groups, such as the United Red Army, have shown a greater tendency to use violence and must be presumed to be more likely to kill their hostages if their demands are not met. This appears to have been the assumption the French government worked under during the siege of the French Embassy in the Hague by the United Red Army in 1974 when they agreed to enter into negotiations with the hostage-takers only after it was learned that other members of the same group had previously been responsible for the killing of 25 Puerto Rican pilgrims at Lod Airport in 1972.

Despite the increasing linkages between groups and the occasional "revolutionary conference" they hold, there is no evidence to suggest all groups share a common long-term goal. Admittedly, a superordinate goal has bound diverse groups together for a specific action, such as the United Red Army attacking Lod Airport in the name of the Palestinian revolution, but this is the exception rather than the rule. Even the PLO, who perceive themselves to be a government-in-exile of the Palestinian people, do not always display a commonality of purpose and have experienced frequent outbursts of acrimony among its constituent factions, if not outright belligerency. Neither is there any reason to believe that a worldwide coalition or a "terror international" exists or is even feasible.

The name chosen by a group is often heavily imbued with symbolism. It is frequently a commemoration of some past achievement or defeat. For example, one of the smallest and most secretive South Moluccan factions was the Action Group January 18 named after the first meeting between the South Moluccans and the Vietnamese Liberation Front. Conversely, Black September and Black June were named after months during which devastating offensives had been mounted against Palestinian strongholds in Jordan in 1970 and Lebanon in 1976 respectively. Groups with names such as these can be expected to intensify their activities during the symbolic times in an attempt to restore their prestige and revitalise their self-esteem. A particular date may also be chosen for an operation if it commemorates some occurrence in the group's past, especially a defeat. This was the case with the date chosen for the siege of the Saudi Arabian Embassy in Paris by Black September exactly one year after their defeat at Furstenfeldbruck Airfield outside Munich. Moreover, for this particular operation, Black September used the *nom de guerre* of *al-Icab* (Punishment).

This, then, represents the fifth operational restriction on a host government's response options: who are the terrorists and what is known of them?

F. Nature of host government policy

The final restrictive variable is host government policy and specifically the relationship between policy and systemic norms. Although certain norms may vary from one system to another and from one society to the next, the most universal is the maintenance of order. It has been argued that every society will seek to sustain order through the pursuit of three primary goals:

> First, all societies seek to ensure that life will be in some measure secure against violence resulting in death or bodily harm. Secondly, all societies seek to ensure that promises, once made, will be kept or that agreements, once undertaken, will be carried out. Third, all societies pursue the goal of ensuring that the possession of things remain stable to some degree and will not be subject to challenges that are constant and without limit.[58]

The first goal of ensuring that life will be secure against violence has an immediate and obvious applicability for policy formulation against political hostage-taking. A host government must prevent indiscriminate acts of violence against all those within its territory. Every government possesses the sole monopoly on the use of force within its jurisdiction. Any act of a similar nature committed by actors other than those appointed by the government may serve to undermine its stability and call into question its ability to protect itself and this monopoly. Accordingly, accurate and continuous intelligence-gathering is required to prevent such acts from occurring. Once plans for an incident have been uncovered, police and government agents must ensure it is thwarted and those responsible apprehended. More importantly, the population must be informed of both the plans and the fact they were foiled.

A good example of this was the announcement in 1975 that Dutch police had stymied a South Moluccan plan to occupy the Royal Palace and hold Queen Juliana hostage. It cannot be overstressed that such announcements are vital if the government is to retain the "hearts and minds" of its people.[59] Should the violence still break out and an incident still occur, intelligence-gathering must continue in an effort to identify the hostage-takers and learn their apparent motive. This will enable decision-makers more accurately to appraise the credibility of the hostage-takers' threat and respond more realistically. Once an incident occurs, the government must have trained personnel immediately available to respond, such as fire suppression teams, assault teams and hostage negotiators. Untrained personnel should not be allowed to become closely involved and play only supportive roles, if a disastrous outcome is to be avoided.

Once the incident is over, the government must be capable of remedying the effects of the violence as promptly as possible. This must be done by providing wounded hostages and the relatives of hostages who were killed with the means of seeking compensation through such organisations as the Criminal Injuries Compensation Board of the United Kingdom.

The second goal of ensuring that agreements are kept is also applicable to policy formulation. A host government should only engage in good faith bargaining with the terrorists and should keep promises made during the negotiations. It has been argued:

> Bad faith bargaining is seen to be a harmful tactic, not only because it diminishes public trust and confidence in the state, but also because of its possible effect on subsequent incidents, either precipitating additional, retaliatory incidents or causing future offenders to employ measures (i.e. retention of women, children or sick hostages) to ensure meeting of demands and fulfilment of promises.[60]

The final goal of ensuring the possession of things is also applicable. If social order is to be maintained a host government must ensure that the lawful possession of things is not abrogated by giving in to demands. It readily follows from this that the government itself must not relinquish possession of anything it controls. Neither can it allow any of its citizens to do so either. In some countries, this has been codified by making the payment of ransom illegal. Should the terrorists be successful in gaining possession of something they have demanded a precedent will have been established which may not only undermine social order but may also serve to invite future incidents.

Determination to uphold law

Although these three goals are the most important for the maintenance of social order, they are not the only ones around which policy must be formulated. Various authors have argued that a government of the type found in Western Europe must also base its policies on several other principles if public trust and confidence are to be retained.

One such principle is "firmness and the determination to uphold constitutional authority and the rule of law."[61] Decisions on policy and its implementation must remain the sole responsibility of those democratically elected to do so. It must not be shared with special departments invested with unlimited powers

79

and no public accountability. The Constitution itself must not be temporarily abrogated for a select few, no matter what. Moreover, the policy finally adopted must be within the law. In some countries this has necessitated a change in the legal code. In West Germany, for example, at the time of the Munich Olympics siege in 1972, police were forbidden by law to "shoot to kill". At the same time, laws must not be changed to the extent they become repressive. This, it has been argued, may be precisely the response the terrorists are hoping for, as one of their major objectives may be "to provoke a Government to ill-judged measures of repression that will alienate public opinion."[62] Similarly, the response must be part of an overall strategy and not be conducted by individuals solely motivated by revenge, such as the 1978 kidnapping of Father Hugh Murphy in Ulster by an RUC sergeant and constable in retaliation for the kidnapping and subsequent murder of Constable William Turbitt, a fellow RUC officer, the day before.

A further fundamental principle for a government in Western Europe is the necessity of being "seen to act in order to restore confidence."[63] This, of course, does not diminish the importance of intelligence-gathering, neither does it preclude hostage negotiation in favour of an assault. Rather it refers to a requirement that a "Government must be seen to be doing all in its power to defend the life and limb of its citizens."[64] This is most readily accomplished by the simple process of responding.

Every policy which is finally adopted will have evolved from a number of factors, such as the government's previous experience; the desire to be seen as supporting some specific regional or international norm or value, such as taking a resolute stand against political terrorism or providing aid to national liberation movements; the necessity of reconciling long-term goals with the exigencies of the moment; the perceptions and personalities of key decision-makers and their concomitant desire to increase personal status and self-esteem; an appreciation of the public's demands and an estimation of what measures they will accept and tolerate; as well as a basic recognition of the general principles outlined above. The policy itself can be placed on a continuum ranging from a no-concessions stance, such as the position of Turkey, to a more flexible response, such as that adopted by the Netherlands, through to outright capitulation, such as the original policy of Austria which has since been modified as a result of international pressure. There is, however, no clear evidence in Western Europe to suggest that one form of policy has a greater deterrent effect than any other. A deterrent is only effective if the terrorists allow themselves to be deterred and the extent of such deterrence remains a matter for speculation.

This, then, represents the sixth and final operational restriction on a government's options: what is the host government's policy for handling such incidents and what is the political cost of the response likely to be?

There is one final factor which although not restrictive in the above sense will play an important part in determining the likely success or failure of a host government's response. Luck, or alternatively bad luck, has often been the sole explanation of why an incident ended as it did. It certainly explained the massacre at Furstenfeldbruck after the Munich Olympics siege. It need not play so large a part in future.

NOTES

[1] Kurt Waldheim, Secretary-General of UN, during his request for an urgent meeting of Security Council to discuss the US–Iran crisis at the UN on 25 November 1979. Quoted in *The Times*, 26 November 1979.

[2] The chronology utilised here was developed from the following sources: *Le Monde, L'Express, Le Figaro, International Herald Tribune* and *Christian Science Monitor* of France; *Frankfurter Allgemeine Zeitung, Die Welt* and *Die Zeit* of West Germany; *The Times, Financial Times, Sunday Times, Daily Telegraph, Sunday Telegraph, Observer, The Guardian* and *Daily Mail* of the United Kingdom; *New York Times* and *Washington Post* of the US; *Egyptian Gazette, Egyptian Mail, al-Ahram* and *al-Gumhuriyah* of Egypt; *al-Nahar* and *al-Safa* of Lebanon; and the *Jerusalem Post* of Israel. *Time Magazine, Newsweek*, the *Economist, Life, 8 Days, Arab Report and Record, Events, Arab World, US News and Foreign Report* and *al-Hawadess* of Beirut. Miscellaneous sources were *Times Index; Keesing's Contemporary Archives; The Annual of Power and Conflict*, ed. by Brian Crozier (London: Institute for the Study of Conflict), 1971–78; *Political Terrorism*, 2 volumes, ed. by Lester A. Sobel (Oxford: Clio Press, 1978); Brian Michael Jenkins and Janera Johnson, *International Terrorism: A Chronology, 1968–1974* (Santa Monica: Rand Corporation, R-1597-DOS/Arpa, March 1975); Brian Jenkins, Janera Johnson and David Ronfeldt, *Numbered Lives: Some Statistical Observations from 77 International Hostage Episodes* (Santa Monica: Rand Corporation, P-5905, July 1977); US House of Representatives, *Political Kidnappings, 1968–1973*, staff study prepared by the Committee on Internal Security, 93rd Congress, 1st Session (Washington, D.C.: US Government Printing Office, August 1973); *Chronology of Attacks upon Non-Official American Citizens, 1971–1975* (Washington, D.C.: US Department of State, 20 January 1976); *Chronology of Significant Terrorist Incidents Involving US Diplomatic/Official Personnel, 1963–1975* (Washington, D.C.: US Department of State, 20 January 1976); *Foreign Broadcast Intercept Service* and *the Summary of World Broadcasts*.

[3] *International Herald Tribune*, 29 February 1983.

[4] Jenkins, Johnson and Ronfeldt, *Numbered Lives*, p. 1.

[5] For useful typologies of terrorist groups, see Brian Crozier's testimony in *Hearings before the Sub-Committee to Investigate the Administration of the Internal Security Act and Other Internal Security Laws, of the Committee on the Judiciary*, US Senate, 94th Congress, 2nd Session, Part 4 (Washington, D.C.: US Government Printing Office, 14 May 1975), pp. 182–83; Paul Wilkinson, *Political Terrorism* (London: Macmillan Press, 1974), pp. 32–44; and Richard Schultz, "Conceptualizing Political Terrorism: A Typology", *Journal of International Affairs*, Vol. 32, No. 1 (1978), pp. 9–10.

[6] *International Herald Tribune*, 29 February 1983.

[7] Charles A. Russell and Bowman H. Miller, "Profile of a Terrorist", *Terrorism: An International Journal*, Vol. 1, No. 1 (1977), p. 26.

[8] However, see Gustave Morf, *Terror in Quebec: Case Studies of the FLQ* (Toronto: Clarke, Irwin and Co., Ltd., 1970); Gideon Fishman, "Criminological Aspects of International Terrorism: The Dynamics of the Palestinian Movement", in Marc Riedel and Terence P. Thornberry (eds.), *Crime and Deliquency: Dimensions of Deviance* (New York: Praeger Publishers, 1974); Guy Richmond, *Shadows of a Violent Mind* (Surrey, British Columbia: Antonson Publishing Ltd., 1979), especially Chap. 9; and John B. Wolf, "Organization and Management Practices of Urban Terrorist Groups", *Terrorism: An international Journal*, Vol. 1, No. 2 (1977), pp. 169–86.

[9] In fact, it has been argued "that organisation for criminal behaviour is shaped by the same system problems and concerns as organisation for any other form of behaviour" (A. K. Cohen, "The Concept of Criminal Organisation", *British Journal of Criminology*, Vol. 17, No. 2 (1977), p. 105).

[10] Conrad Hassel, "The Hostage Situation: Exploring the Motivation and the Cause", *Police Chief* (September 1975), p. 55.

[11] Sigmund Freud, *Group Psychology and the Analysis of the Ego* (London: Hogarth, 1922), p. 85.

[12] Abu Iyad, *Falastini Bila Hawiyah* (Kuwait: Kazimah Publications, n.d.), p. 173.

[13] Irving L. Janis, "Group Identification Under Conditions of External Danger", in Dorwin Cartwright and Alvin Zander (eds.), *Group Dynamics* (New York: Harper and Row, 1968), p. 82.

[14] *Sunday Telegraph*, 18 February 1976.

[15] Dr Harvey Schlossberg quoted in "Patient Sieges: Dealing with Hostage-Takers", *Assets Protection*, No. 3 (1975), p. 22.

[16] "Final Synthesis: Summary and Conclusion", in Ronald D. Crelinsten and Danielle Laberge-Altmejd (eds.), *Hostage-Taking: Problems of Prevention and Control* (Montreal: University of Montreal, Monograph, October 1978), p. 266.

[17] Paul Wilkinson, *Terrorism and the Liberal State* (London: Macmillan Press, 1977), p. 81.

[18] This is the first of three categories of hostage-taker presented in "Hostages—A Viewpoint", *R.C.M.P. Gazette*, Vol. 38, No. 10 (1977), p. 1.

[19] That the hostage-takers hold the initiative during a kidnapping has been noted as a fundamental advantage of this form of hostage-taking. See Richard Clutterbuck, *Kidnap and Ransom* (London: Faber and Faber, 1978), p. 66. See also Jenkins, Johnson and Ronfeldt, *Numbered Lives*, p. 9.

[20] This is the second of four categories of hostage-taker presented in International Association of Chiefs of Police, "Hostage Incident Response", Training Key No. 234, reprinted in *R.C.M.P. Gazette*, Vol. 38, No. 10 (1977), p. 12.

[21] *Ibid.*

[22] *Life*, 10 June 1970.

[23] *The Guardian*, 29 September 1973.

[24] *Observer*, 15 February 1976.

[25] See, for example, D. W. Greig, *International Law* (London: Butterworths, 1976), p. 210.

[26] *Ibid.*

[27] *Ibid.*, p. 580.

[28] R. Y. Jennings, "The Limits of State Jurisdiction", *32 Nordisk Tidsskrift for International Ret*, 212, quoted in Sami Shubber, *Jurisdiction Over Crimes on Board Aircraft* (The Hague: Martinus Nijhoff, 1973), p. 54.

[29] Statement by the representative from Chile during the 57th meeting of the 6th Committee on 29 November 1976, *General Assembly Official Records*, 31st Session, Sixth Committee, Sessional Fascicle, A/C.6/31/SR.57, p. 14, para. 66.

[30] *United Nations Treaty Series*, Vol. 75, No. 973, p. 287.

[31] *General Assembly Official Records*, 32nd Session, Annexes, A/32/144, Annex 1, p. 53.

[32] However, at its 59th meeting on 4 December 1979, the 6th Committee adopted 11 formal recommendations by the Ad Hoc Committee on International Terrorism relating to practical measures of co-operation against international terrorism by a vote of 96 to one (Israel) with 20 abstentions.

[33] Although the League of Nations did adopt a Convention on the Prevention and Punishment of Terrorism on 16 November 1937, this was ratified by only one country (India on 1 January 1941) and was subsequently never entered into force.

[34] On 2 February 1972, the OAS adopted the Convention to Prevent and Punish Acts of Terrorism Taking the Forms of Crimes Againt Persons and Related Extortion That Are of International Significance by a vote of 13 to one (Chile) with two abstentions (Bolivia and Peru).

[35] For the text of the Convention, see *General Assembly Official Records*, 34th Session, Annexes, A/34/39, pp. 23–29.

[36] For a more detailed examination of this Convention and the reasons why it remains an ineffectual international legislative instrument, see Clive C. Aston, "The United Nations Convention Against the Taking of Hostages: Realistic or Rhetoric?", *Terrorism: An International Journal*, Vol. 5, Nos. 1 and 2 (1981), pp. 139–60.

[37] George Orwell, *Animal Farm* (London: Penguin Books, 1975), p. 104.

[38] Paul Wilkinson, "Terrorism Versus Liberal Democracy: The Problems of Response", *Conflict Study No. 67* (London: Institute for the Study of Conflict, January 1976), p. 11. See also, Wilkinson, *Liberal State*, pp. 80–92.

[39] An exception was the Havana Convention on the Status of Aliens of 1928. For the text of the Convention, see *League of Nations Treaty Series*, Vol. 132, No. 3045, p. 301, especially Art. 5.

[40] Georg Schwarzenberger, *A Manual of International Law* (Milton, Oxford: Professional Books Ltd., 1976), p. 84. See also Hans Kelsen, *Principles of Internationalk Law*, rev. and ed. by Robert W. Tucker (New York: Holt, Rinehart and Winston, Inc., 1966), p. 366 and Shigeru Oda, "The Individual in International Law", in Max Sorensen (ed.), *Manual of Public International Law* (New York: St. Martin's Press, 1968), p. 485.

[41] P. O'Connell, *International Law* (London: Stevens and Son, 2nd ed., 1976), p. 941.

[42] *Ibid.*, p. 943.

[43] For a more detailed examination of this issue, see C. F. Amerasinghe, *State Responsibility for Injuries to Aliens* (Oxford: Clarendon Press, 1967), Chaps. 5–8.

[44] James Murphy, "The Role of International Law in the Prevention of Terrorist Kidnapping of Diplomatic Personnel", in Cherif M. Bassiouni (ed.), *International Terrorism and Political Crimes* (Springfield, Illinois: Charles C. Thomas, 1973), p. 286.

[45] *Ibid.*, p. 287.

[46] Francis Deak, "Organs of States in Their External Relations: Immunities and Privileges of State Organs and of States", in Sorensen (ed.), *Public International Law*, p. 387.

[47] *United Nations Treaty Series*, Vol. 1, No. 4, p. 15, General Convention on the Privileges and Immunities of the United Nations, Art. IV, s. 9(g).

[48] *Ibid.*, Art. V, s. 19.

[49] Murphy in Bassiouni (ed.), *Political Crimes*, p. 296.

[50] For a detailed examination of this new field see Ronald D. Crelinsten (ed.), *Dimensions of Victimization in the Context of Terroristic Acts* (Montreal: University of Montreal, Monograph, September 1977).

[51] Walton T. Roth, "Psychosomatic Implications of Confinement by Terrorists", in *Ibid.*, p. 48.

[52] Franck Ochberg, "The Victim of Terrorism—Psychiatric Considerations", in *ibid.*, p. 27. See also, Brian Michael Jenkins, *Hostage Survival: Some Preliminary Observations* (Santa Monica: Rand Corporation, P-5627, April 1976), p. 6. For interesting descriptions of this syndrome by ex-hostages, see Geoffrey Jackson, *People's Prison* (Newton Abbot: Readers Union, 1974), pp. 59–72 and C. Burke Elbrick, "The Diplomatic Kidnappings: A Case Study", in *International Terrorism: Proceedings of an Intensive Panel to the Fifteenth Annual Convention of the International Studies Association, Institute of World Affairs* (Milwaukee: University of Wisconsin, June 1974), No. 16: Global Focus Series, pp. 45–55.

[53] Ochberg in Crelinsten (ed.) *Victimization*, p. 27.

[54] Abraham Miller, "Hostage Negotiations and the Concept of Transference", in Yonah Alexander, David Carlton and Paul Wilkonson (eds.), *Terrorism: Theory and Practice* (Boulder, Colorado: Westview Press, 1979), p. 114. See also Ochberg in Crelinsten (ed.), *Victimization*, p. 28.

[55] Patrick Mullany, "Panelist's Report", in Crelinsten (ed.), *Hostage-Taking*, p. 139. See also Brooks McClure, "Hostage Defense Measures", *Hearings Before the Subcommittee to Investigate the Administration of the Internal Security Act and Other Internal Laws, of the Committee on the Judiciary*, US Senate, 94th Congress, 1st Session, Part 5 (Washington, D.C.: US Government Printing Press, 25 July 1975), p. 264.

[56] H. H. A. Cooper, testimony before the US Senate Criminal Laws and Procedures Subcommittee, 21 July 1977, quoted in Sobel, *Political Terrorism*, Vol. 2, p. 19.

[57] Edward F. Mickolus, "Negotiating for Hostages: A Policy Dilemma", *Orbis*, Vol. 19, No. 4 (Winter, 1976), p. 1318.

[58] Hedley Bull, *The Anarchical Society: A Study of Order in World Politics* (London: Macmillan Press, 1977), pp. 4–5.

[59] For a more detailed examination of the "hearts and minds" approach, see Frank Kitson, *Low Intensity Operations: Subversion, Insurgency and Peacekeeping* (London: Faber and Faber, 1971).

[60] "Final Synthesis", in Crelinsten (ed.), *Hostage-Taking*, pp. 269–70.

[61] Wilkinson, *Liberal State*, p. 123.

[62] Andrew Pierre, "The Politics of International Terrorism", *Orbis*, Vol. 19, No. 4 (Winter, 1976), p. 1255.

[63] "New Dimensions of Security in Europe", *ISC Special Report* (London: Institute for the Study of Conflict, May 1975), p. 45.

[64] Wilkinson, *Liberal State*, p. 124.

First published 1984.

Diplomatic Immunities
and State-sponsored Terrorism

Frank Brenchley

  Extracts from the Vienna Conventions on Diplomatic/Consular Relations, where relevant, appear (in distinctive typefaces) on pages facing the author's text.

FRANK BRENCHLEY

INTRODUCTION

The shooting in London's St. James's Square in April 1984, in which a policewoman was killed and a number of Libyan anti-Qadhafi demonstrators wounded by automatic fire from the Libyan diplomatic mission, focused world attention on State-sponsored terrorism and the problem of dealing effectively with it under existing conventions. A police siege of the mission ended with the evacuation, under diplomatic immunity, of all the occupants – including the unidentified gunman.

Concern shown over the unprecedented nature of the London outrage was reflected in initiatives discussed at several international conferences in the ensuing weeks.

Britain's Home Secretary, Leon Brittan, who had to handle the affair, told the Madrid conference of European ministers of justice that they should unite to combat such terrorism, and urged that they should agree not to accept diplomats expelled by any other country. He pointed out that nations were now faced not only with individual terrorists but with terrorist States, seeking the elimination of opponents outside their own frontiers – "and doing so openly, with little fear of effective retaliation".

Conference approved a concerted campaign against terrorism and abuse of diplomatic privileges, and agreed to set up, under the aegis of the Council of Europe, an *ad hoc* ministerial body to consider ways of improving the exchange of information on terrorism, including abuses of diplomatic privileges as well as violence against diplomats.

A declaration issued by Heads of State and Governments at the London Economic Summit expressed a resolve to combat international terrorism "by every possible means, strengthening existing measures and developing effective new ones". The statement added: "They view with serious concern the increasing involvement of States and Governments in acts of terrorism, including the abuse of diplomatic immunity", emphasising the obligations entailed by international law.

In July 1984, the discovery in two crates at Stanstead Airport near London of the drugged body of a kidnapped Nigerian ex-minister and three Israelis was made possible because the crates, although addressed to the Ministry of Foreign Affairs in Lagos and accompanied by a Nigerian official to supervise their loading, did not in all respects comply with the normal rules for the authentication of diplomatic baggage. This dramatic incident, coming so soon after the Libyan shooting affair, reinforced public concern over the abuse of diplomatic privileges and immunities.

The relevant provisions of the conventions governing the conduct of diplomatic and consular missions, the immunities granted reciprocally for their protection and the obligation on diplomats to observe the laws and regulations of the host country are examined below. I have tried to demonstrate the difficulties inherent in dealing with breaches of the diplomatic code, particularly with "grave crimes" which are not defined in the conventions and to consider ways in which the regulations to prevent terrorism might be tightened.

EXTRACTS FROM UK DIPLOMATIC PRIVILEGES ACT 1964

2.(1) Subject to section 3 of this Act, the Articles set out in Schedule 1 to this Act (being Articles of the Vienna Convention on Diplomatic Relations signed in 1961) shall have the force of law in the United Kingdom.

3.(1) If it appears to Her Majesty that the privileges and immunities accorded to a mission of Her Majesty in the territory of any State, or to persons connected with that mission, are less than those conferred by this Act on the mission of that State or on persons connected with that mission, Her Majesty may by an order in Council withdraw such of the privileges and immunities so conferred from the mission of that State or from such persons connected with it as appears to Her Majesty to be proper.

6.(1) No recommendation shall be made to Her Majesty in Council to make an order under section 2 of this Act unless a draft thereof has been laid before Parliament and approved by resolution of each House of Parliament; and any statutory instrument containing an Order under section 3 of this Act shall be subject to annulment in pursuance of a resolution of either House of Parliament.

The Articles of the Vienna Convention set out in Schedule 1 to the Act are the following: 1, 22, 23, 24, 27, 28, 29, 30, 31, 32, 33, 34, 35, 36, 37, 38, 39, 40.

Section. B.

EXTRACT FROM UK CONSULAR RELATIONS ACT 1968

1. (1) Subject to sections 2 and 3(2) of this Act, the provisions set out in Schedule 1 to this Act (being Articles or parts of Articles of the Vienna Convention on Consular Relations signed in 1963) shall have the force of law in the United Kingdom and shall for that purpose be construed in accordance with subsections (2) to (11) of this section.
    (2) In those provisions—
        "grave crime" shall be construed as meaning any offence punishable (on a first conviction) with imprisonment for a term that may extend to five years or with a more severe sentence.

EXTRACTS FROM THE VIENNA CONVENTIONS

ARTICLE 29

The person of a diplomatic agent shall be inviolable. He shall not be liable to any form of arrest or detention. The receiving State shall treat him with due respect and shall take all appropriate steps to prevent any attack on his person, freedom or dignity.

ARTICLE 31

1. A diplomatic agent shall enjoy immunity from the criminal jurisdiction of the receiving State. He shall also enjoy immunity from its civil and administrative jurisdiction, except in the case of
    (a) a real action relating to private immovable property situated in the territory of the receiving State, unless he holds it on behalf of the sending State for the purposes of the mission;
    (b) an action relating to succession in which the diplomatic agent is involved as executor, administrator, heir or legatee as a private person and not on behalf of the sending State;
    (c) an action relating to any professional or commercial activity exercised by the diplomatic agent in the receiving State outside his official functions.
2. A diplomatic agent is not obliged to give evidence as a witness.

ARTICLE 44

The receiving State must, even in case of armed conflict, grant facilities in order to enable persons enjoying privileges and immunities, other than nationals of the receiving State, and members of the families of such persons irrespective of their nationality, to leave at the earliest possible moment. It must, in particular, in case of need, place at their disposal the necessary means of transport for themselves and their property.

THE CURRENT IMMUNITIES: AN ANALYSIS

The immunity of diplomatic envoys has a long pedigree. Historically, it can be traced back with certainty for some three millennia and may well be even older. This is in itself a strong indication that some such immunity is indispensable.

The Vienna Convention on Diplomatic Relations 1961 and the Vienna Convention on Consular Relations 1963 were therefore largely codifications of pre-existing international law and practice. The British Government played a prominent part in their negotiation and took early steps to ratify them. They entered into force for the United Kingdom on 1 October 1964 and 8 June 1972 respectively. The British Government also ratified in each case an Optional Protocol concerning the Compulsory Settlement of Disputes. These Protocols provide that disputes arising out of the interpretation or application of the Conventions fall within the compulsory jurisdiction of the International Court of Justice.

The Convention on Diplomatic Relations was implemented in the United Kingdom by the Diplomatic Privileges Act 1964, to which was annexed as a Schedule eighteen Articles from the Convention, including all the main Articles relevant to this present analysis. The wording of the Act is interesting for the emphasis it places on a fundamental principle which oddly enough is hardly mentioned in the Convention itself, although it pervades its provisions as an underlying assumption. This principle is that diplomatic privileges and immunities rest on a basis of reciprocity.

The immunities can be grouped conveniently into four categories: immunities of persons; of premises; of communications; and of possessions (archives, diplomatic/consular bags and personal baggage). By coincidence, the beneficiaries also fall into four groups: diplomatic staff; administrative/technical staff; service staff; and consular staff. There are significant differences between the immunities of these groups, particularly those of diplomatic and of consular staff members.

(a) Immunities of persons

In the Convention on Diplomatic Relations, the Articles concerned with immunities of persons are numbered 23, *29*, *31*, 32, 33, 34, 35, *37*, *38*, 40 and *44*. Those reproduced here have been italicised and will be analysed below. Those not reproduced deal with such subjects as exemptions from dues and taxes, from social security provisions and from personal service and military obligations; with waivers of immunities; and with privileges of diplomatic personnel in transit.

The first sentence of Article 29 strikes the keynote: "The person of a diplomatic agent shall be inviolable". The words "inviolable" and "inviolability" ring out at intervals throughout the Convention. They are the strongest expressions employed in it, subsuming in themselves a series of immunities which are also individually spelled out. In this case, inviolability of the person

ARTICLE 37

1. The members of the family of a diplomatic agent forming part of his household shall, if they are not nationals of the receiving State, enjoy the privileges and immunities specified in Articles 29 to 36.

2. Members of the administrative and technical staff of the mission, together with members of their families forming part of their respective households, shall, if they are not nationals of or permanently resident in the receiving State, enjoy the privileges and immunities specified in Articles 29 to 35, except that the immunity from civil and administrative jurisdiction of the receiving State specified in paragraph 1 of Article 31 shall not extend to acts performed outside the course of their duties. They shall also enjoy the privileges specified in Article 36, paragraph 1, in respect of articles imported at the time of the first installation.

3. Members of the service staff of the mission who are not nationals of or permanently resident in the receiving State shall enjoy immunity in respect of acts performed in the course of their duties, exemption from dues and taxes on the emoluments they receive by reason of their employment and the exemption contained in Article 33.

4. Private servants of members of the mission shall, if they are not nationals of or permanently resident in the receiving State, be exempt from dues and taxes on the emoluments they receive by reason of their employment. In other respects, they may enjoy privileges and immunities only to the extent admitted by the receiving State. However, the receiving State must exercise its jurisdiction over those persons in such a manner as not to interfere unduly with the performance of the functions of the mission.

ARTICLE 43 (CONSULAR)

Immunity from jurisdiction

1. Consular officers and consular employees shall not be amenable to the jurisdiction of the judicial or administrative authorities of the receiving State in respect of acts performed in the exercise of consular functions.

2. The provisions of paragraph 1 of this Article shall not, however, apply in respect of a civil action either:

   (a) *arising out of a contract concluded by a consular officer or a consular employee in which he did not contract expressly or impliedly as an agent of the sending State; or*

   (b) *by a third party for damage arising from an accident in the receiving State caused by a vehicle, vessel or aircraft.*

ARTICLE 41 (CONSULAR)

Personal inviolability of consular officers

1. Consular officers shall not be liable to arrest or detention pending trial, except in the case of a grave crime and pursuant to a decision by the competent judicial authority.

2. Except in the case specified in paragraph 1 of this Article, consular officers shall not be committed to prison or liable to any other form of restriction on their personal freedom save in execution of a judicial decision of final effect.

3. If criminal proceedings are instituted against a consular officer, he must appear before the competent authorities. Nevertheless, the proceedings shall be conducted with the respect due to him by reason of his official position and, except in the case specified in paragraph 1 of this Article, in a manner which covers immunity from "any form of arrest or detention" (Art. 29); from "the criminal jurisdiction of the receiving State" and with minor exceptions from its "civil and administrative jurisdiction" (Art. 31.1); and from being "obliged to give evidence as a witness" (Art. 31.2). Moreover, similar immunities are enjoyed by "the members of the family of a diplomatic agent forming part of his household", provided they are not nationals of the receiving State (Art. 31.1). These immunities persist "even in case of armed conflict" (Art. 44).

The term "diplomatic agent" used in Article 29 is defined in Article 1 as the "head of the mission (in other words, an Embassy, legation etc.) or a member of the diplomatic staff of the mission". Diplomatic agents are thus (for practical though not necessary legal purposes) the persons listed, with their ranks, in the Diplomatic List published at intervals in each capital by the Government of the receiving State. But missions also have non-diplomatic staff, not so listed, who enjoy lesser but still considerable immunities (set out in Article 37), provided they are not nationals or permanent residents of the receiving State. Thus, "members of the administrative and technical staff" (clerks, radio operators, security guards, etc.) also enjoy inviolability of person, except that their immunity from "civil and administrative jurisdiction" "shall not extend to acts performed outside the course of their duties". Note that this limitation is not applied to their immunity from criminal jurisdiction. However, "members of the service staff of the mission" (drivers, cleaners, etc.) have immunity only "in respect of acts performed in the course of their duties". Offences committed by them in their private capacities could therefore be subject both to criminal and to civil/administrative jurisdiction.

So far, there has either been no limitation on personal inviolability or a limitation based on the criterion of on-duty and off-duty acts. However, the Convention on Consular Relations (negotiated two years later than that on Diplomatic Relations) follows a significantly (almost startlingly) different course. The on-duty/off-duty criterion remains "Consular officers and consular employees shall not be amenable to the jurisdiction of the judicial or administrative authorities of the receiving State in respect of acts performed in the exercise of consular functions" (Art. 43.1). But there is a quite different criterion in respect of personal inviolability: "Consular officers shall not be liable to arrest or detention pending trial, except in the case of a grave crime and pursuant to a decision by the competent judicial authority" (Art. 41.1).

In the context of the remainder of the texts of these two Conventions, this is really a surprising provision. The term "grave crime" is not defined in the convention (though it is in the UK Consular Relations Act, 1968) and could clearly be a contentious point. To the extent that a judgment on gravity is subjective, it would presumably be decided by the receiving State, whereas the on-duty/off-duty criterion, if in doubt, would tend rather to be ruled on by the sending State. There is also a possible conflict between the passages quoted from Articles 41 and 43. What would happen if a "grave crime" were committed by a consular officer on duty? The possibility is not inconceivable.

That aside, Articles 41 and 42 make it clear that a consular officer, admittedly in what should be rare circumstances, could be arrested, detained pending trial, tried and committed to prison. The only constraints, in such a case, are that the *will hamper the exercise of consular functions as little as possible. When, in the circumstances mentioned in paragraph 1 of this Article, it has become necessary to detain a consular officer, the proceedings against him shall be instituted with the minimum of delay.*

ARTICLE 42 (CONSULAR)

Notification of arrest, detention or prosecution

In the event of the arrest or detention, pending trial, of a member of the consular staff, or of criminal proceedings being instituted against him, the receiving State shall promptly notify the head of the consular post. Should the latter be himself the object of any such measure, the receiving State shall notify the sending State through the diplomatic channel.

ARTICLE 70 (CONSULAR)

Exercise of consular functions by diplomatic missions

1. The provisions of the present Convention apply also, so far as the context permits, to the exercise of consular functions by a diplomatic mission.
2. The names of members of a diplomatic mission assigned to the consular section or otherwise charged with the exercise of the consular functions of the mission shall be notified to the Ministry for Foreign Affairs of the receiving State or to the authority designated by that Ministry.

ARTICLE 22

1. The premises of the mission shall be inviolable. The agents of the receiving State may not enter them, except with the consent of the head of the mission.
2. The receiving State is under a special duty to take all appropriate steps to protect the premises of the mission against any intrusion or damage and to prevent any disturbance of the peace of the mission or impairment of its dignity.
3. The premises of the mission, their furnishings and other property thereon and the means of transport of the mission shall be immune from search, requisition, attachment or execution.

ARTICLE 30

1. The private residence of a diplomatic agent shall enjoy the same inviolability and protection as the premises of the mission.
2. His papers, correspondence and, except as provided in paragraph 3 of Article 31, his property, shall likewise enjoy inviolability.

ARTICLE 45

If diplomatic relations are broken off between two States, or if a mission is permanently or temporarily recalled:
- (a) the receiving State must, even in case of armed conflict, respect and protect the premises of the mission, together with its property and archives;
- (b) the sending State may entrust the custody of the premises of the mission, together with its property and archives, to a third State acceptable to the receiving State;
- (c) the sending State may entrust the protection of its interests and those of its nationals to a third State acceptable to the receiving State.

proceedings should be conducted "with the respect due to him by reason of his official position" and "in a manner which will hamper the exercise of consular functions as little as possible". The proceedings must be instituted "with the minimum of delay" and the consular officer's superiors must be notified "promptly". Fine words, but a long way from the inviolability of a diplomatic agent.

Of course, and for this very reason, sending States minimise the number of their consular officers at such risk. It has become a widespread practice for the staffs of Consulates General or Consulates in capitals to be declared as members of the diplomatic mission, with appropriate titles (a practice authorised by Article 70 of the Convention on Consular Relations). There thus appear in Diplomatic Lists, Counsellors, First, Second or Third Secretaries and Attaches with (Consular Affairs) after their ranks. In reality they are Consuls-General, Consuls, Vice-Consuls and Consular Clerks but they are in this way protected from the judicial consequences of any "grave crimes" they may happen to commit. However, outside the capitals, independent consular posts do fall under the provisions of the Convention on Consular Relations. In such cases *caveat Consul*!

It is only fair to add that the great majority of consular officers (as indeed of diplomatic agents) live highly respectable lives (apart perhaps from minor motoring offences). So trials of consular officers are of the utmost rarity.

(b) Immunities of premises

The relevant Articles in the Convention on Diplomatic Relations are numbered 21, *22, 30* and *45*; again, those italicised are reproduced. Article 22.1 opens with the keynote phrase: "The premises of the mission shall be inviolable". Moreover, the receiving State has "a special duty to take all appropriate steps to protect" them (Art. 22.2). The same is true of a diplomatic agent's private residence which "shall enjoy the same inviolability and protection as the premises of the mission" (Art. 30.1).

In the event of a breach in diplomatic relations some hold that this inviolability is automatically terminated. Others argue that it passes to the protecting power if one has been appointed: "the sending State may entrust the custody of the premises of the mission . . . to a third State acceptable to the receiving State" (Art. 45(b)). Even war between the two States is not sufficient to wipe out a degree of immunity: "the receiving State must, even in case of armed conflict, respect and protect the premises of the mission" (Art. 45(a)).

Consular premises have a less absolute inviolability. The Convention on Consular Relations gives inviolability only to "that part of the consular premises which is used exclusively for the purpose of the work of the consular post" (Art. 31.2). So private residences, even forming part of the Consulate building, are by implication not inviolable. And in the event of "fire or other disaster requiring prompt protective action", the authorities of the receiving State may enter consular offices; in such cases, a waiver of inviolability by the head of the consular post "may be assumed" (Art. 31.2). There can, it

ARTICLE 31 (CONSULAR)

Inviolability of the consular premises

1. Consular premises shall be inviolable to the extent provided in this Article.
2. The authorities of the receiving State shall not enter that part of the consular premises which is used exclusively for the purpose of the work of the consular post except with the consent of the head of the consular post or of his designee or of the head of the diplomatic mission of the sending State. The consent of the head of the consular post may, however, be assumed in case of fire or other disaster requiring prompt protective action.
3. Subject to the provisions of paragraph 2 of this Article, the receiving State is under a special duty to take all appropriate steps to protect the consular premises against any intrusion or damage and to prevent any disturbance of the peace of the consular post or impairment of its dignity.
4. The consular premises, their furnishings, the property of the consular post and its means of transport shall be immune from any form of requisition for purposes of national defence or public utility. If expropriation is necessary for such purposes, all possible steps shall be taken to avoid impeding the performance of consular functions, and prompt, adequate and effective compensation shall be paid to the sending State.

ARTICLE 27

1. The receiving State shall permit and protect free communication on the part of the mission for all official purposes. In communicating with the Government and the other missions and consulates of the sending State, wherever situated, the mission may employ all appropriate means, including diplomatic couriers and messages in code or cipher. However, the mission may install and use a wireless transmitter only with the consent of the receiving State.
2. The official correspondence of the mission shall be inviolable. Official correspondence means all correspondence relating to the mission and its functions.
3. The diplomatic bag shall not be opened or detained.
4. The packages constituting the diplomatic bag must bear visible external marks of their character and may contain only diplomatic documents or articles intended for official use.
5. The diplomatic courier, who shall be provided with an official document indicating his status and the number of packages constituting the diplomatic bag, shall be protected by the receiving State in the performance of his functions. He shall enjoy personal inviolability and shall not be liable to any form of arrest or detention.
6. The sending State or the mission may designate diplomatic couriers *ad hoc.* In such cases the provisions of paragraph 5 of this Article shall also apply, except that the immunities therein mentioned shall cease to apply when such a courier has delivered to the consignee the diplomatic bag in his charge.
7. A diplomatic bag may be entrusted to the captain of a commercial aircraft scheduled to land at an authorized port of entry. He shall be provided with an official document indicating the number of packages constituting the bag but he shall not be considered to be a diplomatic courier. The mission may send one of its members to take possession of the diplomatic bag directly and freely from the captain of the aircraft.

should be noted, be no such assumption in the case of diplomatic premises, even if the result is that they burn down. Another limitation on the immunity of consular (but not diplomatic) premises arises from "purposes of national defence or public utility". Consular premises may not be requisitioned for such purposes but may, if necessary, be expropriated, subject to payment of "prompt, adequate and effective compensation" (Art. 31.4).

(c) Immunity of communications

This subject is treated rather briefly in both Conventions, and in virtually identical terms, in Article 27 of the Convention on Diplomatic Relations and Article 35 of the Convention on Consular Relations. The general principle is that the receiving State "shall permit and protect free communication on the part of the mission for all official purposes" (Art. 27.1). Specified as permitted are diplomatic/consular couriers and messages in code or cipher. But there is an important limitation: "the mission may install and use a wireless transmitter only with the consent of the receiving State." In practice, though the Convention does not say so, radio transmitters are obviously a matter of reciprocity. Country A, wishing to have a radio transmitter in its Embassy in Country B, would have to apply for permission to install and use it, and could not hope to do so with success unless it were prepared to grant Country B similar facilities in its own capital.

The other relevant provision of the two Conventions is on official correspondence, defined as "all correspondence relating to the mission and its functions". This is dealt with simply and briefly: it "shall be inviolable" (Art. 27.2). Note that this inviolability applies to all official correspondence, however transmitted. But in practice there are many countries in the world where diplomatic missions would not place much trust in the inviolability of letters entrusted to the open mail. Hence the almost universal use of diplomatic/consular bags, which will be dealt with in the next section. The inviolability of a consular post's correspondence is identical (Art. 35.2).

(d) immunities of possessions (archives, diplomatic/consular bags, personal baggage)

Article 24 of the Convention on Diplomatic Relations is brief: "The archives and documents of the mission shall be inviolable at any time and wherever they may be." The last phrase is noteworthy. Almost always, such archives and documents will be in diplomatic premises or in diplomatic bags, which have their own immunities. But even if elsewhere, e.g. shipped in packing cases following closure of a mission for whatever reason, the immunity of archives and documents is absolute. Article 33 of the Convention on Consular Relations uses exactly the same wording, with no qualification, regarding the inviolability of consular archives and documents. This is notable since on many other points consular immunities tend to be less absolute than diplomatic immunities. Not so for archives.

Perhaps surprisingly, the word "inviolable" is not used in the main Articles

ARTICLE 24

The archives and documents of the mission shall be inviolable at any time and wherever they may be.

ARTICLE 35 (CONSULAR)

Freedom of communication

2. The official correspondence of the consular post shall be inviolable. Official correspondence means all correspondence relating to the consular post and its functions.

3. The consular bag shall be neither opened nor detained. Nevertheless, if the competent authorities of the receiving State have serious reason to believe that the bag contains something other than the correspondence, documents or articles referred to in paragraph 4 of this Article, they may request that the bag be opened in their presence by an authorized representative of the sending State. If this request is refused by the authorities of the sending State, the bag shall be returned to its place of origin.

4. The packages constituting the consular bag shall bear visible external marks of their character and may contain only official correspondence and documents or articles intended exclusively for official use.

5. The consular courier shall be provided with an official document indicating his status and the number of packages constituting the consular bag. Except with the consent of the receiving State he shall be neither a national of the receiving State, nor, unless he is a national of the sending State, a permanent resident of the receiving State. In the performance of his functions he shall be protected by the receiving State. He shall enjoy personal inviolability and shall not be liable to any form of arrest or detention.

6. The sending State, its diplomatic missions and its consular posts may designate consular couriers ad hoc. In such cases the provisions of paragraph 5 of this Article shall also apply except that the immunities therein mentioned shall cease to apply when such a courier has delivered to the consignee the consular bag in his charge.

7. A consular bag may be entrusted to the captain of a ship or of a commercial aircraft scheduled to land at an authorized port of entry. He shall be provided with an official document indicating the number of packages constituting the bag, but he shall not be considered to be a consular courier. By arrangement with the appropriate local authorities, the consular post may send one of its members to take possession of the bag directly and freely from the captain of the ship or of the aircraft.

ARTICLE 36

1. The receiving State shall, in accordance with such laws and regulations as it may adopt, permit entry of and grant exemption from all customs duties, taxes, and related charges other than charges for storage, cartage and similar services, on:
   (a) articles for the official use of the mission;
   (b) articles for the personal use of a diplomatic agent or members of his family forming part of his household, including articles intended for his establishment.

2. The personal baggage of a diplomatic agent shall be exempt from inspection, unless there are serious grounds for presuming that it contains articles not covered by the exemptions mentioned in paragraph 1 of this Article, or articles the import or export of which is prohibited by the law or controlled by the quarantine regulations of the receiving State. Such inspection shall be conducted only in the presence of the diplomatic agent or of his authorized representative.

about diplomatic and consular bags (although, as has already been seen, official correspondence in such bags would be inviolable). Instead Article 27.3 of the Convention on Diplomatic Relations says: "The diplomatic bag shall not be opened or detained." This wording makes it at least arguable that a diplomatic bag could, without breach of the Convention, be subjected to treatment which did not detain it, nor of course open it. It might, for instance, be passed through an X-ray machine (though measures are available for shielding from X-rays). Kuwait has in fact recently begun to X-ray diplomatic bags and diplomatic missions there are divided on whether this is acceptable.

As for Article 35.3 of the Convention on Consular Relations, it begins with virtually identical wording about the consular bag: it "shall be neither opened nor detained". However, it goes on to provide that if "the competent authorities of the receiving State" suspect, or rather "have serious reason to believe", that the bag contains something other than official correspondence and documents or articles intended exclusively for official use, they may ask for it to be opened in their presence by "an authorised representative of the sending State" and if that is refused may return it to its place of origin. This is a very interesting limitation on the immunity of the consular bag, which will merit later consideration.

Personal baggage is dealt with in the Convention on Diplomatic Relations in the context of exemption from customs duties and from customs inspection. Articles "for the personal use of a diplomatic agent or members of his family" enjoy immunity from "all customs duties, taxes and related charges" (Art. 36.1(b)). However, its exemption from inspection is not absolute: it "shall be exempt from inspection, unless there are serious grounds for presuming that it contains articles not covered by the exemptions mentioned in paragraph 1 of this Article, or articles the import or export of which is prohibited by the law or controlled by the quarantine regulations of the receiving State" (Art. 36.2). In such a case, the customs officials could inspect the baggage, but "only in the presence of the diplomatic agent or of his authorised representative".

The Convention on Consular Relations has an identical provision on inspection (Art. 50.3). But it also has one limitation not applied to diplomatic agents: the "articles intended for consumption" included in the personal baggage of a consular officer or members of his family "shall not exceed the quantities necessary for direct utilization by the persons concerned". Members of the administrative and technical staff of a diplomatic mission and likewise consular employees, enjoy similar privileges to those of their seniors, but only "in respect of articles imported at the time of first installation" (Art. 37.2 and Art. 50.2 respectively). This rather pettifogging limitation is of long standing but it is not clear that it serves any really useful purpose, except to remind junior staff of their juniority. It has a certain nuisance value, but in practice it is easily (and almost universally) evaded.

OBLIGATIONS OF DIPLOMATS

Balancing the many Articles on the privileges of diplomatic and consular personnel, there is just one Article in each of the Conventions on their

ARTICLE 50 (CONSULAR)

Exemption from customs duties and inspection

1. The receiving State shall, in accordance with such laws and regulations as it may adopt, permit entry of and grant exemption from all customs duties, taxes, and related charges other than charges for storage, cartage and similar services, on:

    (a) articles for the official use of the consular post;

    (b) articles for the personal use of a consular officer or members of his family forming part of his household, including articles intended for his establishment. The articles intended for consumption shall not exceed the quantities necessary for direct utilization by the persons concerned.

2. Consular employees shall enjoy the privileges and exemptions specified in paragraph 1 of this Article in respect of articles imported at the time of first installation.

3. Personal baggage accompanying consular officers and members of their families forming part of their households shall be exempt from inspection. It may be inspected only if there is serious reason to believe that it contains articles other than those referred to in sub-paragraph (b) of paragraph 1 of this Article, or articles the import or export of which is prohibited by the laws and regulations of the receiving State or which are subject to its quarantine laws and regulations. Such inspection shall be carried out in the presence of the consular officer or member of his family concerned.

ARTICLE 41

1. Without prejudice to their privileges and immunities, it is the duty of all persons enjoying such privileges and immunities to respect the laws and regulations of the receiving State. They also have a duty not to interfere in the internal affairs of that State.

2. All official business with the receiving State entrusted to the mission by the sending State shall be conducted with or through the Ministry for Foreign Affairs of the receiving State or such other ministry as may be agreed.

3. The premises of the mission must not be used in any manner incompatible with the functions of the mission as laid down in the present Convention or by other rules of general international law or by any special agreements in force between the sending and the receiving State.

ARTICLE 55 (CONSULAR)

Respect for the laws and regulations of the receiving State

1. Without prejudice to their privileges and immunities, it is the duty of all persons enjoying such privileges and immunities to respect the laws and regulations of the receiving State. They also have a duty not to interfere in the internal affairs of that State.

2. The consular premises shall not be used in any manner incompatible with the exercise of consular functions.

3. The provisions of paragraph 2 of this Article shall not exclude the possibility of offices of other institutions or agencies being installed in part of the building in which the consular premises are situated, provided that the premises assigned to them are separate from those used by the consular post. In that event, the said offices shall not, for the purposes of the present Convention, be considered to form part of the consular premises.

obligations. Article 41.1 of the Convention on Diplomatic Relations says: "Without prejudice to their privileges and immunities, it is the duty of all persons enjoying such privileges and immunities to respect the laws and regulations of the receiving State." The effect of this wording is very clear: there is an obligation corresponding to immunities, but if the obligation is broken the immunities still persist. The wording of Article 55.1 of the Convention on Consular Relations is identical. (Sad to say, there are diplomats who pay little attention to Article 41, at least in regard to laws and regulations which they find troublesome and think unimportant, such as parking regulations. Their own head of mission should put a stop to such undisciplined behaviour, but it is clear that not all do so.)

Some disturbing figures about the frequency of serious crimes committed by foreign diplomats in London was released by the Foreign Office on 20 June 1984. A Select Committee of the House of Commons was informed that in the preceding 10 years there had been 546 serious offences (those punishable with a six months or longer prison sentence) believed to have been committed by diplomatic agents possessed of personal immunity. This somewhat startling figure turns out on analysis to consist mainly of shoplifters and drunken drivers (serious enough in all conscience, but on a different plane from State-sponsored assassins), with a sprinkling of sexual offenders. However, there were 36 cases involving violence and five in which firearms were involved. Set against a figure of 50,000 diplomat-years this is a small minority, but is nevertheless inexcusable. There can be no doubt that there has been a decline in standards of diplomatic behaviour in recent years, but arguably not beyond the bounds which can be contained by summary expulsions. In most cases, the heads of mission concerned take this action themselves; in the relatively few remaining cases, the *persona non grata* system can be and is invoked.

ARTICLE 2

The establishment of diplomatic relations between States, and of permanent diplomatic missions, takes place by mutual consent.

ARTICLE 4

1. The sending State must make certain that the *agrément* of the receiving State has been given for the person it proposes to accredit as head of the mission to that State.
2. The receiving State is not obliged to give reasons to the sending State for a refusal of *agrément*.

ARTICLE 10

1. The Ministry for Foreign Affairs of the receiving State, or such other ministry as may be agreed, shall be notified of:
   (a) the appointment of members of the mission, their arrival and their final departure or the termination of their functions with the mission;
   (b) the arrival and final departure of a person belonging to the family of a member of the mission and, where appropriate, the fact that a person becomes or ceases to be a member of the family of a member of the mission;
   (c) the arrival and final departure of private servants in the employ of persons referred to in sub-paragraph (a) of this paragraph and, where appropriate, the fact that they are leaving the employ of such persons;
   (d) the engagement and discharge of persons resident in the receiving State as members of the mission or private servants entitled to privileges and immunities.
2. Where possible, prior notification of arrival and final departure shall also be given.

ARTICLE 7

Subject to the provisions of Articles 5, 8, 9 and 11, the sending State may freely appoint the members of the staff of the mission. In the case of military, naval or air attachés, the receiving State may require their names to be submitted beforehand, for its approval.

ARTICLE 11

1. In the absence of specific agreement as to the size of the mission, the receiving State may require that the size of a mission be kept within limits considered by it to be reasonable and normal, having regard to circumstances and conditions in the receiving State and to the needs of the particular mission.
2. The receiving State may equally, within similar bounds and on a non-discriminatory basis, refuse to accept officials of a particular category.

RIGHTS AND POWERS OF RECEIVING STATES

Receiving States have some not insignificant powers to protect themselves against abuse of diplomatic privileges. They include the following (Articles cited are from the Convention on Diplomatic Relations)

(a) A State can refuse to establish diplomatic relations with another State or can refuse the mutual opening of permanent diplomatic missions (Art. 2). In practice this rarely happens except in cases where one State refuses to recognise the legitimacy of another.

(b) Diplomatic relations may be broken off. This is a sanction which some States use freely to show disapproval of a particular Government or indeed of a particular line of policy. British practice has been to resort to this sanction very rarely (three times only since 1945), on the principle that lines of communication should be kept open even with Governments with which relations are for the time being cold.

(c) If relations are broken off, the Convention provides for the appointment of protecting powers. The third States chosen for this role (usually different States in the two capitals, although the same State can act in both) are selected by the sending States, but must be acceptable to the receiving States (Art. 45). So the receiving State could ban a particular selection (difficult in practice since to do so would be likely to impair its relations with the third State concerned).

(d) A receiving State has a veto on the accreditation of a head of mission, and need give no reason for refusing *agrément* (Art. 4). It does sometimes happen that *agrément* is refused, though rather rarely. The procedure for seeking *agrément* is such that a refusal need not become public knowledge.

(e) For members of the staff of the mission other than its head, there must be notification to the receiving State of their appointment, their arrival and their final departure (Art. 10.1). The Convention does not stipulate that there must be prior notification in all cases, but says that there shall be "where possible" (Art. 10.2). In the case of appointments and arrivals, prior notification should in practice always be possible, so there seems no reason why a receiving State should not insist on it, either for all missions or for particular missions. It could then use its other powers to frustrate any appointment it had reason to dislike (e.g. because the person nominated had abused his or her diplomatic status elsewhere). This would *prima facie* be a breach of Article 7, which says that the sending State "may freely appoint the members of the staff of the mission", and which makes an exception only for military, naval or air attachés, in whose case "the receiving State may require their names to be submitted beforehand, for its approval". But administratively a receiving State could by asking for prior notification of all appointments put itself into a position to give tacit approval to appointments of all staff, and so could in practice object to a particular appointment and insist that its objection must be heeded. The last sentence of Article 9.1 makes such an objection binding.

Limiting size of mission

(f) Apart from any control on individual appointments, a receiving State may limit the size of a mission (Art. 11.1) and may refuse to accept officials of a

ARTICLE 47

1. In the application of the provisions of the present Convention, the receiving State shall not discriminate as between States.
2. However, discrimination shall not be regarded as taking place:
   (a) where the receiving State applies any of the provisions of the present Convention restrictively because of a restrictive application of that provision to its mission in the sending State;
   (b) where by custom or agreement States extend to each other more favourable treatment than is required by the provisions of the present Convention.

ARTICLE 12

The sending State may not, without the prior express consent of the receiving State, establish offices forming part of the mission in localities other than those in which the mission itself is established.

ARTICLE 9

1. The receiving State may at any time and without having to explain its decision, notify the sending State that the head of the mission or any member of the diplomatic staff of the mission is *persona non grata* or that any other member of the staff of the mission is not acceptable. In any such case, the sending State shall, as appropriate, either recall the person concerned or terminate his functions with the mission. A person may be declared *non grata* or not acceptable before arriving in the territory of the receiving State.
2. If the sending State refuses or fails within a reasonable period to carry out its obligations under paragraph 1 of this Article, the receiving State may refuse to recognize the person concerned as a member of the mission.

ARTICLE 26

Subject to its laws and regulations concerning zones entry into which is prohibited or regulated for reasons of national security, the receiving State shall ensure to all members of the mission freedom of movement and travel in its territory.

particular category (Art. 11.2). The size-limiting powers are occasionally used. For instance, on the famous occasion when 105 Soviet citizens, the majority of them diplomats, were simultaneously expelled from the United Kingdom for espionage, the Soviet authorities were informed that the size of their mission in London must be reduced by the number of diplomats expelled, so preventing their replacement. This was feasible because the staff of the Soviet Embassy in London was much more numerous than that of the British Embassy in Moscow. It is a tactic which (despite the non-discrimination provisions of Article 47) could be used more often, not necessarily at the time of expulsions, to limit the size of troublesome missions to a level of reciprocity. The separate power to exclude officials of a particular category (e.g. service attachés) has not been found to be very useful and is virtually a dead letter. The most frequently employed sanction of all is that in Article 9, the right to declare a diplomat *persona non grata* (or a non-diplomat not acceptable). The receiving State may do this "at any time and without having to explain its decision", even, as already mentioned, in advance of arrival of the person concerned. Usually, such expulsions are for espionage (often euphemised as "conduct incompatible with diplomatic status"), but they are sometimes for other forms of unacceptable behaviour and this sanction could be used more freely.

The drawback, of course, is that the sending State regularly protests that such expulsions are unjustified (not least when it knows the contrary) and takes "tit-for-tat" action against perfectly law-abiding members of the mission of the aggrieved State. There is normally no satisfactory defence against such a riposte; further reciprocal action could lead to a chain effect which would eventually cripple both missions. It would of course be possible for the receiving State to threaten to break off relations entirely if it suffered tit-for-tat expulsions, but only if ready to carry out the threat. Short of that, the size-limitation sanction could be threatened as a reprisal for such expulsions (see (f) above). This could be effective where there is a discrepancy in the size of the two missions.

(h) One Article which the Soviet Union in particular notoriously fails to observe is Article 26, which provides that "the receiving State shall ensure to all members of the mission freedom of movement and travel in its territory". The exception to this provision is "zones entry into which is prohibited or regulated for reasons of national security", an exception which the Soviet Union exploits so widely as to frustrate the primary purpose of the Article. Here again there is no very satisfactory defence against such abuse. Counter-restrictions on movement are sanctioned by Article 47.2(a) and are normally applied, but that is really no solution to the problem. In the end it comes down to a decision on whether it is still worth while to have diplomatic relations with a State which notoriously limits the movement of diplomats in its territory, and so far the answer to that question has been a reluctant "yes".

(i) Mention has already been made of the right of the receiving State to refuse consent for a mission to "install and use a wireless transmitter" (Art. 27.1). This is a right of only marginal importance and is obviously subject to considerations of reciprocity. It is on its way to becoming a dead letter.

(j) Also already mentioned is the right to inspect the personal baggage of a diplomatic agent when there are "serious grounds for presuming" that it contains forbidden articles (Art. 36.2). But there is no right to inspect "articles for the official use of the mission" (Art. 36.1). So this is a sanction against an individual diplomat breaking the laws of the receiving State (e.g. by smuggling drugs), but gives no protection against abuses by the sending State itself.

EMERGENCE OF STATE-SPONSORED TERRORISM

It is only in recent years that the world has experienced the phenomenon of heads of State or Government or other leading politicians, usually of dictatorial and "revolutionary" regimes, announcing an intention to liquidate the regime's opponents abroad as well as at home. Colonel Qadhafi of Libya has been the prime example, but not the only one, and there has been evidence that this is in fact the policy of certain regimes which have not publicly announced it.

In the nature of things, a regime which adopts such a policy will be one which has bitter opponents and fanatical supporters. Otherwise the policy would be unnecessary or ineffective. The opponents will include exiles from their country, some of whom may have been granted political asylum, while others may be living abroad ostensibly as tourists or students. To liquidate them will require the presence of assassins and weapons in the foreign country concerned, and diplomatic privileges can be abused to this end.

On the whole, it is unlikely that assassins will be sent in as members of a diplomatic mission (although the possibility cannot be entirely excluded). The mission staff members are more likely to be charged by the terrorist Government with the tasks of identifying the targets (probably under cover of consular concern with the welfare of nationals) and briefing the assassins on these targets' whereabouts and habits. The assassins would probably arrive on brief visits, ostensibly as tourists or businessmen, ready to leave quickly after accomplishing their tasks. False passports would be used to disguise the identity, and often the nationality, of the assassins (diplomatic passports, which all too many States issue to non-diplomats, might be used, but are perhaps more likely to be avoided as drawing too much attention to the visitors).

The other task of the diplomatic mission would be to arm the assassins after their arrival in the foreign country (obviously they would avoid bringing weapons with them, since detection by customs officers could frustrate their tasks). Hand guns imported through the diplomatic bag, under cover of its immunity, constitute the most obvious source of such arms.

POSSIBLE CHANGES IN THE CONVENTIONS

The texts of the two Vienna Conventions contain no procedures for their amendment; nevertheless they could be amended, or new Conventions could be negotiated to supersede them. It goes without saying that to do so would be a difficult and lengthy business. The United Nations would have to be the forum and a consensus of all, or virtually all, of its members would be required.

However, if the objective is desirable, these practical difficulties should not be allowed to stand in the way of making the attempt. It might take 10, 20, 30 years to bring better texts into force (and by then new problems might have arisen), but if the new texts really would be better then the effort would be worthwhile. The International Law Commission has in fact spent the last three years examining the Article on diplomatic bags, so far with little result.

There would be a choice between two main ways of proceeding. One would be to redraft key Articles here and there throughout the text to increase the powers of receiving States in particular cases. The other would be to swing the whole balance of the Conventions so as to increase the obligations on members of diplomatic and consular staffs and to reduce their immunities in the event of breach of such obligations.

To take the latter case first, the key provision is Article 41.1 of the Convention on Diplomatic Relations (and the corresponding Article 55.1 of the Convention on Consular Relations). The Article begins: "Without prejudice to their privileges and immunities, it is the duty of all persons enjoying such privileges and immunities to respect the laws and regulations of the receiving State." This could be redrafted on the lines of: "It is the duty of all persons enjoying privileges and immunities to respect the laws and regulations of the receiving State and a failure to do so renders such privileges and immunities null and void."

No doubt the newly worded Article would then have to be elaborated (probably into a whole chapter) to specify the procedures to be followed and the safeguards to be applied, but that is detail (important detail of course, but still detail). It is the principle of the balance between immunities and obligations which is crucial. And that balance needs to come down firmly on one side or the other: any attempt to leave it evenly suspended would produce such uncertainty that chaos would result (almost certainly to the disadvantage of the law-abiding).

The other approach would be to leave the immunities prevailing over obligations as in Article 41.1 at present, but by amending certain other important Articles to make the immunities themselves less absolute. With State-sponsored terrorism in mind, the key Articles would be those on the diplomatic bag, on immunity of diplomatic agents from judicial process, and perhaps on inviolability of diplomatic premises. An interesting way of approaching such an objective would be to reduce diplomatic immunities to the lower level of consular immunities.

As was brought out above in the analysis of the provisions of the Convention on Consular Relations: "if the competent authorities of the receiving State have serious reason to believe that the bag contains something other than official correspondence and documents or articles intended exclusively for official use, they may request that the bag be opened in their presence by an authorised representative of the sending State. If this request is refused by the authorities of the sending State, the bag shall be returned to its place of origin" (Art. 35.3).

Again, with regard to immunity from judicial process, the Convention on Consular Relations provides: "Consular officers shall not be liable to arrest or detention pending trial, except in the case of a grave crime".

Only the limitation on inviolability of consular premises seems inadequate to enable the receiving State to cope with State-sponsored terrorism, since this limitation applies only "in case of fire or other disaster requiring prompt protective action" (Art. 31.2). A link with the concept of "grave crime" would be more apposite, and wording for this would have to be worked out.

Provided these three provisions were modified on these lines, there would seem to be no good case for watering down other immunities, such as the inviolability of archives and of official correspondence (when opening of diplomatic bags was requested, it would be in search for quite different contents, such as weapons, and correspondence would remain inviolate). It follows that in principle there need be no interference with the legitimate functioning of diplomatic missions.

LIVING WITH THE CONSEQUENCES

If the Convention on Diplomatic Relations were amended along either of the two lines examined above, what would be the consequences for the missions of States innocent of State-sponsored terrorism? What, to take the specific example, would be the consequences for British Embassies and for their staffs? In the nature of things, this must be a matter for personal judgment amounting to little more than guesswork, but there is some experience to draw on.

Even with the present panoply of immunities to protect them, diplomats in certain countries sometimes suffer harassment from the officials of receiving States. There have been, in particular, a considerable number of recorded cases of their being arrested and held for quite long periods (say 24 to 48 hours) for interrogation. This is illegal under Article 29, and yet it happens. How much more often would it happen if that Article were made less absolute? The likelihood is that in certain countries it would become quite a frequent experience. If, for instance, the concept of "a grave crime" were introduced into the Article, then, however carefully that term were defined, there would be some countries which would twist the facts to suit their own interpretation of the definition.

At least at present those illegally arrested are ultimately released, after vigorous protests by their heads of mission and their Governments. But under an Article similar to Article 41 of the Consular Convention, there would be a real risk of some quite innocent diplomat being arrested, tried and sentenced to prison on a trumped up charge. The object might be, for instance, to set up a bargaining position to secure an exchange of prisoners. This is not totally unknown already in espionage cases, below the diplomatic level.

Improper advantage could also be taken of a change in the wording of the Article on the diplomatic bag (Art. 27). It must be realised that the bag is not just a sack of letters. It can include packing cases, even whole railway wagons. (The Soviet lorry recently turned back by the Swiss Government was rejected as diplomatic baggage not because of its size but because it had strayed from its direct route into suspicious proximity to a Swiss airfield.) There are many things besides official correspondence which missions quite properly need to import under diplomatic franchise. One of the most sensitive of these, in this technological age, is the cypher machine. Even a quick glimpse of the size and shape of the exterior of such a machine could give an expert of the receiving State, disguised no doubt as a customs officer, a vital starting-point for efforts to break the cypher concerned. This obviously could not be tolerated. But consider the alternative. Suppose the authorities of the sending State refused permission for the bag to be opened and it were "returned to its place of origin". The result could be that an Embassy might be left for a considerable time without the protection of cyphers for its telegrams, so either frustrating much of its work or compelling it to operate insecurely.

Article 47.2(a) of the Convention on Diplomatic Relations gives a receiving State the right to withhold any immunity from a sending State which does not itself grant that immunity to others. Ironically (and tragically in the light of the events of 17 April 1984 in London), this provision for negative reciprocity would have authorised the UK Government to deny to Libya the immunity of the diplomatic bag provided by Article 27.3 of the Convention, since the Libyan Government (like certain other Arab Governments) had itself excluded acceptance of this provision from its adherence to the Convention. This was revealed to Parliament by the Foreign Office Legal Adviser in evidence given to a Select Committee of the House of Commons on 20 June 1984. But Libya had not put its exclusion of this immunity into practice, and for the sake of the *de facto* immunity of the UK diplomatic bags to and from Tripoli, Libyan bags had been allowed into and out of London unsearched. This decision seems likely to attract retrospective criticism, but for the reasons just discussed it was surely right. A diplomatic mission really cannot function without an immune diplomatic bag. Removal of the immunity of the bag is therefore bound to lead ultimately to withdrawal of the diplomatic mission concerned. This can be achieved more straightforwardly by a breach of diplomatic relations, which is the course the UK finally adopted towards Libya.

Again, consider the consequences of a weakening of the provisions for inviolability of diplomatic premises (Art. 22). If, under pretext of suspicion of a "grave crime", officials of the receiving State could enter an Embassy without prior permission, such an entry could be staged as cover for surreptitious "bugging" of the premises (microphones can be minute in size these days and be planted in an instant).

These are not figments of a heated imagination, but real possibilities which were surely taken into account when the present Convention on Diplomatic Relations was drafted. They point to the moral that living with the consequences of a weakened Convention could be extremely unpleasant, even dangerous, for the missions of law-abiding States.

If changes to particular Articles have such drawbacks, the alternative discussed above of altering Article 41.1 of the Convention on Diplomatic Relations and the corresponding Article 55.1 of the Convention on Consular Relations is surely a complete non-starter. The effect of making the obligation "to respect the laws and regulations of the receiving State" take precedence over the privileges and immunities of diplomatic agents and consular officers would in practice mean that there were no immunities when they were needed.

An expert on the subject has described a Convention so revised as "a bridge which is designed to collapse when the first person crosses it".

CONCLUSIONS

I conclude that:

(a) No attempt should be made to amend the Vienna Convention on Diplomatic Relations 1961. To do so would not only be difficult and time-consuming but, if accomplished, would on balance do harm. There is no future in (to use T. S. Eliot's phrase) "dreaming of systems so perfect that no one will need to be good".

(b) To combat the use of diplomatic privileges and immunities for the purposes of State-sponsored terrorism, more vigorous and much earlier use should be made of the rights of receiving States under the present Convention. In particular:

  (i) The size of suspect missions should be limited, or else the threat of limitation should be held over the mission as a penalty for any malpractice.

  (ii) The missions of suspect States should be instructed to give prior notice of the names and dates of arrival of all their staff, both diplomatic and non-diplomatic. If any of them is believed (perhaps from activities elsewhere) to be a potential assassin, or a trainer or organiser of assassins, he or she should be declared *persona non grata* (or unacceptable) prior to arrival.

  (iii) If adverse information about a member of the staff of a suspect mission comes to light after that member's arrival, or if he or she is reported to be acting suspiciously (particularly in relation to the mission's own nationals in the receiving State), the *p.n.g.* procedure should be used immediately without waiting for evidence to accrue.

  (iv) If, despite the above sanctions against individuals, the mission is still believed to be planning or engaging in terrorism, diplomatic relations should be broken off without delay.

(c) Such measures against State-sponsored terrorism should to the extent possible be co-ordinated with like-minded law-abiding States. In particular, full information about persons declared *p.n.g.* and their activities should be circulated rapidly through liaison channels.

(d) It must be recognised that a receiving State which takes the initiative on the lines of (b) above to pre-empt State-sponsored terrorism must be ready to suffer retaliation (however unjustified) from the sending State. This is unavoidable and is a price which must be paid, but there should be advance planning on how to minimise its consequences, e.g. in the commercial field, as soon as any State becomes suspected of practising State-sponsored terrorism.

First published 1984.

Part Two

Terrorist Tactics in Western Europe

Four Case Studies

Terrorism in France

Edward Moxon-Browne

INTRODUCTION

Until recently, terrorist activity in France has not been sufficiently serious to warrant much attention from either academic analysts or policy makers. In a book on European terrorism, published as recently as 1981, the contributor on France was able to comment that "in the 1970s France was relatively free from the kind of classic terrorism that predominates elsewhere".[1] In the five years from 1972 to 1977 only eleven people died in France as a result of terrorist incidents. In contrast, no fewer than fifteen people were victims of terrorism in a four-month period in 1982 (May–August). By the end of 1982, the French government was facing criticism not only from its own supporters in France but also from abroad. For example, in early August, the judge in charge of the inquiry into the kidnapping of Aldo Moro by Red Brigades terrorists in 1978, Ferdinando Imposimato, launched a scathing attack on the French authorities:

> For a long time now, we in Rome have had evidence that terrorism has rooted itself in France and that Paris has become a remarkably well-organised base for terrorist operations . . . We deplore the fact that the French authorities have not reacted with more interest to our information and warnings . . . International terrorism has been strangled in Germany, and has suffered serious setbacks in Italy. Driven out, or almost from these countries, it has taken refuge and is recuperating in Paris.

The apparent laxity of the French government is related to both the novelty of the problem and its inherent complexity. In the first place, France has had a long tradition of welcoming foreigners to its soil. Around 120 different nationalities are represented among the inhabitants of France amounting to eight per cent of the total population. Since 1945, one million foreigners have obtained French citizenship. Among the many foreigners in France, there are about 150,000 political refugees the vast majority of whom respect the condition that political asylum excludes political activism let alone political violence. Nevertheless, a small minority of political refugees abuse the hospitality of the French State, and the same can be said of a few diplomats accredited to embassies in Paris. This latter phenomenon led to calls for a "purge of the embassies" in April 1982 after a serious terrorist incident near the Champs Elysées. The existence of large numbers of foreigners and French citizens of foreign extraction makes it particularly difficult for the police to weed out foreign terrorists. The steady influx of political refugees keeps political life in France in a state of constant ferment; and the conspiratorial

---

[1] P. G. Cerny, "France: Non-Terrorism and the Politics of Repressive Tolerance" in J. Lodge (ed.) *Terrorism: A Challenge to the State* (Oxford: Martin Robertson, 1981), p. 103.

111

activities of exiled groups in Paris are not only an accepted fact of life but have, until recently, been seen as a worthy attribute of France's pluralist democracy.

Foreign groups, of every persuasion, do not find it difficult to blend in with France's rich and diverse political culture. The kaleidoscopic political arena provides ample opportunity for every conceivable political opinion to express itself, and for foreign political dissidents to latch on to ideologically sympathetic groups. The breadth of the political spectrum reduces the temptation to resort to extra-systemic activities (i.e. violence) and the groups that do succumb to the temptation are those that are too insignificant to make an impact in any other way and who are, generally speaking, extremely marginal to French society. It is from the edges of French society, among individuals who have a variety of grudges, grievances and burning aspirations, that French terrorism emanates.

If French public opinion has appeared, until recently, to be rather casual about terrorism, one has to remember that in a historical context, the concept of "terrorism" has not always been antipathetical to the "state" or the "nation". Frenchmen are readier than most Europeans to judge terrorism by its aims; and thus less willing to condemn all terroristic methods out of hand. If Frenchmen regard the Revolution of 1789 as the birth date of their liberties and republican form of government, such an event is not easily divorced in the public conscious-ness from the "state terror" of Robespierre and the Jacobins that followed. In the twentieth century, terrorist methods have sometimes been identified with extreme forms of patriotism e.g. in the heroism of the *maquisards* in World War II or the campaign of the OAS to keep Algeria French. Such an overlap robs "terrorism" not only of its fear-inducing qualities but more importantly of the automatically pejorative overtones that the words "terrorism" and "terrorist" convey in other parts of Western Europe.

If public policy in extending hospitality to political refugees, and the multi-faceted political culture of France, make the country vulnerable to terrorism, the same is true of its geographical location. A glance at the map shows France to be at the crossroads of Western Europe. Its thousands of miles of borders touch seven other countries and the borders themselves are all too easily penetrated by the terrorist-in-transit. Thus it is that although much of French terrorism stems from an unresolved ethnic conflict (i.e. Corsica) most of the rest is not indigenous but imported. France's long frontiers, its international airports, and its good communications with Western Europe all conspire to render the country vulnerable to foreign terrorism. An added bonus is the amount of media representation in Paris which guarantees maximum publicity for acts of terrorism that are, in many cases, a settling of scores between foreign groups abusing the hospitality of France as the traditional *terre d'asile*.

As there is rarely an obvious personal link between the terrorist and his victim – the latter is normally a symbolic target – the work of the police in curbing this kind of violence is extremely difficult. *A fortiori*, any serious academic analysis of terrorism in France comes up against the sheer complexity of the phenomenon. Terrorist groups in France are both numerous and small but they often overlap in methods and membership. Analysis is further complicated by the willingness of groups with diametrically contrary objectives to display temporary solidarity in the achievement of a short-term goal. The existence of this pragmatism makes it risky to assume that the use of similar weaponry denotes the involvement of similar groups or that attacks on related targets necessarily denote related ideological goals. In fact, groups with quite divergent aims may attack almost identical targets. For example, an attack on the British-owned ICL computer firm's premises in Toulouse on 20 May 1980 was the work of a left-wing group Comité Liquidant ou Détoumant les Ordinateurs (Clodo—Committee Liquidating or Stopping Computers) whereas the attack on Marks and Spencer in Paris on 1 May 1981 was inspired by Irish Republican Army (IRA) sympathisers supporting the hunger strike of Bobby Sands; and the bombing of a Rolls Royce showroom in December 1981 was claimed by the extreme left Action Directe. The Ministry of Education was the target of a Corsican separatist group in February 1981; the Ministry of Overseas Co-operation was machine-gunned by Action Directe in March 1980; and the Palace of Versailles was seriously damaged by Breton extremists in June 1978. The task of disentangling the various terrorist groups from each other is made harder, however, by the fact that more than one group may claim responsibility for a particular incident. For example, a bomb explosion at the Ministry of Finance in Paris in February 1979 was claimed by both the Corsican separatist Front de la Libération Nationale de la Corse (FLNC) and by an obscure left-wing group calling itself the Autonomous Fighters Against Capitalism. The bombing of the Intercontinental Hotel in Paris in August 1981 was claimed by no fewer than six different groups but was eventually attributed by the police to Action Directe. At the other extreme are atrocities for which no group claims responsbility. Among these are incidents involving several fatalities e.g. a bomb on the Paris--Toulouse express in March 1982 (five deaths) and a bomb outside a Paris synagogue in October 1980 (four deaths).

The categorisation of terrorist groups in France is not an easy task. One possible distinction is between those groups that seek regional autonomy (e.g. the FLNC) and those that have ideological motives (of the right or left) e.g. Action Directe; but such a neat division ignores the socialist leanings of some regional groups e.g. the Breton, Armée Républicaine Bretonne (ARB). A neat dichotomy between "right" and "left" groups is elusive since Action Directe (usually characterised as "extreme left") has recently adopted anti-Jewish tactics (normally associated with the extreme right); and groups with "national-ist" aspirations such as the FLNC (and nationalism is normally valued on the extreme right) also toy with left-wing objectives such as decentralised decision-making and decolonisation. In this perversity, terrorist groups in France share in the general perversity of the political culture which is replete with anomalies. The Communist Party (PCF) participates fully in the bourgeois parliamentary system of the Fifth Republic; and the right-wing Gaullists are fully committed to economic planning.

In the analysis that follows we shall deal first with "ethnic terrorism", that is the violence inspired by separatist movements within France. Then we shall turn to examine other groups that operate in France making a distinction where possible between "foreign" groups and those with indigenous roots.

EDWARD MOXON-BROWNE

"ETHNIC TERRORISM"

The term "ethnic terrorism" is used here to denote the violence perpetrated by various groups in France to secure either complete separation from, or a degree of autonomy for their region within, the French state. We shall be concerned with two regions, Brittany and Corsica, that have produced most violence in support of separatist aims in the last decade. However, separatist movements exist in other areas e.g. the Occitan, Haute Savoie and the Basque country.

Violence, of the kind generated in Brittany and Corsica, arises from cultural differences that are exacerbated by perceptions of economic deprivation or exploitation. The "internal colonialism" thesis[2] argues that peripheral and economically deprived regions of a nation-state may be kept in a condition of dependence by systematic exploitation for the benefit of the richer areas. Certainly, in both Corsica and Brittany, there has been an awareness that the resources of each region were being "exported" to the more advanced parts of the country and very little of the resulting profits were being ploughed back into the two regions. Added to this, in each case, were poor communications and a higher-than-average unemployment rate. Both regions have also traditionally suffered from heavy emigration of their younger inhabitants with the result that badly needed skills were in short supply. At face value, the "internal colonialism" thesis seems to fit the bill in both Corsica and Brittany. However the fact is that violence flared up in both regions in the 1970s, a decade that saw the pace of economic activity quicken in France generally, and in particular saw a narrowing of the gap between the "core" areas and the "periphery". A revised version of the internal colonialism thesis suggests that perceptions of relative deprivation are more likely to be sharpened at a time of rapid economic growth; since it is at these times that feelings of "being left behind" may be exacerbated as indications of conspicuous consumption become more obvious.

In both Brittany and Corsica, in the 1970s, pre-existing cultural differences of long standing were thrown into sharper focus as socially mobile groups believed that their regions were relatively worse off in a period of economic expansion. Those who became activists in the separatist movements (violent and non-violent) were more than likely to be students, teachers and intellectuals. These groups were most likely to experience the anomie that results from upward social mobility; and also most likely to embrace some new form of group identity in the shape of ethnic militancy. On this argument, activists in Corsica and Brittany are consciously putting down ethnic roots to replace the social roots that have been torn up by sudden upward mobility.

Several further factors encouraged separatist movements in the 1970s. The loss of Algeria had shown that "integral" parts of the French state could achieve independence. In other parts of Europe, ethnic activism seemed to be paying dividends e.g. the Basque region of Spain, and Scotland. Paradoxically, perhaps, in view of its long attachment to administrative centralisation, the French state itself encouraged notions of regional identity. Regional planning

---

[2] For a discussion, in the French context, see W. R. Beer, *The Unexpected Rebellion* (New York: New York University Press, 1980), pp. 55–86.

areas were established of which Brittany and Corsica were just two examples. The Deixonne Law of 1951 had sanctioned the teaching of ethnic languages in schools, and legislation in the 1970s actually made provision for it. Finally, the Socialists (in opposition until 1981) made promises of greater self-rule (*autogestion*) for the regions; and steps in this direction have, in fact, been implemented under Mitterrand's presidency.

Brittany

Brittany is a distinctive geographical and cultural region in north-western France. The administrative region today is comprised of four *departements*: Finistère, Cotes-du-Nord, Morbihan, Ille-et-Vilaine although historically the region also encompassed Loire-Atlantique. Brittany has about 2½ million inhabitants, and a land area of 27,184 sq km. As a result of steady emigration, the Breton population now constitutes 4·9 per cent of the national total compared with 6·5 per cent at the turn of the last century. The principal economic activities are agriculture, fishing and tourism. The contribution made by Breton farmers to national food production is substantial (28 per cent of national pigmeat production; 14 per cent of national milk production, for example) and on the increase. Although fishing occupies only 2 per cent of the Breton population, their catch represents 45 per cent of the French total. In the coastal areas, tourism is an important source of income with about two million visitors coming to Brittany each year. New industries have come to the region since the 1960s. Cars are assembled at Rennes; steel is made at Lorient; and electronic industries can be found at Lannion, Rennes, Brest and elsewhere. At the same time, older industries are in a state of chronic decline: footwear at Fougères, shipyards at Lorient and Brest.

Brittany's cultural boundaries are less distinct than those of the administrative region. The Breton language, akin to Welsh, Manx and Gaelic is spoken by about 500,000 people although many more claim a Breton identity by virtue of speaking a dialect of French called Gallo, or by having a Breton surname. Brittany shares cultural links with other Celtic regions. For example, bagpipes evoke the music of Scotland; and cider-making the orchards of south-west England.

Up until 1532, Brittany was an autonomous, political entity and only became part of France in that year after a royal marriage between the Duke of Brittany's daughter and the French King, Louis IX. The marriage was sealed by a Treaty whose terms paid some lip service to Breton autonomy. Nominally, taxes could not be raised without Breton consent, and the Breton assembly was allowed to continue in existence until 1790 when it was abolished and Brittany officially became an integral part of the French state. The constant inroads by French central authority before the Revolution of 1789 had always met with opposition and, even after the Revolution, Brittany played a fierce and defiant role in the general counter-revolutionary insurrections that swept Western Europe from 1793 onwards.

Breton political activity during the nineteenth century was virtually dormant. In the twentieth century, the political pulse quickened. In 1911, the first Breton separatist party (Strollad Broadel Breiz) was founded. The inter-war period was marked by the emergence of a multiplicity of small groupings and considerable infighting. The Parti Autonomiste Breton emerged as one of the more significant groups and produced a journal called Breiz Atao (Brittany Forever). In 1932, the Parti Nationaliste Breton (PNB) was forged from a handful of smaller groups and, as World War II approached, became fascistic in tone and a dissident faction within it resorted to bombing.

It was, however, only in the 1970s that the Breton separatist movement spawned a serious terrorist problem. While the Mouvement pour l'Organisation de la Bretagne (MOB) sought autonomy for Brittany within the French state by peaceful means, the armed struggle passed to the Front de Libération de La Bretagne – Armée Républicaine Bretonne (FLB – ARB) which was outlawed in 1974. The ARB "faction" represents a more militant Marxist-oriented wing of the movement but both factions are committed to violent methods.

Although there were isolated terrorist incidents before 1976, it was in that year that the campaign of violence really began. Most of the incidents have been confined to Brittany itself, and the targets have almost invariably been ones symbolising French authority in the region. Thus legal, military, transport and administrative buildings have been very much in the front line. There has been a meticulous policy of minimising the threat to life and limbs; and the occasional injuries have been clearly accidental.

At the start of the bombing campaign, the principal targets were buildings and property connected with the maintenance of law and order. In June 1976, lawyers' offices were damaged in Quimper by a bomb made from a bottled gas container. In January 1977, the court house in St Malo sustained 10,000 francs worth of damage in an explosion and, the following month, five police vehicles were wrecked by explosions in St Brieuc. At about the same time, other targets – most notably those connected with French national administration – came under the attention of the FLB – ARB. A new TV and radio licence centre in Rennes was partly immobilised by two bombs and a third inflicted serious damage at administrative offices in Redon. The co-ordinated nature of these bomb attacks became apparent in October 1977 when five explosions in a single night across Brittany affected a number of buildings connected with French governmental authority in the region. Two of the bombs affected military installations in the west; two more, in the northern *departement* of Côtes-du-Nord caused 250,000 francs worth of damage while the fifth, in the southern *departement* of Loire-Atlantique, was placed in a tax office. At about the same time, the FLB – ARB alienated a good deal of Breton public opinion by blowing up a TV relay mast at Pré-en-Pail, thus depriving most of the region of TV programmes for several weeks.

1978 was to prove the turning point in the campaign of the FLB – ARB since it now extended its activities outside Brittany and, in turn, provoked a clamp-down by the police that virtually spelt the end of militant Breton nationalism. In May bombs blasted the offices of the government broadcasting studios in Rennes; and a police van and the town hall in Dinard were damaged. In the same month the police headquarters in St Brieuc was attacked and in

Nantes the Shell headquarters was bombed. The latter incident was evidence of a growing identification of the FLB – ARB with environmentalist groups in the wake of the Amoco-Cadiz disaster. On 26 June, however, came the single most spectacular attack mounted by the FLB – ARB and marked the climax of its campaign of violence. At about 2 a.m. a bomb explosion ripped a gaping hole in the south wing of the Palace of Versailles. A full inspection at first light showed that ten rooms had been damaged, and three completely destroyed. Ten huge paintings, including some of the most famous depicting Napoleon, were ripped to pieces, statues were shattered, furniture was destroyed, crystal chandeliers were smashed, and nearly every window in the wing had been blown out. President Giscard d'Estaing called the explosion "lamentable damage to a part of France's heritage".

From the viewpoint of the FLB – ARB, the attack had not only wrought significant material damage (estimated at about £500,000) but, more importantly, had made a spectacularly symbolic gesture in the heart of France. That the FLB – ARB should have selected an exhibition devoted to Napoleon was particularly appropriate since Napoleon represents the relentless centralisation of government to which Breton separatists, and all separatists in France, are firmly opposed. Versailles is to many Frenchmen the symbol of their heritage and thus, in itself, an appropriate target for a militant group dedicated to the preservation of Breton culture in its various manifestations. A month before the attack the FLB – ARB issued a pamphlet which, among other things, threatened attacks on the "symbols and representatives of French imperialism in Brittany and throughout France". This message was underlined by a communiqué issued by FLB – ARB (in fact, left for police in a lay-by near Rennes) immediately after the Versailles attack:

> The Breton people is oppressed; the land of Brittany is occupied by French military camps; the Breton language and culture are denied and destroyed by the imperialist French power.

The attack on Versailles marked not only a new departure for the FLB – ARB inasmuch as it had selected a major target outside Brittany, but it also led to a gradual disintegration of the group as many of its leading members came to face arrest and trial. However, there were a few more violent incidents despite a growing crackdown by the police. In December 1978, a bomb in a Paris department store was claimed by the FLB – ARB. In 1979, electricity pylons were bombed in Finistère; electricity showrooms in both Paris and Brittany were damaged; and police stations were targets in Brest and St Brieuc.

By 1980, Breton militancy had become quiescent. Only four days after the Versailles explosion in 1978, police picked up Lionel Chenevière and Patrick Montauzier (both aged 28) in Rennes; and six others were arrested the same weekend. Less than a month later 14 Breton separatists were on trial in Paris. Further arrests were made after an arms cache was discovered in Brittany in January 1979. In May, four men were arrested; and at the end of September a trial of 25 Breton separatists opened in Paris. They were charged with involvement in some 40 bombings between May 1974 and June 1978. The defendants ranged in age from 22 to 63 and a wide range of occupations were represented including a printer, a sales representative, a mechanic, some students, a farmer, and several white collar workers. To the defence argument that the Treaty of 1532 rendered the Court incompetent to try the case, the judge ruled that the Treaty had been rendered null and void by the Revolution of 1789 which had established the "unity of French national territory". The sentences were pronounced on 20 September 1979. Eighteen of the accused were jailed for periods ranging from two to 15 years, and six were acquitted. These sentences were generally regarded as lenient, and they undoubtedly took into account the fact that the FLB – ARB, in the course of over 300 bombings since 1966, had successfully avoided killing a single person. The trial marked the virtual end of the violence inspired by Breton separatists. The government in Paris has turned to other sources of terrorism, most notably in Corsica, and on the streets of Paris.

In considering the demise of the FLB – ARB, it is also worthy of note that the sense of economic deprivation experienced in Brittany had largely evaporated by 1979. The visit of Giscard d'Estaing to the region in 1977 was the occasion of a "cultural charter" which, among other things, accelerated the programme of instruction in the Breton language in schools from the primary level upwards. Already sensitive to the need for more Breton language programmes in the media, the broadcasting authorities clocked up 144 hours of Breton language output on the radio, and 11½ hours on TV. On the economic front, the region's traditional problems have been tackled in a determined way by the government. A new port was built at Roscoff. New industries have come to towns like St Brieuc and Rennes. The region is now the leading food producing area in France and the gap between average earnings in Brittany and the rest of the country is closing fast. For the first time in this century the flow of people out of the region has been stemmed, and reversed as new job opportunities are created. The sense of being cut off from the rest of the country has been largely removed by better communications. An *autoroute* between Paris and Rennes was completed in 1981; and new express trains cover the 220 miles from Rennes to Paris in just under three hours. The sentiment of the French government, as expressed by former President Giscard d'Estaing, is even more applicable today: "Brittany is no longer isolated from France. There is no contradiction in being entirely French and living your own culture".

Corsica

Corsica is the fourth largest island in the Mediterranean, and lies just over 100 miles from the coast of mainland France. To the south it is separated from the Italian island of Sardinia by the ten-mile-wide Strait of Bonifacio. The land area of Corsica is about 8,680 sq km almost all of which is made up of rugged mountainous terrain.

The island became part of metropolitan France in 1769 and was made a *departement*, at the request of its inhabitants, twenty years later. A long history of exploitation and control by outside powers has served to forge a keen sense of Corsican nationalism. Prior to 1769, the island endured about four hundred years of almost unbroken Genoese rule. This period culminated in a national Corsican rebellion (1729–69) during which the Genoese were effectively expelled from the island. A written constitution, enshrining the principle of self-government, was adopted in 1755 and, with it, a legislative assembly most of whose members were elected by universal suffrage. The assembly, in turn, elected an executive council that was answerable to it; and Pasquale Paoli (still revered today in Corsica as the embodiment of national independence) became life-president of the council until the annexation of the island by the French in 1769.

The population of the island today is just over 200,000, about a third of whom live in the two main towns, Ajaccio and Bastia. The majority of the inhabitants are Corsican-born but a substantial, and growing, minority are immigrants from North Africa – both French settlers who came following Algerian independence and, more recently, a workforce composed of Moroccans, Tunisians and so on. There is also a community of some 10,000 Italians. At the same time, many younger Corsicans emigrate to France (about 2,000 a year) to seek work with the result that the ratio of old inhabitants to young is increasingly weighted towards the former, and the ratio of Corsican-born inhabitants continues to decline. The island's birth-rate (1·61 per cent) is rather lower than that of mainland France (1·74 per cent). The population density is heavily weighted in favour of the coastal towns and, overall, there is insufficient population to guarantee expanding prosperity without considerable economic inducements from the French government.

The island's two principal economic activities are tourism and agriculture. The latter contributes about 11 per cent of the island's revenue with profit coming only from the coastal farms. Agriculture has suffered from emigration, falling markets, outdated methods, and the division of land by inheritance (only a third of Corsican farms exceed 25 acres). As a tourist destination, Corsica has many natural advantages and although tourism contributes about 16 per cent of the island's income, it is handicapped by lack of investment, and poor marketing. Half a million tourists visit the island annually but there is scope for considerable expansion especially in the relatively underdeveloped interior. Corsica is heavily dependent on direct financial payments from the French government (46 per cent of the island's revenue comes in the form of retirement pensions, state salaries, and social security benefits).

Local government is based on the *departement*, as in the rest of France. In January 1970, the island was detached from the Region Marseilles-Côte d'Azur-Corse and instituted as a separate *region*. In 1975 the island was divided into two *departements*: Corse-du-Sud and Haute-Corse. The island's administrative centre is Ajaccio, while the judiciary is seated in Bastia. The Foreign Legion has bases at Calvi, Corte and Bonifacio; and there is a military air base at Solenzara on the east coast.

Culturally, the island is quite distinct from the rest of France. Although all Corsicans are able to speak French, the Corsican language (directly derived from Latin) is still in common use by most of the island's indigenous population. There is considerable interest in, and financial support for, the island's cultural heritage (especially archaeology); and this interest is reflected in the number of museums dedicated to the preservation of artifacts and the written record of the island's history.

The economic, demographic and cultural factors, discussed above, combine to form an invaluable backcloth against which the violence of separatist groups has to be viewed. In the context of the French state, Corsica remains a highly marginal society. It is marginal in the sense of being economically passive (it absorbs more wealth than it creates). Corsica shares with Brittany a sense of being relatively deprived in economic terms and this tests further the already strained loyalty to central institutions in Paris. It is marginal in the cultural sense of being "not really French". This politico-cultural distinctiveness is epitomised by the slogan "Francesi fora" ("French out") daubed on walls throughout the island. In the case of Corsica, these factors are accentuated by geographical distance and historical experience. The island's rugged terrain has resulted in a society scarcely penetrated beyond the coastal fringe by external influences. As we saw earlier, Corsica was annexed by France in the eighteenth century after a short fling at self-government and a long experience of being under control other than French. Corsica is, therefore, the most recent and probably the most reluctant, addition to the French Republic.

As in the case of Brittany, a wide variety of groups has competed for the attentions of regional opinion in the struggle to "renegotiate" the relationship with the central government in Paris. Broadly speaking, the Corsican groups can be divided into two groups: those who believe that autonomy can be won within the French state, and those, on the other hand, who believe that complete separation, or independence is the only solution to Corsica's problems. By the end of 1976, two rival organisations had come to be the leading exponents of these two possible scenarios for Corsica's future. The Associu di Patrioti Corsi (APC) was established in January 1976 to succeed the banned Action pour la Renaissance de la Corse (ARC). The APC and its ARC predecessor maintained an ambiguous attitude towards violence, usually arguing that it should be avoided, but circumstances sometimes make that impossible. The APC has been dominated by the Siméoni brothers, both doctors, who participated in violent incidents in the early 1970s, but have since mellowed and attempt to plot a peaceful path towards autonomy for the island within the French state. In strong contrast to the APC is the Front de la Libération Nationale de la Corse (FLNC) which was formed in May 1976 out of militant elements from the Fronte Parisann Corsu di Liberazione (FPLC) and Giustizia Paolina. The FLNC (and its forebears), believe in complete separation for the "Corsican nation" from France, and in violent methods to achieve that end. In fact, the FLNC has been the single most violent terrorist group affecting the security of the French state during the period since 1976. Before examining in more detail the FLNC campaign, it should be pointed out that violence is endemic in Corsica. Although most violence is claimed by, or can be attributed to the FLNC, there are small splinter elements also engaging in violence. There are also counter-separatist groups among which the Front d'Action Nouvelle contre l'Indépendance et l'Autonomie (Francia–New Action Front against Independence and Autonomy for Corsica) is most active. Other attacks may or may not be political: some are undoubtedly carried out for reasons of personal revenge or business rivalry with the perpetrators relying on the background of violence to escape detection.

The principal targets of the FLNC are related to the separatists' main grievances. Military installations have been attacked because the stationing of troops in Corsica is regarded as evidence of the island's "colonial" status. Tourist facilities are a frequent target because tourism is seen as being detrimental to the island's environment, and of no real benefit to its economy. Police and judicial buildings are obvious objects of violence representing, as they do, French authority in Corsica. The homes of French settlers are occasionally damaged or destroyed because the French are regarded as "foreigners" and there is a certain resentment at their sometimes superior entrepreneurial talents. Banks are attacked because of the generous loans given to French settlers, and because of the widespread belief that the banks are more interested in making a profit for their parent organisation (invariably on the French mainland) than in developing the island for the benefit of the indigenous population.

The following summary of the FLNC campaign from 1976 to the present day is not intended to be exhaustive but rather to indicate the range and extent of its targets. Among the first incidents instigated by the newly formed FLNC were a series of bombings in May 1976. The worst explosion occurred at Ajaccio on the west coast where a shop was totally destroyed and damage was estimated at about 1 million francs. In August, bombs damaged a bank, a chemist's shop and business offices in the southern port of Porto Vecchio. Tourism and the military were targets in the same month; a nightclub was destroyed in Corte, and a water tower belonging to the Foreign Legion was put out of action. The most serious incident of the year was the blowing up of an Air France airliner at Ajaccio in September. No one was hurt as the 181 passengers were forced to disembark just as the plane was about to leave for Paris. In 1977, the most serious attacks were on a Club Méditerranée camp (a favourite target for the FLNC) when nine bungalows were completely destroyed at Cargese in April; and on a television transmitter which robbed the island of television programmes for several weeks. This latter attack was an attempt to reduce the impact of a rally of moderate autonomists in the town of Furiani although a less mundane motivation emerged at the trial of an FLNC member accused of complicity in the transmitter explosion:

> (I)t transmits throughout our country, all of French culture, all that alienates and destroys the language and culture of Corsica, the collective memory of our people.[3]

Although most FLNC violence takes place in Corsica, there were, from the early stages, attacks in southern France: in May 1976, for example, FLNC bombs exploded outside a Marseilles courthouse, and near a Nice electricity relay station. At the end of 1977, the FLNC announced (at a clandestine press conference) that the struggle in Corsica would be intensified, and extended to the French mainland. The FLNC spokesmen said they found themselves faced by the policies of the state and the forces of occupation which made it necessary

---

[3] *Le Monde*, 14 June 1979.

for them to take tougher measures. The Foreign Legion bases on the island were specifically mentioned as targets. The FLNC would "chase them from our soil". Only a few weeks later, on 14 January 1978, an armed group of ten FLNC terrorists blew up vital radar installations at the Solenzara air base on the island's east coast about 100 km south of Bastia. Solenzara is the biggest French air base outside the French mainland and is used jointly by the French and Belgian Mirages for target practice. The publicity value of the attack was substantially enhanced by the almost simultaneous attack by Breton separatists on a military base at Quimper. In a statement, released after the Solenzara attack, the FLNC promised to "continue the struggle against the army of occupation and the colonialism that it reinforces". The FLNC message then went on to point out the wider implications of the Solenzara base:

> (It is) an instrument of under-development imposed on Corsica . . . The presence of these installations in time of war could attract sudden reprisal attacks on Corsica because Solenzara is one of the staging posts for nuclear bombers . . . Solenzara allows western imperialism to threaten the free and progressive countries of the Mediterranean: a base for intervention and aggression against the Palestinian people in 1967, hand-in-glove with fascist and bloody regimes in Iran and South Africa who send their pilots to train at Solenzara . . . Our people are threatened; free people are too. The Front will continue the political and military struggle which is the only way the Corsican people can throw off colonialism.

Following Solenzara, the frequency of violent incidents increased as 1978 progressed. Two attacks over the Whitsun weekend caused widespread resentment in the island. An explosion at the gas and electricity board offices in Ajaccio provoked a protest demonstration by the staff; and the burning down of a farm building in which about a thousand goats were being housed was widely condemned by the farming community. The visit of Giscard d'Estaing to the island in June aroused protests ranging from peaceful demonstrations to violence. A gendarme, one of hundreds flown to the island to help keep order, was fired on in his police van in the eastern part of the island. An explosion, meanwhile, demolished the garage of Col. Erulin, the commander of the Second Parachute Regiment which was due to be honoured by Giscard d'Estaing for its role in the liberation of Kolwezi. On one night in July, the FLNC were responsible for 33 bombings, the highest number so far in a single 24-hour period. At the end of 1978, as a prelude to a visit to the island by Prime Minister Raymond Barre, further violence erupted. A chief fire officer had to have a leg amputated when a bomb exploded in his car; and several police stations were bombed in various parts of the island.

From 1979 up to the present, FLNC violence on the mainland has increased. In February 1979, the Ministry of Finance in Paris was damaged by a bomb explosion which, according to an FLNC statement, marked an "intensification of the Corsican people's struggle". In March, targets included many banks both in Paris and Corsica. In statements issued after the attacks, the FLNC said that banks had multiplied in Corsica during the 1960s. They were keen to lend money for a short period at high interest rates, but what Corsican agriculture needed, according to the FLNC, were long-term loans at low rates of interest. In April came an attack on the Palais de Justice in Paris. Damage was serious but there were no injuries. In a statement, the FLNC said that it did not recognise French justice, which it regarded as simply a tool of repression in the hands of the French State. "Our fight is legitimate and is in the tradition of struggle of our people to preserve their liberty. Only our descendants and history will judge us." In May 1979, the FLNC celebrated its third anniversary by attacking about 30 targets across the island: tourist projects, estate agents, holiday homes. At a clandestine press conference, FLNC spokesmen vowed to go on with the struggle. "Our land is being surrendered to property speculators supported in their depredations by the colonial administration". To coincide with the trial in Paris of their colleagues, FLNC activists struck at various targets in the French capital in May and June: banks, travel agencies, shops and Government buildings.

In 1980, the most serious incident was a siege of the Hôtel Fresch in Ajaccio but this was the work of the Unione di u Populu Corso (UPC – successor to the non-violent autonomist APC). Ironically, it resulted in three deaths – a young man, a young woman and a policeman – all of whom died in cross-fire during a demonstration near the hotel. During the year the FLNC continued its violent campaign in Corsica and mainland France: Nice was affected by FLNC actions, and the Paris Hôtel de Ville was bombed on 14 March. In April a co-ordinated FLNC bomb campaign in Paris, Nice and Corsica on a single night suggested a certain organisational sophistication despite inroads made by police arrests. A policeman was deliberately shot by the FLNC in May (the group's first deliberate shooting) and in September a bombing raid was carried out on Bastia's police station.

In 1981, there was little violence from the FLNC due to a truce called in late April following Mitterrand's electoral promise to give Corsica a "new deal". However, earlier in the year, in response to prison sentences for FLNC members, 46 bombs went off in one night in Corsica in mid-February and, on 16 April, a bomb at Ajaccio airport (minutes after Giscard d'Estaing arrived from Paris for an official visit) killed one person and injured seven. In Paris, the Ministry of Education was damaged by an FLNC bomb attack in February. 1982 was only six weeks old when the FLNC truce ended, apparently due to disappointment with the measures announced for Corsica by the new Socialist government under President Mitterrand. A member of the Foreign Legion was shot dead by the FLNC in February (the FLNC's first fatal victim) and a few days later, 19 separate bomb attacks were carried out in the Paris region. Pressure on French settlers in Corsica was stepped up in the succeeding weeks by the means of "suitcase or coffin" letters (i.e. the addressees were told to either pack their suitcases and leave the island or risk ending up in a coffin). By the day of the elections for the island's first regional assembly (6 August) there had been almost 300 bomb attacks since the beginning of the year: a rate of nearly two a day. This rate continued so that, by the end of the year, about 800 explosions had been reported in the island. Pressure on the "continentals" (i.e. citizens of mainland France) focused on teachers as the year ended with the aim of intimidating them to leave the island, and especially their jobs, behind them. A sinister new development was the "revolutionary tax" that the FLNC began to demand in a tract distributed at the end of December 1982. It was this new intimidation, coupled with an escalating bomb campaign, that led the government to declare the FLNC illegal in the first few days of 1983.

Government response

What has been the response of French governments to the campaign of the FLNC? Under the government of Giscard d'Estaing, the policy was one of economic aid but no concessions on political autonomy, let alone separatism. Corsica has long enjoyed special fiscal privileges that make tobacco, for example, cheaper than on the mainland. A great deal of investment has gone towards agriculture and towards developing tourist facilities. The argument of the separatists is that much of this money goes to French settlers. Their liking for hard work – not a Corsican virtue – arouses resentment and envy among the indigenous population. The island has subsidised transport links with the mainland. The aversion of the Giscard government to any kind of regional assembly for Corsica was well-expressed by Prime Minister Barre during his visit to the island in December 1978. He said he was "profoundly opposed" to a directly-elected assembly for the island or for any mainland region in France. But clearly the frustrations in Corsica have stemmed more from this lack of local control over the island's destiny than from sheer economic neglect. In crude economic terms, the island has done well from the French government. Investment in the island rose from 150 million francs in 1975 to 466 million in 1979. This represented four times the amount invested per capita in other French regions. Another way of looking at it is to reflect on the fact that for every franc Corsica gives to France, France returns 4·66 francs to Corsica.

The advent of a Socialist government in France in 1981 altered the whole picture. The Socialists are not wedded to centralisation for its own sake and promised greater *autogestion* (self-rule) for France's regions. As we have seen, these promises resulted in an FLNC cease-fire for most of 1981. However when the violence resumed, it was evident from an FLNC statement, that the government's proposals had not gone far enough to appease separatist opinion as represented by the Front and its supporters:

> Concrete political acts wiping out the symbols of colonialism should have been announced, with their implementation well under way. There has been nothing of the sort . . . The new Government must rapidly acknowledge the national rights of the Corsican people.

What the government was in fact proposing was a regional assembly for Corsica, to be elected by proportional representation. From the viewpoint of Paris, the proposals seemed both generous and risky in the implications that might be drawn in other French regions. The government's own supporters in Corsica, the Socialists, warned Mitterrand in July 1982 that opinion in the island expected more and labelled the plan an "empty shell". The elections were held on 6 August 1982 and the 70 per cent turnout was in itself a triumph for the government since the island's political apathy had traditionally kept turnout figures below 50 per cent. The results of the election saw parties of the Left (23 seats) and the Right (26 seats) evenly poised with the UPC (7 seats), led by the Siméoni brothers and standing for non-violence and autonomy within France, holding the critical balance.

There is no doubt that opinion in the island favours peaceful politics and more autonomy. The extent of support for general strikes (e.g. "Operation Dead Island" in 1976 on the occasion of Dr Edmond Siméoni's trial in Paris which paralysed the island) and peaceful rallies has been evident over the past eight years or so. As the Siméoni brothers have moved from participation in violence towards participation in the electoral process (via the UPC), the FLNC, with perhaps 4 per cent of public opinion behind it, has found itself increasingly isolated but still able to call on passive acquiescence in its campaign. The problem for the French government is to encourage moderate opinion in the autonomist camp (about 40 per cent of public opinion) without appearing to appease violence. At the moment, the frustration of moderate opinion is forcing many young unemployed Corsicans to join the ranks of the FLNC.[4] Even UPC leaders realise the danger. As recently as 1979, Dr Siméoni admitted in an interview with *El Pais* that young Corsicans were being driven into the FLNC by a mixture of repression and frustration:

> Violence is inevitable because of a block of the situation maintained by Paris with growing repression . . . Repressions of every kind are exercised by Paris, a public repression under the pretext of fighting the FLNC . . . The Court of State Security which judges us is not the court of a democratic country. In Corte there are 680 police for 4,000 people. We're besieged by police and soldiers . . . The FLNC is not exploited by foreigners, I know them, they are patriots helped by Corsicans.[5]

A few months earlier, another moderate and respected Corsican nationalist, Admiral Sanguinetti, had expanded on the same point in an interview for the *Irish Times*:

> Today's violence is a direct result of successive denials of our national and cultural rights by the most centralised, industrialised, state in the world . . . Repression instead of a political solution provides further solidarity among Corsicans, and above all pushes them all further towards a radical stand.[6]

The following year, Dr Siméoni was distancing himself from the FLNC by stating his unambiguous opposition to violence:

> We consider violence as very dangerous because it threatens public safety and is totally useless because it is not the sort of thing that will make the State give in.

Although the election results in August 1982 were a boost for the moderate UPC and a blow for the FLNC, it looks as if disappointment with the new Assembly, in practice, will once again play into the hands of those who advocate violence. Even though there are only about 200 FLNC activists, and despite the abhorrence for violence that most Corsicans feel, the FLNC continue to find

---

[4] But by no means all FLNC militants are unemployed. Among FLNC members appearing before the State Security Court in June 1979 were a wine-producer, a farmer, a psychiatric nurse, a philosophy lecturer, a policeman and a student. A leading French newspaper called them "un echantillon sociologique de la population corse" ("a cross-section of the Corsican population"). See *Le Monde*, 14 June 1979.

[5] *El Pais*, 5 September 1979.

[6] *Irish Times*, 16 January 1980.

refuge among a populace that expects the destiny of Corsica to be in Corsican hands. On 5 January 1983, deciding that the FLNC could never be bought off with constitutional changes, Mitterrand sent the former head of France's Serious Crime Squad, Robert Broussard, to the island to tackle both the violence and intimidation that seemed to have become endemic. It remains to be seen what effect *superflic* Broussard will have on the escalating terrorist problem.

IMPORTED TERRORISM: UNWANTED GUESTS

As we have seen, most of the terrorism in France is caused by the FLNC. Like the FLB – ARB, the FLNC, has confined most, but by no means all, of its activities to towns and cities far from Paris. The dubious reputation that Paris has now won for itself as a "haven for terrorists" can be attributed largely to terrorism connected with the politics of the Middle East and Turkey. This type of terrorism perpetrated either by diplomats abusing their immunity, or political refugees abusing the hospitality of the French government, is a rather complex phenomenon. Broadly speaking, we can divide it, for the sake of convenience, into three categories. Firstly, there are incidents that involve the "settling of scores" between two factions within one Middle East country. Secondly, there are incidents that settle scores either between two Middle East governments or between an ethnic minority and a government. Thirdly, there are incidents unconnected with the Middle East. This third category usually involves dissident exile groups protesting against their home government. In all three categories, the choice of French soil for the violence is tangential to the issues involved: it is simply a case of France providing the stage for a drama that could, in theory, be played out anywhere in the world. Occasionally, the terrorism in these three categories is intended to have, or may incidentally have, an effect on the action of the French government but, in most cases, the choice of Paris as the scene for violent incidents is attributable to the policy of welcoming political exiles to France and that welcome then being abused by the individuals or groups concerned.

The first category, involving a "settling of scores" between factions within a single country is epitomised by the violence that has been generated between Iranian pro- and anti-Khomeini groups in Paris. For example, Khomeini supporters occupied the Iranian Embassy in January 1979; and police had to eject students from the Embassy in July of the following year. In the same month, a former Prime Minister under the Shah, Shahpour Bakhtiar, who was living in exile at Neuilly, narrowly escaped an assassination attempt outside his home. However, two people (including one policeman) were killed in the shoot-out. In 1981, tension between France and Iran was heightened by the granting of political refugee status to ex-President Bani-Sadr. This tension was reflected in clashes between supporters and opponents of Khomeini in the streets of Paris. One man died in a clash between the two factions; and in late November a student denouncing the Khomeini regime outside the Iranian Embassy was shot dead by a security guard. At Marseilles, an Iranian gunboat was hijacked, but the hijackers later gave themselves up. In 1982, there was less violence attributable to Iranian factions clashing in Paris. There was a protest march against massacres in Iran in January and, in early July, an Iranian was arrested at Orly airport while trying to smuggle in plastic explosives for an attempt on the life of ex-President Bani-Sadr.

Our second category of imported terrorism is exemplified by the efforts of Armenians to draw attention to grievances suffered at the hands of the Turkish government; and the continuing strife between various Palestinian groups and the Israeli government. The most active group of Armenian exiles has been the Secret Army for the Liberation of Armenia (ASALA), based in Beirut, whose activities relate to the alleged massacre of over one million Armenians by Turkey between 1915 and 1922 and, more relevantly, to a campaign for self-determination for the Armenian people most of whom nowadays live within the borders of the Soviet Union. In late 1979, ASALA members bombed three airline offices in Paris and assassinated the Director of the Turkish Tourist Office, 31-year-old Ylmaz Colpan. In 1980, the most serious incident perpetrated by ASALA was the injuring of three people at the Turkish Consulate in Lyons; and a Turkish press attaché was seriously wounded in an attempt on his life at Boulogne–Billancourt in September. Another Turkish diplomat had a lucky escape when a bomb went off under his car in January 1981. Less fortunate was Resat Moral, Labour attaché in Paris, who was gunned down in the Rue Amelot in March of the same year. In September 1981, ASALA militants held several hostages for a time at the Turkish Embassy's cultural centre. Although a guard was killed in the attack beforehand, the hostages themselves were released unharmed. In early 1982, some ASALA terrorists in a French jail won political status after a hunger strike and, consequently, ASALA announced a cease-fire on French territory. However, later in the year, further violent incidents instigated by Armenians were reported. An Armenian was killed by his own bomb in July and, in August, ASALA placed a bomb in a Paris telephone exchange but gave sufficient warning for it to be defused.

France has also been the scene of violence directly related to the Arab–Israeli conflict. A particularly serious incident was the killing of four people at Orly airport in May 1978 when a Palestinian group, calling itself the Sons of Southern Lebanon attacked El Al passengers in a departure lounge in protest at the Israeli invasion of Southern Lebanon earlier in the year. In July 1982, Fadl Dani, deputy head of the Palestine Liberation Organisation office in Paris, was killed in a bomb explosion. He was the seventh victim among leading PLO representatives in France in ten years. In April 1982, the second Secretary at the Israeli Embassy was shot dead as he was returning home. The murder was claimed by a hitherto unknown group, the "Movement of Revolutionary Arab Brigades" although the PLO was blamed; and calls for the PLO office in Paris to be closed were in fact resisted by the French Government. Another attack blamed on the PLO but denied by the organisation and possibly attributable to a splinter faction of another group, was the machine-gunning of a Jewish restaurant in Paris in August 1982 leaving six dead and 21 injured. These examples suffice to illustrate the "overspill" effect of the Middle East conflict into France. In fact, the "overspill" extends beyond merely PLO and Israeli targets. Iraqi, Syrian and Lebanese nationals have also been involved in acts of terrorism in the streets of Paris during the past five or six years.

Our third category of imported terrorism covers all those actions carried out by foreign dissidents not connected with the Middle East. In most cases, these groups are seeking either autonomy, independence or political change from the governments they select as targets. Again a few examples suffice to indicate the wide range of foreign groups active in France during the past decade. Ukrainian nationals bombed Soviet Embassy cars in November 1979. The Togolese Embassy was the target of a student demonstration in January 1980. Later the same year, Bolivian expatriates protested at a military coup in their country outside the Bolivian Embassy. In early 1981, a bomb at a Chanel showroom was claimed by the Guadeloupe Armed Liberation Group and another bomb, this time at Charles de Gaulle airport in October, was claimed by a hitherto unknown New Caledonian independence group. In the autumn of 1982 the Brazilian Embassy suffered an arson attack claimed by a group called "Toukou".

ANTISEMITIC TERRORISM

Antisemitism in France has a history going back to the late nineteenth century. Prior to that, French public opinion regarded the Jewish minority in much the same way as Catholics did in other countries i.e. it was a doctrinal distaste based on the Jews' rejection of Christ. From the 1880s onwards, Jews were attacked as radical subversives with dangerous cosmopolitan connections that compromised their loyalty to France. The key to the Dreyfus affair was not so much that Dreyfus was a Jew but that he was less than totally French, and that the secrets of the army (the one uncompromised force in national life) had been betrayed from within. In the inter-war period, antisemitism was more of an intellectual vogue than a mass movement: it was part of a wider academic dialogue. However, in World War II, the antisemitic tradition had become firmly rooted enough for the French authorities to collaborate with the Germans in the rounding up of French Jews, 75,000 of whom were to perish in concentration camps. A sense of shame and guilt still pervades the French political conscience today, although antisemitism still survives (even thrives) on the far right of the political spectrum.

The emergence of a new intellectual tradition on the political right, known as the *Nouvelle Droite*, has provided a cloak of "respectability" for various violent groups to commit crimes against minorities in France such as the Jews. The vanguard of the Nouvelle Droite is a group called the Groupement de Recherche et d'Etudes pour la Civilisation Europeene (Grece) which has managed to get its views expressed through *Figaro-Magazine* and its own publishing house Copernic. The leading exponent of the new ideas is Alain de Benoist. The aim of groups like Grece is to penetrate decision-making circles in France and peddle an ideology based on the racial superiority of Indo-Europeans and the inferiority of such minorities as Jews, Corsicans, Arabs and blacks.

Not surprisingly, perhaps, certain groups feed on this neo-fascism. Prominent among these is the Fédération d'Action Nationale Européene (Fane) which emerged in 1966 and had, by 1980, about 200 active members. Its journal *Notre Europe* acted as a vehicle for racist ideas. In its pages, it was argued that immigrants should be repatriated; that Christian ecumenism was a threat to mankind; that Hitler had been misunderstood and could not be held responsible for the extermination of Jews; and that race was the only proper basis for nationhood. Fane, and several similar terrorist groups, were responsible for attacks on buildings frequented by Jews or having connections with Israel. The offices of *Le Monde* (generally reckoned by the political right to be too liberal) were bombed by a group calling itself the league of French Fighters Against Jewish Occupation in April 1979. Later the same year, the well-known author and Jewish activist, Pierre Goldman, was assassinated in Paris.

In 1980, there was a distinct upsurge in right-wing terrorism. Two synagogues were fired on in late September and on 3 October a bomb outside a synagogue in the Rue Copernic killed four and injured twenty. By this time, the government had outlawed Fane (3 September) and the Fane leader, a 43-year-old bank clerk, Marc Fredrikson had been charged in court with inciting racial hatred through his articles in *Notre Europe*. The attack on the synagogue in the Rue Copernic marked the climax of a four-month period of antisemitic terrorism during which more than 30 Jewish targets had been either bombed, burnt or raked with gunfire. Rabbi Michael Williams, the rabbi in charge of the Rue Copernic synagogue, said "There is a cancer of antisemitism in this country and people do not take it seriously enough". A Freudian slip of the tongue by Prime Minister Barre demonstrated how deeply antisemitic attitudes had become ingrained in French society. Referring to the attack in the Rue Copernic, Barre said it had been "directed against Jews attending the synagogue, which hit innocent French passers-by". Many in the Jewish community pondered on whether the Jews in the synagogue had been "less innocent" or "less French" than the passers-by.

The banning of Fane had led to no diminution in right-wing violence. The Faisceaux Nationales Européens (FNE) took its place before the Rue Copernic explosion; and in the following year (1981) antisemitic acts of terrorism continued. The director of a Jewish cultural centre in Paris escaped a car bomb explosion in April and, in the same week, dozens of Jewish graves were desecrated near Paris. Slogans daubed at the cemetery included "Nuremberg soon avenged" and "Death to Israel"; and the symbol of Fane was much in evidence in black paint on several tombstones.

The worst anti-Jewish atrocity since World War II occurred, however, in August 1982. Six people were killed in a Jewish restaurant in the Rue des Rosiers, and 22 were injured, when gunmen opened fire at close range. The difficulty the police have had in tracing suspects for this atrocity and, indeed, for the Rue Copernic explosion, led critics of the police in the Jewish community to suggest that the police themselves have right-wing sympathies. In fact, in 1980, a young police inspector, M. Durand, had been suspended for neo-fascist tendencies and, although he denied Fane membership, he had contributed articles to the Fane journal *Notre Europe*. When Fane was banned in

September 1980, about a fifth of its active members were found to be police officers. A right-wing group, calling itself l'Honneur de la Police had been responsible for the murder of Jewish activist Pierre Goldman in the previous year. The relatively light sentence received by Fane leader Fredrikson, six months in jail, did nothing to reassure the Jewish minority that racialism was being tackled seriously in France.

The extent of antisemitic sentiment in France can be gauged from an opinion survey carried out for the magazine *L'Express*[7] a few days after the Rue Copernic explosion in October 1980. The poll found that although 87 per cent thought "a Jew is just as French as any other French person", 57 per cent of those questioned felt that antisemitism was either "very widespread" or "fairly widespread" in France today. On the more specific question of the police response to right-wing groups, only 19 per cent thought that the police had done "all that they ought to have done" while 57 per cent thought that they had not.

ACTION DIRECTE

Having discussed the principal sources of terrorism on the extreme right, we now consider terrorism on the extreme left. This has become increasingly important since 1979, as a new and more virulent strain of terrorism in France has appeared in the form of a group calling itself Action Directe (AD) which was declared illegal in August 1982. Although the beginnings of this group are believed to stem from a merger of GARI (Group d'Action Révolutionnaire Internationaliste) and NAPAP (Noyaux Armes pour l'Autonomie Populaire); it has since extended both its membership and its aims to encompass broader sympathies on the extreme left. The principal aim of GARI had been to overthrow the Franco regime in Spain while NAPAP was essentially a small Maoist group of urban guerrillas along the lines of the Brigate Rosse in Italy with whom indeed it shared close links and similar tactics.

The activities of AD in the last three years have shown both its ruthless (in a French context) lack of concern for human life and its wide range of targets. One of the earliest themes in AD attacks was French intervention in Africa. This was the subject of AD leaflets distributed after an attack with automatic weapons on the Ministry of Overseas Co-operation in March 1980. The neo-colonial activities of the French government, designed to preserve her existing economic benefits, were condemned in general terms. French involvement in Tunisia, Chad, Djibouti and the Central African Republic were mentioned specifically and AD concluded by asserting that to "struggle against French imperialist politics in Africa" was to "struggle against the French state in its world institutions"; and that now was the time "to take up arms against the slave-making state".

Another preoccupation for AD appears to have been unemployment. In fact the first incident claimed by AD was a bomb explosion at the French Employers Federation in Paris on 1 May 1979, but in September of the same year there

---

[7] *L'Express*, 18 October 1980.

were attacks on the Ministry of Labour and on a labour exchange in the Ile de France. In February 1980, two factory inspectorates were attacked. Other targets have included American and Jewish-owned buildings in Paris. In June 1982, an American school at St Cloud was bombed. Although there were no injuries, there was considerable damage and slogans daubed on walls clearly linked the attack to AD. An earlier attack on the Bank of America also had the hallmarks of an AD incident. These events, and others, were a response to the visit of President Reagan to Paris. Events in the Middle East in the spring and summer of 1982 also caused a rash of attacks by AD. In March, the Israeli mission was machine-gunned and on 1 August, a diplomat at the Israeli embassy had his car machine-gunned. Documents seized by police at a "squat" occupied by AD activists clearly linked AD with Middle East terrorism and especially the "Waddi Haddad" dissident breakaway faction from the PLO. A communiqué issued by AD after the attack on the Israeli diplomat's car confirmed the anti-Zionist tendency of AD which has become a pronounced feature of the group in the past year. "We reject" the AD communiqué said, "genocide of Palestinians by Israeli troops . . . We will not allow the Palestinian people to be exterminated in West Beirut."

Police activity against AD intensified during 1980 and generated a series of reprisal attacks. A police station was damaged by an AD bomb in Toulouse on 30 March. This was obviously in response to the arrest of 28 AD suspects two days earlier, and was designed to counter police claims that the movement was broken. In early August 1980, AD mounted a raid on a police station in the 14th arrondissement of Paris and got away with a useful haul of passports, identity cards and other paraphernalia essential to international terrorists requiring a "new identity". An attack on the Intercontinental Hotel on 29 August 1981, in which ten people were injured, was specifically aimed at persuading the authorities to release AD suspects who had not benefited from the new government's recent amnesty.

Another target, one that is peculiar to AD, is any firm connected with computers. In April 1980, for example, there were two attacks on computer firms in Toulouse. In the first, the target was Philips and the raid showed that the terrorists had some knowledge of computers since the machines had been scientifically neutralised without any visible damage. Police implicitly acknow-ledged this when they said the AD attackers were not vandals. Nevertheless, the damage was estimated at about £250,000. AD justified the attack on the grounds that military secrets were kept there. Only four days later, the offices of the computer firm CII-Honeywell-Bull Co. were destroyed in an arson attack. This attack, claimed by a group called Clodo (Comité Liquidant ou Détoumant les Ordinateurs), and under the umbrella of AD, was later "explained" in a statement asserting that computers were "the favoured tool of people who dominate. They serve to exploit, to document, to control and to punish".

What kind of movement is AD? Its membership is unusual in two respects for a terrorist group operating in France: the high proportions of foreigners and women, respectively, who play a leading role in the organisation. In one of AD's earliest actions, the bank raid at Condé sur L'Escaut (Nord) on 28 August 1979, the gang had participants from Italy and Spain as well as France. In the police round-up on 28 March 1980, there were some Italians (members of Brigate Rosse and wanted in connection with the murder of Aldo Moro) among the 28 suspects held. At a "squat" raided by police in the 20th arrondissement in April 1982, an Algerian was held. Among the leading fifteen AD members indicted in the State Security Court on 4 April 1980, five were female. Eye-witnesses have, on several occasions, reported the part played by female terrorists in AD attacks. The best known of the AD women is Nathalie Menigon who, with her colleague, Marc Rouillan, evaded police capture until September 1980. She first came to public attention in the March 1980 attack on the Ministry of Overseas Co-operation when eye-witnesses saw her, with an accomplice, fire 30 bullets from an automatic weapon and, when her gun jammed, calmly fit a new clip and resume the attack. The nature of this, and other similar attacks, where women have played leading roles, underlines the similarity and close links between AD and other urban guerrilla movements e.g. Baader-Meinhof. Definite links between AD and the two Italian groups, Brigate Rosse and Prima Linea, and the Basque separatist movement Euskadi ta Askatasuna (ETA), were uncovered by the police in raids on AD "safe" houses in Paris, and in the Ardeche, in 1980.

The international links between AD and other European groups underline an important fact about its structure. It is not a tightly-knit or coherent organisation. On the contrary, it is a network of "groupuscules" with broadly left views and centrifugal links with both "ideological" and "separatist" organisations abroad. Indeed, the links sometimes become so close as to become examples of "dual membership". In other words, some members of AD are members of other foreign groups temporarily "resting" in France. The "network" structure of AD is expressed in the various names used by "groupuscules" operating under the AD "umbrella": among the best known of these *sous-groupes*, besides Clodo (already mentioned in connection with the computer attacks at Toulouse) are Jeune Taupe (Young Mole); Casse-Noix (Nutcrackers); Moutons Enragés (Angry Sheep). The members of AD tend to be young and unemployed but they are rarely uneducated. Among AD members appearing in court in April 1980, occupations cited included a student, a plumber, a pharmacist, a compositor and more than one bank employee.

The AD "network" draws on an unusually wide assortment of ideological themes normally associated with the extreme left. As we have seen, its targets included computer firms, labour exchanges, police stations, a hotel, banks, and various agencies concerned with overseas trade, aid and development. An explosion at Orly airport on 12 June 1980, in which seven immigrant workers were injured, is normally attributed to AD but seems to have been something of an aberration. Possibly, the explosives, hidden in left luggage lockers, were either in transit or awaiting collection.

AD has never been short of either money or equipment. The bank raid at Condé L'Escaut in August 1979 had netted the organisation 16 million francs in unused notes. Weapons used in AD attacks suggest ready access to sources outside France. In April 1982, an AD arms cache in the 20th arrondissement included machine-guns, pistols, revolvers, and bullet-proof vests. In September of the same year, police found $1\frac{1}{2}$ tonnes of explosive at a remote rural commune in the Ardeche.

CONCLUSIONS

Our survey of the principal sources of terrorism in France today suggests that the problem is far from being overcome. Despite the upsurge in terrorism (especially in Corsica) in 1982 and 1983, the French government has held back from taking panic measures since there is widespread public distaste, on both sides of the political spectrum, for anything even mildly reminiscent of "state terrorism". However, French governments have traditionally had at their disposal a range of constitutional and judicial devices for tackling threats to the security of the state.

Under Article 36 of the constitution, the government can proclaim a "state of siege" which allows the army to take over essential police powers. At a more mundane level, marches and demonstrations can be banned by government authority exercised through the Prefect or Mayor. A law of 1936 allows the government to ban organisations that are a threat to the security of the state, groups that:

> provoke armed demonstrations in the streets . . . racial discrimination, hatred or violence against a person or group of persons because of their origin, ethnic group, race or religion.

By 1980, fourteen groups of the right and fourteen of the left plus five autonomist groups had been banned, under the Fifth Republic. However banning groups is not a very effective measure since their members often reconstitute themselves under a new label: Fane was replaced by the FNE; and the Corsican autonomist group ARC was succeeded by the APC.

Among special judicial procedures, there is that of *flagrant delit* (literally "caught in the act") which allows police special powers if a crime is in the process of being carried out, and an accelerated court procedure thereafter. From 1963, the State Security Court was set up to cope with the upsurge of terrorist attacks linked to the Algerian conflict. Its jurisdiction covered the whole territory of France and suspects brought before it could be held for six days beforehand (instead of the usual 48 hours) and for unlimited periods of remand thereafter.

Following a period of relative calm and in an effort to soften what were considered by the Socialists to be the harsh law and order policies of the previous regime, the Mitterrand government effected several important changes that were likely to make the fight against terrorism more difficult. On 18 September 1981, the National Assembly voted to abolish capital punishment. A month earlier the State Security Court had been abolished after eighteen years' service. Hundreds of prisoners in jail were granted an amnesty by the new government which had the effect of putting unrepentant terrorists back on the streets and provoking acts of violence from colleagues of other terrorists kept behind bars. Finally, the new government reiterated France's traditional policy of remaining a *terre d'asile* where political refugees would be welcomed to a safe haven. This implied that there would be no relaxation of the previous government's policy of refusing to extradite "politically motivated" suspects to other European jurisdictions.

By late 1982 these policies of concessions and tolerance were yielding a bitter harvest for President Mitterrand. Neighbouring European governments, and in particular the Spanish government, were critical of the French refusal to extradite wanted terrorists; an exchange of visits at ministerial level between Paris and Madrid achieved only promises of stricter controls on the Franco–Spanish border. Even within France public opinion grew restive as Paris was clearly becoming "a haven for terrorists".

After the wave of attacks during the summer, the French government felt compelled in August 1982 to take some tougher measures to prevent further escalation of terrorist incidents. These measures included the creation of a post of Secretary of State for Public Security, the establishment of a centralised anti-terrorist data bank, new laws on the sale of certain weapons, the banning of AD, heavy reinforcement of police services dealing with public security and closer co-operation with other European police forces. Within the government, a "Council of terrorism" was established to keep a watching brief on the situation. It was announced that stricter controls on immigration would be implemented; and foreigners under suspicion in France would be watched more closely by the police. As the Interior Minister, G. Defferre put it, "we will discourage them from coming to settle their scores on our territory". The expulsion of two Syrian diplomats in 1982 marked the first time for ten years that Arab diplomats had been compelled to depart from France – a sure sign of the growing concern at "imported terrorism". A much publicised disagreement over tactics between the Justice Minister, M. Badinter, and the Interior Minister, M. Defferre, was not calculated to instil confidence into the public. M. Badinter resisted M. Defferre's call for the police to be able to mount spot identity checks, and to use firearms on occasions other than self-defence.

Although Breton nationalism is now quiescent, Corsican separatism is likely to continue as a serious problem for the foreseeable future. The most constructive strategy for the French government will be to enhance the political importance of the regional assembly so that the widespread public support in the island for autonomy within the French state will have a forum that effectively embodies these aspirations. Such a strategy would be likely to isolate the 4 per cent of Corsicans who support separatism and violence and who rely on the passive connivance of much of the indigenous population for their campaign.

On the French mainland, the central problem is that of "imported terrorism". It is clear that co-operation with neighbouring states, especially Spain, will have to be further improved and the reluctance to extradite considerably modified. Secondly, frontier controls (the principle of free movement in the EEC notwithstanding) will have to be tightened up. Thirdly, judicial procedures will have to be devised (e.g. longer holding periods for suspects) to assist the police in the fight against terrorism. Finally, the case in France for a special anti-terrorist police force has been recognised with a view to obviating the problems, inherent in the present structure, of divided responsibility by making it answerable to one person.

Spanish Separatism:
ETA's Threat to Basque Democracy

Peter Janke

Within the decade of the 1970s no single political achievement in Europe can compare in importance with the peaceful transformation of Franco's Spain into a modern constitutional monarchy. It was brought about by the political mastery exercised by King Juan Carlos and his youthful prime minister Adolfo Suárez: their skill in containing violence from the political right-wing, whilst dismantling the structures of an authoritarian régime and replacing them by democratic institutions, saved Spain from the historic cycle of revolution to which, after one of the bloodiest civil wars Spain had known, General Franco put a stop in 1939.

Of the many problems which the government confronted during the period of political reconstruction (1975–80) none was as pregnant with danger as the regional issue. On it the civil war (1936–39) had been fought in the Basque country; furthermore the Spanish military had been taught to consider itself the guardian, the custodian even, of Spain's unity. The military were therefore particularly sensitive to political developments which threatened the state in this way. Basque demands for autonomy had to be channelled into institutions loyal to the crown and to Spain.

If this were not hard enough, the existence of a Basque separatist group, *Euskadi ta Askatasuna* (ETA), skilled in the practice of political violence, complicated still further the government's task. Yet by 1980 the process was largely complete, the institutions existed and were functioning: and still violence from a tiny minority persisted. This study charts the course of that violence from its timid beginnings to its dramatic heights, examines its aims and support, assesses the threat it poses to the nation, and recounts how the state responded to the challenge.

THE BASQUE PEOPLE

The Basque country lies in the north-west corner of Spain, tucked into the Bay of Biscay and cut off by mountains from the plains of Castile. Originally a mountain and a fishing people, the Basques straddle the Pyrenees, extending into the fertile French departments of Basse-Navarre, Labourde and Soule. On the Spanish side the two most fiercely Basque provinces, Guipúzcoa and Vizcaya, lie on the rocky Atlantic coast; inland are Alava and Navarre.

More Basque is spoken in Spain than in France, but all told probably fewer than half a million inhabitants speak this ancient and undocumented language[1] at all, and fewer still with any fluency. In any case pronunciation and spelling differ widely within the region, and the relatively small base

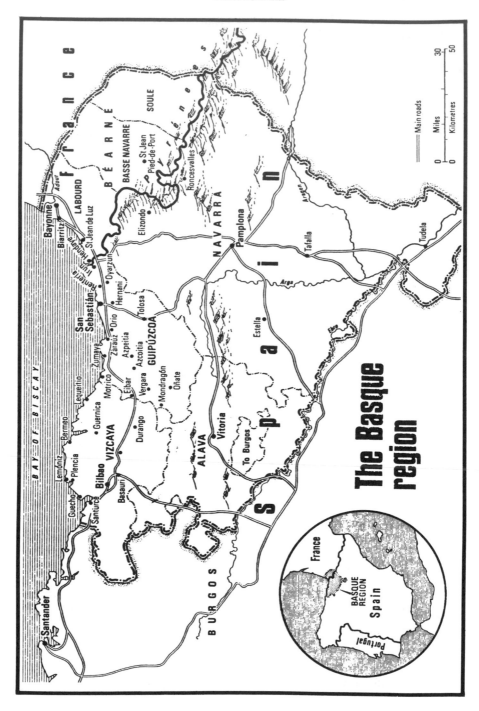

The Basque region

vocabulary limits the use of Basque as a vehicle for modern expression or scientific analysis, although the practice of borrowing words from Spanish lends it some flexibility. Hardworking, independent, resourceful and self-reliant by nature, the Basque people created for themselves a standard of living second to none in Franco's Spain.

The provinces have long been knitted into the institutional fabric of the Spanish monarchy so that royal administration relied heavily upon outstanding services lent by loyal Basques. Serving at court, they rose to the highest offices of state: nor under Franco was there any noticeable impediment to the career of a diligent Basque. True, many Basques turned their back on Madrid; as a city it did not attract them, and their business, anyway, was transacted in Paris and London. They are industrialists, manufacturers of ships and steel workers, and tackle their livelihoods with a Victorian ethic in banking halls built with nineteenth-century wealth. Open as they are to the sea and therefore to outside influences, Madrid appears to them provincial.

In common with the rest of Spain Basques have a deep attachment to the Roman Catholic Church and a passion for bullfighting—that other sacrifice—although the sport looks out of place in the steep green valleys and cloud-laden skies. More typical are *pelota*, a fast ball game akin to fives or squash and played in every village by priest and boy alike; wrestling; the *aizkolari*, sturdy men who compete in tree-trunk chopping; and races at sea, in which every fishing village sports its oarsmen. Inland, teams of oxen, used on the land where the tractor overturns, are driven to compete in dragging mammoth weights short distances; and rams are pitted in combat. Such sports, with their emphasis upon strength, and more besides, distinguish the Basque from the Castilian and the Andalusian, whom the European romantic movement made "typical" of Spain.

Physically, the Basque can be recognised still as a distinct race, fairer haired than "Spaniards", taller, sometimes with blue eyes, a fairer skin and—most characteristic of all—a noble nose. Sartorially, his beret and his umbrella, taken everywhere and with good reason, set him apart. Successful in their industry, these people have attracted to their factories in greater Bilbao and in the smaller industrial towns, of which there are many, families from the traditionally poor south. Indeed, so many have settled in the region that the Basque risks losing something of his identity. Some feel it a threat to their existence and resent the intrusion.

There are of course sectors where the foreigner has made no impact—for instance fishing and farming, the produce of which provides the Basque with the finest tables in Spain. In comparison the Castilian has only his pride, albeit a pride that strengthens rather than debilitates character, yet even in this the Basque is strong.

MOMENTOUS ASSASSINATION

Madrid in the early 1970s was a capital like no other in Europe. Although growing rapidly to some three million inhabitants it preserved its provincial

137

nature, the occasional tractor in the street, the weekend influx of country folk drawn by the bright lights, a homogeneous society, where the foreigner or stranger was still very much an oddity, an object of curiosity and a subject for comment. For a while he could remain anonymous by moving from one to another of the numerous lodging houses, but each time he would have had to fill in a form for the police, and if he came home after 11 o'clock he would have called the local night watchman to open the main door to the block in which he was staying.

As long as the stranger had no police record he passed, quite naturally, unnoticed by the authorities. So it was in 1972 when two members of ETA travelled down from the northern Basque country to verify for the terrorist organisation a piece of intelligence which had been passed anonymously to it: namely, whether or not Admiral Carrero Blanco, the *eminence grise* of General Franco's régime, heard Mass every day at the same hour in the same church.

It turned out to be true, and the regularity gave ETA its chance to plan the kidnapping of the one man capable of ensuring the survival of Franco's system of government after his death. Four young men, very different in character, were entrusted with the operation, aimed at securing the release of some 150 ETA militants who were serving sentences of ten years or more for terrorist offences against the Spanish state.

They arrived in Madrid quite unprepared, wrongly dressed, with no contacts, no previous knowledge of the city or of its customs. They looked the Admiral up in the telephone book to discover his domicile and bought a street map to find the way. As often as not they could not find in the labyrinthine streets of old Madrid pre-determined meeting places, and because of their strong Basque accents were soon teased by unsuspecting neighbours with membership of ETA.

Once they had settled down in an apartment rented for a year and had satisfied the curiosity of the street as to their business in Madrid, they all set to work on a plan. Without guidance or help from the widespread clandestine communist party (PCE) apparatus or any of the other illegal networks which flourished at the time in Madrid's political underworld, a safe house was prepared for the Admiral. As chance would have it, before the operation could be put into effect thieves broke into the apartment only to be discovered by the caretaker, who called the police.

By the time the group had found other suitable accommodation the hot weather was upon them, and the government prepared to depart for the Basque coast to the summer capital of San Sebastián. Furthermore, in July 1973 Franco nominated Carrero Blanco as Prime Minister and it was thought his new office might well cause him to change his habits and certainly lead the police to tighten the security surrounding him. ETA accordingly abandoned its plans until the autumn.

When the unit returned to Madrid its members had everything set up and prepared. They began once again to observe the Admiral's habits. As the days passed the four kept fit by doing an hour's gymnastics after orange juice but before an English breakfast. For target practice they often went out by car to the utter loneliness of the mountains surrounding the capital.

Amateur tunnellers

At home one member would read Dickens and Russian novels, another texts on guerrilla warfare. Of the four only one was practical by nature, preferring to occupy himself with his hands, experimenting with inks and printing equipment for forgery, and only one was deeply concerned to rationalise the group's actions in accordance with revolutionary dialectics. Indeed, his "scientific" analysis cut little ice with the others, who nonetheless appreciated the need for rigour, even if in practice each for lack of experience or training was found wanting.

They were after all amateurs, the product of a gentle, local environment and certainly not schooled in the tough brutalities of power by Moscow or Peking. Hardly surprising, therefore, that in the handling of firearms accidents occurred indoors. It was not unknown for members to relax to the point of forgetfully leaving their weapons wrapped in swimming towels on bar stools, and in street cafes. Their lack of mechanical knowledge led them to invest in a second-hand car which proved a mechanical failure. Physically they were quite unhardened, coming as they did from comfortable middle-class backgrounds, nor had they been psychologically prepared for terrorism.

They lacked neither courage nor initiative or determination, but their resilience had never been tested in the professional world of killing. Their minds were still young and impressionable: their driving motivation was fierce nationalism.

Surprisingly, ETA had no contacts in Madrid for this particular undertaking. Attempts had been made to link up with dissident bodies in other provinces and indeed national networks, but these people saw the national question from a different angle, and were sceptical towards the armed struggle. As the PCE and the labour movement in the capital was pretty well penetrated by the authorities, and since in the Basque country itself the security forces had waged a successful campaign in 1973 against ETA, it was perhaps the autonomous nature of the unit which allowed it to escape detection. That and the sheer unpredictability characteristic of amateurs allowed them to slip through the larger meshes of the security net, to find that on the ground remarkably little precaution was taken to protect the Spanish Prime Minister; itself an indication of the amazing stability of Franco's Spain.

It was clear in the autumn that to kidnap Carrero Blanco was no longer an option: the security was too tight. The unit itself decided therefore upon a political assassination "on behalf of the people". By chance behind the Jesuit Church which the Admiral attended was a semi-basement flat to let. One member of the group, posing as a sculptor, hired it in early November with the idea of digging out from it a passage underneath the road, which might then be blown up as the Admiral's car passed above it.

The work began on 7 December and was completed five days later. Even at this stage the group displayed its lack of preparation. They were unprepared for the foul stench of gas-soaked earth which seeped from the flat to the irritation of neighbours, and which clung to their clothes and hair to the point that people moved away from them in bars. They had the wrong tools and put the stinking soil into plastic bags which broke. One member had to buy a tape measure to discover if they had dug far enough. Another had to gain an elementary knowledge of tunnel supports from mining manuals on sale to engineers, so as to prevent the road from caving in. Their health suffered from the bad air, which caused frequent fainting and allowed them to dig for no more than a maximum of ten minutes each.

With the digging completed, 80 kilos of industrial explosives were driven south and collected by the group, who packed it into the T-shaped chamber which extended over seven metres. The idea was to detonate it from the end of the street. In cold rain three of the group arrived, dressed as electricians, to run the cable out of the flat's window and along the street. On 20 December, having heard Mass, the Prime Minister entered his car. The charge was detonated and the car was hurled spectacularly over a five-storey building to land on an inner courtyard balcony on the second floor. The Admiral's death changed the face of Spain.

Those involved in the assassination escaped by car to Salamanca and crossed into Portugal, where they took ship for France arriving at Nantes.[2] Confident in its exploits, ETA organised in Bordeaux a meeting with representatives of the press, when in a childish fashion, the night before Christmas eve, the murderers recounted their deeds.

For the occasion ETA used the home of a Basque engineer[3] who was conveniently on holiday, and had their masked representatives photographed in front of nine posters depicting ETA members killed in shoot-outs.[4] It was the first time that ETA had operated outside the Basque country and the first time that it had exploited the media in the fashion popularised by the Tupamaro terrorists a few years earlier in Uruguay. It was also the first time that a European prime minister had been assassinated since the death in 1939 of Rumania's premier Calinesco. In Spain one has to go back to 1921, when Conservative leader Eduardo Dato died as anarchists riddled his car with bullets.

NATIONALISM AND IDEOLOGY

Terrorism in Europe sprang to life in the late 1960s in Ireland, Italy, France and Germany and in Spain. Scandinavia remains untouched by political violence, and so to a very large extent does Portugal, having recovered from its revolution in the mid-1970s. Switzerland and the Low Countries have also escaped. The causes for the widespread upsurge of violence in Europe were multifold, but invariably ran deep in the veins of political life; from country to country the causes differed, and although attempts on occasions were made, no one successfully orchestrated European terrorist groups. Sometimes indeed there were common factors, and certainly cheap and easy travel, automatic telecommunications and media coverage encouraged international contacts between groups. Yet the principal motivation of these groups remained singularly personal.

Two overriding currents motivate European terrorism: the gut feeling of nationalism and the influence of an intellectually constructed ideology on the so-called left or extreme left of the political spectrum. Neither, for one reason or another, depending upon the state, can be accommodated within the existing political framework; in other words the currents run outside consensus politics, beyond the reach of compromise, so that to include them would in some form break the dominant consensus. Rejecting conformity, some men and women are stung to action and—perhaps encouraged by irresponsible outsiders who exploit them politically and commercially—embrace violence with the intolerance of the fanatic to impose their selfish ends upon the overwhelming moderate majority.

Nationalism lies at the root of the Irish troubles, as it does in the Basque country. It accounts also for the actions of the Corsican separatists, who feel threatened by French mainlanders settling on the island and destroying Corsica's traditional way of life. On the other hand the mainspring behind Italy's *Red Brigades* and behind the German successors to Andreas Baader and Ulricke Meinhof in the *Red Army Faction* is ideology, in fact a transient and intellectually weak derivative of Marxism–Leninism.

In ETA nationalism and ideology are confused, and the confusion has led to endless feuding and splits since the movement began in 1959. In origin it sprang from the Basque Nationalist Party (PNV)[5] which throughout Franco's long years of dictatorship had maintained a government-in-exile in France following upon the defeat in 1939 of the Republican forces in the Spanish civil war. A group from the party's youth section, *Euzco-Gaztedi*, travelled to Paris in 1957 to try to persuade the party elders, headed by the *Lenda-kari*, José Mariá Leizaola, to embark upon armed struggle. They failed.

Disappointed, they returned home and drew close to a circle of university students, who some years earlier had founded a clandestine and irregularly circulated journal called *Ekin* (Action).[6] Before long the police moved in to break up the group. A new organisation was needed, and ETA was born on 31 July 1959[7] from a fundamentally patriotic conviction of young people principally concerned about the survival of their language and with researching their own history. Their political convictions were democratic.

ETA's first assembly took place in May 1962 to review the effect of the earliest timid steps towards terrorism, inspired especially by the example of Fidel Castro in Cuba, but also by national liberation struggles against colonialism. "Violence is necessary. A destructive contagious violence which supports our struggle and which has been taught us by the Israelis, the Congolese and the Algerians."[8] Again the police had stepped in, making many arrests, forcing the leaders to cross into France. There, to resist capture in future, they determined to set up in the Spanish Basque country a three-man cell system and defined ETA as "a revolutionary movement of national liberation". Its sole object was to obtain rapidly the independence of the Basque country by whatever means necessary, including violence.

Maoism and Marxist–Leninism

But that year the first conflict over motivation occurred. A Spanish Basque, José Echevarrieta Ortiz (22), studying law in Paris, read the works of Mao Tse-tung and was so impressed that he enthused others within the Basque movement. It was to exclude such people from ETA that the founders called a further assembly in March 1963. Whilst their views predominated no split occurred. Yet shortly afterwards the militants compiled their own manual, *Insurrection in Euskadi*, which was influenced by Maoist ideas, although it called for an urban rather than a rural guerrilla campaign.

Written by Goiztiri (a pseudonym), the pamphlet proudly asserted the existence of an older order, which pre-dated Gallic or hispanic law, and which was Basque. It spoke of embarking upon a revolutionary war—

> For the militant *gudari* (soldier) intent upon waging revolutionary warfare, far from being ignoble, to deceive, to force and to kill is essential. We are intransigent so far as our idea, our truth and our goal are concerned. The targets from which we can choose amount to thousands. To us is reserved the luxury of attacking when and where we want. In the moment of attack, through concentrating our forces, we shall be stronger and more numerous than the enemy. The form is to charge like a bull, to defend like a boar and to flee like a wolf.

Goiztiri imagined that the Spanish state would react blindly, "like a colossus stung by bees", and that such action would arouse the indignation of a hitherto passive population, which would turn with sympathy towards ETA. Sympathy would grow to achieve support and admiration for the militant "who must appear as the exponent of the peoples' aspirations." Yet in all this there was an element at best of nineteenth-century romanticism, at worst of narcissistic theatricality. "Power is taken by fascination. Justice can enthuse, liberty produces heroes, but neither the one nor the other fascinate. Only the invocation and the imminent fact of a grand collective tragedy is capable of arousing fascination."

In 1964 the third assembly finally broke with the old nationalist PNV and, under the influence of the "Maoists" within ETA, defined the movement as "anti-capitalist" and "anti-imperialist". Yet the predominant line was still not Marxism–Leninism; rather, as Alvarez Emparanza explained, the primacy of the human person and of his rights was the basis for any political action. At this time the French government took action against the ETA founders on their soil, removing them from the Spanish frontier. As the direction necessarily passed from the founders' hands[9] into those of the militants in the field—especially Francisco Iturrioz and José Luis Zalbide—ETA's ideology veered to the left.

For ETA national liberation was in the mid-1960s still the predominant intellectual concept. The black French sociologist Frantz Fanon, through his book *The Wretched of the Earth*, wielded an important influence and inspired the writing of *A Letter to the Intellectuals*. The thinking behind this document dominated the proceedings of the fourth assembly held in Brussels in the summer of 1965. By this time ETA leaders had come into contact with orthodox communist party members both abroad and at home, and a debate had begun within the movement as to whether it was advisable or not to link up. No decision was taken on this important point in 1965.

Behind Goiztiri's approach lay the childish temper which, unrebuked, expressed itself in the absurdly intolerant language of the totalitarian:

> We must destroy the apparatus of oppression, known as administration, by setting up parallel hierarchies, that is to say our own administration. Such is the beginning of our final triumph. In our view the principal objective of revolutionary warfare is to pulverise the enemy administration. Law and order must be torn down, and legality transformed into uncontrollable chaos. We must create a state of disorder and insecurity: the one and the other paralyses a country's life . . . On the one hand believing order can no longer defend it and on the other feeling enslaved by that very order, the masses will come of age and join our side.

The movement's founders had to fight not only the influence of the powerful PCE but also the Trotskyists, who made a determined bid to infiltrate ETA through employing "entryist" tactics. Most of these people were students from San Sebastián: in 1966 they were expelled and went off to found eventually the Trotskyist Communist Movement of Spain (MCE). To them there was no Basque "national" question, but the majority of those attracted to ETA identified themselves with patriotic struggles in Kurdistan, Quebec, Algeria and even in Croatia, where nationalist fervour drove men to organise terrorist campaigns.

It was at the fifth assembly in December 1966 that for the first time ETA met in Spain. Some of those members outside the country returned for the occasion, but they were outnumbered by those on the ground. Together they amounted to no more than 45 people. Discussions were continued in March 1967, by which time ideology mattered. Possibly 13 of the 45 people involved were strongly inclined towards communism. Yet the attraction of Marxism–Leninism was still less than "revolutionary nationalism", which was propagated by an ETA theorist of German origin, Federico Krutwig Sagredo, in the theoretical organ *Branka* (Prow) around this time. He looked to Vietnam as an example and inspiration.

At the second meeting of the fifth assembly ETA defined itself as a "Basque socialist movement of national liberation". Meeting in the tiny fishing village of Guetaria, outside Zarauz, members discussed such things as the concept of a nation, a people or a culture, who actually made up the Basque people, the role of the intellectual within the movement, the ideology of the workers and argued over strategy and ETA's general political line.

Because of the marked turn towards ideology some of the founders parted company after the fifth assembly. Alvarez Emparanza could find no room for his own brand of "humanist socialism" amongst the Marxist–Leninists, nor could the practical Benito del Valle. It was this issue which led to the definitive split within ETA between the followers of the fifth assembly, ETA-V, and those of the sixth, ETA-VI.

Patriotism before socialism

Two words characterised for those involved the differing attitudes displayed by ETA-V and ETA-VI: *abertzale* (patriotic) and *españolismo-marxista* (pan-Spanish-Marxism). The patriots were naturally those who felt Basque before they felt socialist; the ideologists were inspired first by the idea of revolutionary socialism, and since this was a condition which they sought to bring about all over Spain were disparagingly labelled "Spaniards", a term which accused them of having betrayed their real fatherland—*Euskadi.*[10] The final schism did not come about for several years, largely because the police uprooted the organisation in the late 1960s and put the principal members on trial in the famous proceedings at Burgos in 1970. With no organisation, there was nothing and nobody to discuss.

However the Burgos trials gave ETA enormous publicity and attracted a new and younger generation of enthusiasts. Among them was Eduardo Moreno Bergareche (born 1950), who prepared the ideological position papers for the sixth assembly held in Hasparren (France) in the summer of 1973, and which Carrero Blanco's four would-be murderers attended. No more than 20 people were present in all, whereupon on behalf of the whole organisation the majority approved the formal adoption of democratic centralism as the correct procedure to turn ETA into a party:

> The party aspires to convert itself into the vanguard of the oppressed to carry out the revolution. It therefore follows a policy which links it to the masses with a view to winning them over in favour of the programme. It does not need to acquire as members large sectors of the population; it needs compliance and acceptance of the party's leadership.

Such formalisation along Leninist lines led a number of less orthodox communists to leave. A further meeting took place in December—ten days before the Admiral's assassination. The final split came in May 1974. It proved that the ideologists were not strong enough to take over a predominantly nationalist movement or, as they would have it, "it has become impossible to transform ETA into an instrument capable of developing a revolutionary policy which would respond to the interests of the Basque working class". In fact it had proved impossible, at that juncture, to turn ETA into a Marxist–Leninist vanguard party. The attempt nonetheless had been made, but made not so much by fellow travellers as by individuals who had themselves independently arrived at that doctrinal position.

In the early 1970s ETA consisted of no more than three dozen members, who were divided more by their personalities than by their beliefs. Those who were physically practical, determined and daring, the "doers" of this world, were for action and refused to wait upon the long-term development of party structures. Others, more patient and of a reflective nature, although no less committed, gathered around Moreno Bergareche, who believed the armed struggle pursued by "militarists" should go hand in hand with a more general "political-military" programme aimed at strengthening the movement among the workers. Instead of ETA-V and ETA-VI of the early 1970s the division was formulated in ETA-M and ETA-PM.

The militarists explained their position in a special document, *Agiri* (Explanation), in 1974. Their objective was the establishment of a Basque socialist state by armed action. As their model they looked to the IRA, recognising in the ETA-PM ranks an incipient Sinn Fein. The militarists made very clear their fundamental hatred of liberal democracy, which because of its flexibility and capacity to reform threatened their own support and made the violent achievement of their minority aims even less feasible than under the Franco régime.

The Bergareche approach

The position of those who were more analytical in the mid–1970s is best described by their spokesman, Moreno Bergareche:

> One must make clear that the fact that communists militate in ETA does not mean that this organisation is a Communist Party, nor does it transform it into one. There can be no doubt that ETA is a class organisation, but it is not communist through and through. There is a further point: those who define ourselves in this way do not even attempt to work towards this end. I militate within ETA because I understand that within it there is a place for a patriotic communist option, as there is room for other less well-defined positions. And finally I am active in ETA not because it accommodates men of communist persuasion, but because it is the best framework within which to practise proletarian Basque politics.

Speaking still more personally, Moreno Bergareche continued:

> I understand that a communist from an oppressed people, such as Euskadi is, cannot forget his Basque condition. For that reason, because I'm Basque, I try to realise my communist option here, in Euskadi, fighting not only for the triumph of the socialist revolution but for the national liberation of the people to whom I belong. I feel deeply as a Basque, and such patriotism does not stem from internationalism. I am genuinely concerned to provide an answer to the problem of the Basque people as a whole. What might be new in this stance is that the national struggle develops within the communist framework of the class struggle.[11]

And that indeed is the intellectual position which Moreno Bergareche attempted to define and for which political opponents murdered him in 1976. He set out to reconcile with Marxism–Leninism the passionate patriotism which motivated ETA members by adopting and refining further a third course of "revolutionary nationalism". By so doing he hoped ETA might outwit on the right the Basque nationalism which found expression in the PNV, representing the overwhelming majority of Basques, and on the left the so-called "social imperialism" of Moscow-line communism:

> We honestly believe that our problem as Basque workers, our problem as an exploited class in the context of a nationally oppressed and divided people, cannot be solved within the Spanish or French framework. Certainly our liberation as a class would be viable within the framework of a socialist Spain or France. But in our opinion, only an independent power in our own hands, that is to say only a Basque socialist state could guarantee the solution to the other half of the problem, our liberation as members of an oppressed national community: Euskadi.
> Naturally this independence has a socialist content for us: it is separatist with respect to imperialism and to the Spanish and French capitalist states, but unionist with respect to all the other peoples of the world and especially our close neighbours ... We are in

145

favour of the abolition of frontiers when the conditions under which a man exploits another or a people oppresses another no longer exist. Our independence struggle is conceived within the unity of the workers of the world and as a function of the interests of the Socialist Revolution.

We conceive of the armed fight as the supreme form of the struggle of the working class. Our liberation as a class and as a people will be made possible through the armed insurrection of the proletariat and of the rest of the people of Euskadi employing a revolutionary tactic alongside other peoples who make up the Spanish state.[12]

GROWTH OF AN ORGANIZATION

Developing as it did from the older branch of Basque nationalism represented by the PNV, ETA naturally overlapped and sought to use the PNV network. The younger ETA militants quickly found themselves controlling the PNV party organisation in Alava and Navarre and were dominant in Vizcaya and Guipúzcoa. As members of ETA they divided their interests into five branches—publications, responsible for *Zutik* (Stand up), the official organ, and *Berriak* (News); distribution of propaganda; study courses; Basque language encouragement; and legal considerations. A sixth activity was considered, that of violent action, but ETA's main concern was cultural and historical activities, which were taught in six-month courses, at the end of which militants were required to take an oath of silence.

ETA's first executive committee consisted of Julián de Madariaga, Benito del Valle, and Barreño Omaechevarría, who in 1961 fled to Bordeaux in France, where they set up their headquarters in a house belonging to a Bilbao priest. A year later Ignacio Irigaray and José Luis Alvarez Emparanza joined them in France. The leadership was uniquely middle-class, from university backgrounds in engineering, law and administration. The whole organisation numbered less than 65 members.

As the attraction of violent action grew in the early 1960s the need for a clandestine structure became apparent. ETA consequently adopted the three-man cell (*hirurko*—threesome) as its base unit, only one of whose members communicated with a member of another cell. At the second assembly, held in 1963, ETA divided the whole Basque region into five areas of responsibility under a regional leader (*herrialdeburu*). Foreign contacts were established through delegations in Europe and America.

When the French government, alarmed by the ensuing acts of political violence, forced the executive committee members to leave the French Basque country Madariaga and Irigaray went to Algiers to organise military action and training. Alvarez Emparanza preferred Brussels, where the Communist Party lent ETA its premises, and Benito del Valle flew to Caracas (Venezuela) to promote ETA's propaganda.

Faced with the physical absence of the founders, ETA reorganised itself on the ground, for the first time within Spain, in 1966. The fifth assembly, which was attended by 45 activists, in Gaztelu (Guipúzcoa), under Francisco Javier Echevarrieta Ortiz, set up four fronts responsible for political action, cultural action, economic action, and activity amongst the industrial working class. The thought was to provide organisational channels for every

146

type of activity, which together would cumulatively contribute to a popular war of liberation.

It never worked. The reality was very different. "The work undertaken by the various fronts has overlapped, the units of one front doubled so as to act as units for another—in fact we have displayed the utmost organisational disorder. All this, together with the repression which comes with armed activity, has led us to suffer defeat after defeat without ever achieving solid groundwork, other than the armed actions which have been fairly constant."

The despair was justified for ETA had already lost its leader in the field, Echevarrieta Ortiz, a middle-class university-educated teacher from Bilbao. He failed to stop for speeding near Tolosa, and was killed in an exchange of shots with the Guardia Civil. To avenge his death ETA killed the San Sebastián police chief, Melitón Manzanas, outside his home in Irún in August 1968. Such action, quite new to ETA, caused the state to crack down on the organisation. There followed the arrest of 16 people connected with the Irún murder, who were put on military trial at Burgos in 1970. Six received sentences of death, but were reprieved by Franco.[13] Many others fled to France.

With such losses all control within ETA broke down and the remaining militants split into at least three factions, which eventually formed into ETA-V and ETA-VI in the early 1970s. In theory a general assembly (*Biltzar Nagusia*) was supposed to have met every year since the decision to set one up had been taken at the fifth assembly. In fact it never met and power devolved to a tactical executive committee (KET), which was responsible for organising all of ETA's activities in each region. Such a structure did not withstand police action.

Mendizábal's military front

However, from the ashes of the Burgos trial arose a new ETA under the leadership of Eustakio Mendizábal Benito. Consisting of the rump of ETA-V, it became known as the military front. Mendizábal typifies the tragedy overtaking the Basque country in the early 1970s. He displayed a passionate love for his language and feared for its future—he once said that to make a revolution one needed to be a poet. He himself was a *versolari*, practised in the art of spontaneous declamation. Having once studied in Lazacano to become a Benedictine monk he retained a great simplicity and sincerity until his violent death in April 1973 in Algorta, outside Bilbao. At 28 he left two sons, and the negative record of having planned and carried out successfully two kidnappings on behalf of ETA—those of the German consul Beihl and the industrialist Huarte.

Mendizábal could not believe in a Europe of nation states because his gut reaction for things Basque was too strong. He belonged to a people, like the Bretons and the Flemish, who had had the misfortune to be dominated by larger national movements which had forged the unities of Spain and France. He argued that these two nineteenth-century liberal states had imposed their laws upon Euskadi, which had become dependent upon their capitalist interests. The French Basque country was sold out to French tourism, causing the young Basque to be pushed aside socially and economically by the Paris bourgeoisie. As for the Spanish Basque country it had lost out to the centralisation of nineteenth-century Spanish liberalism, which had sold the region to foreign capital—principally British in the case of Bilbao.

Such thinking is common at a certain intellectual level amidst a Basque *petite bourgeoisie* based upon small workshops and family businesses and amongst skilled artisans. It is hostile to big business, which disrupts its way of life, and finds comfort, sympathy and even encouragement in the fierce patriotism of the Basque clergy and members of religious orders.

Up to 1970 Basque militants had not undergone any rigorous training or formation: there had been no organisation to undertake it. True, in the mid-1960s Francisco Javier Zumalde Romero had attempted to set up in the mountains surrounding Oñate an autonomous ETA front, but such a rural campaign was unproductive and he fled to France in 1968. Mendizábal changed all this, and set up a clandestine military front based in Guipúzcoa. His personality and strength of character held the group together: conceivably it amounted to 40 individuals.

Mendizábal financed his operations through bank robberies and bought abroad on the illegal arms network a consignment of 500 Firebird "parabellum" small arms, after outwitting the smuggler who had tried to fool ETA by delivering dummies. From that point on ETA had sufficient arms, which it had never enjoyed before. Militants practised in the foothills of the Pyrenees. Furthermore, they stole large quantities of explosives from local manufacturers and from quarries. Showing an eye for publicity, Mendizábal had filmed four simultaneous attacks upon state trade union premises in Irún, Tolosa, Rentería and Hernani in December 1972. But he will be remembered for his kidnapping exploits, which were undertaken as much to improve workers' conditions as to raise funds.

His followers thought of political violence as the supreme form of the struggle of the working class. Yet it was not a *proletarian* but a popular struggle, for they were careful never to exclude other classes,[14] therein recognising their own social origins and the indispensable contribution they made to ETA: in fact without them it would not have existed, for ETA had made almost no impact at all upon the Basque labour movement in the early/mid-1970s. Militants nonetheless expected to be able to sustain their violent campaign and by so doing radicalise general opinion. "It is therefore an imperative task for revolutionaries to attempt to widen and extend the armed struggle."

After Mendizábal's death in 1973 his organisation crumbled as swiftly as it had been built up: most of its members faced trial that year. Few of these recruits to ETA had seen more than three years' activity. Most were in their mid-20s and unmarried, many were skilled workers and all ended up in prison or across the border in France.[15]

Political–military split

As a result of the armed action, and especially the death of Carrero Blanco in December 1973, the patient non-violent work of Basque dissidents became wellnigh impossible because of rigorous police action. It brought to a head the quarrel within ETA between those who favoured political action amongst the factory workforce and the "militarists", who preferred to blast their way to the conference table. The split between the "workers" front and the "military" front occurred in 1974.

Confronted by total disarray intellectually and militarily, Moreno Bergareche attempted to bring together the two wings by taking a hard look at ETA's organisation. For comparison he turned to the experience of the Tupamaros in Uruguay, but took account of Régis Debray's book *The Critique of Armed Struggle*. Special commando units were set up (*bereziak*—specials) with the objective of undertaking actions specifically aimed at the security forces. They were also instructed to make contact with other revolutionary bodies in Spain—particularly in Galicia, but also in Barcelona and Madrid. Their leader in the field was Ignacio Pérez Beotegui (27) but the initiative soon failed, for he was arrested in July 1975.

Two further "military" leaders were captured that year—Ignacio Múgica Arregui (30) and Félix Eguia Inchaurraga (28); others were shot dead. By the end of 1975 the police had uncovered over 60 "safe houses" used by ETA, leaving only one commando unit intact—in Zaraúz. The new structures had clearly not improved ETA's armed struggle.

Convinced of the hopelessness of armed action without political back-up, Moreno Bergareche in 1976 advocated the creation of a revolutionary vanguard party which did not engage in armed struggle. Political violence would be organised quite separately, but be subordinated to the party, which would elaborate its own theory of revolution based upon the peculiarities of the Basque situation. It would reunite an independent Basque state, thereby resolving the problem of oppression, but it would also be a revolutionary party of the working class so as to establish a socialist society, by violence if necessary. But the party would operate under the new bourgeois democracy (Franco died in November 1975) although governed by the principles of democratic centralism.[16]

Yet there was in Moreno Bergareche's view a place for armed struggle, and there was still in 1980 a place for it in the ranks of ETA-PM, which survived the murder in 1976 of its principal theorist. Indeed the purposes of the armed struggle were "to act as a detonator, to sharpen the contradictions of the régime, to back up the mass struggle and to act as a nucleus for the future people's army".[17]

In the meantime it was suggested that the military structure should imitate the Tupamaro "column" based upon a geographical area. Each column should have ample autonomy, with its own logistical back-up, its hit men, an intelligence function and a propaganda network. But within each column there would be political commissars (*asesores políticos*) to ensure strategic uniformity. All columns were to be subject to the direction of a centralised military staff, which would devise and coordinate strategy. Such a structure did not exist in the mid-70s.

Over 1975 and 1976 the cleavage between ETA-M and ETA-PM grew. Those convinced by Moreno Bergareche understood that the advent of constitutional monarchy in Spain following Franco's death required a change in the method of struggle. The "militarists" did not agree and continued to practise violence in an increasingly destructive manner throughout the late 1970s. Yet despite the hostility between the two branches both in fact developed political fronts in the late 1970s, although efforts to unite ETA-M and ETA-PM came to nothing.

THE POLITICS OF SEPARATISM

General Franco's life had ebbed away slowly: by the time he died on 20 November 1975 the support on which he had built his system of authoritarian government had largely vanished. The Spanish Church had withdrawn its approval—even Rome was critical of Madrid. The official syndicates could no longer speak for the labour force, so that strikes were often settled through the good offices of clandestine trade union structures, which were for the most part, although not entirely, in the hands of the PCE.

Having fought a crusade, as he termed it, against communism (1936–39), Franco found increasingly in the 1970s that the emergence of an apparently democratic Euro-communism required a response more flexible than the intellectual siege mentality with which he had equipped modern Spain. Finally, the Spanish economy had so flourished as to transform the country sociologically: how ironic that in peacetime the traditionalists had in fact buried for good the old Spain for which they had fought in the civil war!

With Carrero Blanco dead, the young King, Juan Carlos, had been left a free hand to pursue a gradualist approach to reform. Many Spanish democrats argued that the restrictive nature of Franco's state had caused in the Basque country the nationalist frustration which had found its only outlet in political violence. There was some truth in this view, but the persistence of terrorism under a democratic constitutional monarchy left many red faces.

Weighing with no little skill the political forces at work, the King retained Franco's Prime Minister, Sr. Arias Navarro, who called upon reformist ministers of the old régime to begin the process of adaptation and change. The old right-wing, no more than a rump but fearful of reform, lost thereby its best moment to strike. They could hardly call upon the military to stage a coup against Franco's appointed successor and against ministers who had served the *generalissimo*.

The government announced reform proposals on 28 April 1976, but implementation was left to Adolfo Suárez, a man chosen by the King and appointed Prime Minister in July. To him should be given the credit for persuading Franco's representatives in the *Cortes* to vote themselves out of politics in November by approving a Bill which opened the lower chamber to electoral representation with direct, universal and secret suffrage. The nation gave overwhelming endorsement in a referendum on 15 December 1976 and elections were set for 1977.

Within the newly emerging democratic framework the King called for a national reconciliation. An immediate royal reprieve on 25 November 1975 commuted death sentences to life imprisonment and reduced all other prison sentences. But the demand in the Basque country throughout 1976 was for an amnesty for the 749 Basques in jail for what their supporters termed political reasons. The call was partially answered in July with an amnesty that allowed many to return from exile. It benefited the original founders of ETA—such men as Madariaga, Benito del Valle and Alvarez Emparanza. Some of these men had long ceased their concern for politics, others joined newly emerging Basque political groups. By the end of the year only about 180 remained in prison.

The call for a total amnesty persisted loudly and clearly from all quarters in the Basque country. Street demonstrations were supported by a significant group of local mayors[18] and by a myriad of non-political groups. In talks which the government attempted to hold with both ETA-PM and ETA M the same insistence was displayed. The government refused to be rushed, but passed further dispensations in March 1977, which left only some 20 hard-core ETA terrorists—all men—behind bars, of whom the most important were Pérez Beotegui and Múgica Arregui, both of whom supported ETA-PM.

The remaining score had with only one or two exceptions been accused of planning or actually carrying out murder. They were for the most part in their mid-20s and unmarried, although five had children. They came from small towns in Vizcaya and Guipúzcoa. The majority were relatively unskilled workers although the group included three students, two clerks, a printer, an electrician, a mechanic, a boiler-maker and a teacher. They finally received their liberty in May 1977 on condition that they left the country; they found refuge in Brussels, Oslo and Vienna.

New separatist coalition

Liberal democracy revived pre-Civil War memories in Spain, so that parties which had been virtually redundant for years sprang once again to life on a national scale. The multitudinous political acronyms were confusing; translated into Basque and added to purely regional political parties they became almost impossible for outsiders to follow. In the Basque country by far the greatest influence was exercised by the traditional following of the PNV, which although weak in Navarre was strong in the remaining Basque provinces of Guipúzcoa, Vizcaya and Alava. In two national elections in 1977 and in March 1979 its following has held up, but it has been unsuccessful in drawing within its nationalist folds the separatist extremists.

Although ETA had political ambitions before Franco's death in 1975, the first Basque party initiative outside the PNV came with the creation in August 1976 of the *Koordinadora Abertzale Sozialista* (KAS—Patriotic Basque Socialist Coalition). It consisted of a number of organisations, and particularly ETA-PM.[19] Whilst each organisation retained its independence, they all undertook to act independently only after submitting and debating their proposals within KAS. Together they aimed to force an alternative political programme for the Basque working people by setting up mass organisations of a working class and popular nature, through which the working class could express itself. The objectives were very much those that Moreno Bergareche had in mind before he was lured to his death a month earlier in Behobie (France).

KAS was an attempt, once more, to fuse Basque nationalism with Marxism–Leninism. As in all capitalist states so in Spain KAS believed the class struggle operated, and it believed in the ultimate primacy of the working class, "because it incarnated the highest degree of social contradictions and because of its internal cohesion". KAS saw no contradiction in these reasons—the proletariat "was clearly destined to become the directing class".

> Both the national and the social aspects of Basque reality are, under different forms, examples of the same dynamic of the class struggle, nor can they be separated, nor resolved independently, the one supporting or holding down the other. It is then the desire of KAS and of those that compose it to further the struggle in a simultaneous and coordinated manner in both fields and yet maintain a strategic and organisational independence in Euskadi.

The long-term objectives which KAS set itself were the creation of a classless Basque society, in a united and independent country. Such a "popular, democratic, socialist republic" would be headed by the workers within a constitutional formula "which guaranteed full and direct popular participation in the overall functioning of Basque society". KAS was "aware that final liberty for Euskadi will only come about alongside that of other peoples in the French and Spanish states, in Europe and in the whole world . . . which can only be achieved by the destruction of the capitalist and imperialist system which exploits and oppresses our people."

Outside KAS there were many other groups on the extreme left,[20] but KAS had a political importance for it overlapped the terrorist fringe and provided the government with the possibility of dialogue, an initiative it undertook secretly in November 1976 in a small hotel in Geneva. ETA-PM showed up; ETA-M, in the person of Juan Manuel Pagoaga Gallástegui, instructed the government to negotiate through KAS. Nothing came of the talks, although KAS played a part in 1977 in the general demand for an amnesty. Alongside those of other groups it sent a representative, Santiago Brouard, to Madrid to plead in April on behalf of those imprisoned.

ETA-PM party

KAS continued to exist, although its usefulness was swiftly overtaken by ETA-PM forming its own party—*Euskal Iraultzako Alderdia* (EIA—Party for the Basque Revolution), first announced in March 1977. The following month the first meeting of an underground separatist party, still at that time illegal, took place in the pelota court of Gallarta (Vizcaya). Some

4,000 people attended and recognised at the event the founding role of Moreno Bergareche, and hailed the imprisoned Pérez Beotegui and Múgica Arregui as heroes and leaders. Tape recordings were played of messages recorded by both men calling for a total amnesty. To thunderous applause the voice of Múgica Arregui concluded "Long live Euskadi, for Euskadi cannot be free whilst it is not red".

Present at the meeting and prominent as spokesmen were Francisco Letamendía and Gregorio López Irasuegui who had been released the previous year from a 30-year prison sentence imposed for his part in the murder of police chief Manzanas. He was one of a number of ETA members in jail who had been persuaded of the need to form a party to politicise the masses and had therefore supported ETA-PM. López Irasuegui summed it up at the EIA founding meeting:

> The fact that ETA lacked political and ideological bases caused a certain ambiguity in the organisation's orientation, leading it to adopt a populist rather than a class basis, even although the precise terms in which it waged its struggle up to now have not required it to adopt such a stance, or indeed to resolve the ambiguity. EIA inherits 15 years of ETA's clandestine struggle, its deaths, its imprisonments, its exiles. In other words we are not starting with a void, although we show our public face only today. We take up the same fight, but using new forms, working politically among the masses.

In fact EIA faced the 1977 elections in a coalition known as *Euskadiko Ezkerra* (EE—Basque Left), whose principal candidates were Juan María Bandrés, a lawyer from San Sebastián who had under Franco courageously defended ETA suspects in the courts, and Mario Onaindía, who at the Burgos trial had been sentenced to death. They dismissed ETA-M as an "elitist" organisation and rejected terrorism as "non-revolutionary". In the elections of March 1979 Bandrés was actually elected and took his seat in the Cortes.

Whilst ETA-PM renounced violence and participated in elections, ETA-M did not. So far as these Basque nationalists were concerned the monarchy had been imposed upon Spain by a dictator and bourgeois elections could not guarantee a new order in Euskadi. ETA-M supported the immediate aims of an alternative eight-point programme put forward by KAS. Given that the government would grant a total amnesty, which did not come about until later that year, and that all Basque political forces were legalised, including ETA-M, the militarists would have had the 26 Basque deputies within the Cortes constitute themselves an "assembly of southern Euskadi" and have had them demand as great a degree of self-government as feasible. Above all it urged that the national police force be withdrawn from the Basque country and that Basques be allowed to police themselves.[21]

Those prominent among the militarists at this time were José Miguel Beñaran Ordenana (29) who, five years to the day since he murdered Carrero Blanco, was himself murdered in Anglet (France) in 1978; Miguel Angel Apalátegui (23), thought by Moreno Bergareche's family to have instigated their son's murder; Domingo Iturbe Abasolo, wounded in Biarritz (France) in May 1979, and Francisco Aya Zulaica, ETA's principal political brain. Following Beñaran Ordenana's death María Dolores González Catarain (24) and Antón Echevestí were believed to have assumed prominent places in ETA-M.

Some compromise had to be made with democratic politics if the militarists were not to be left out in the cold and condemned permanently to a clandestine life of crime. Accordingly ETA-M founded a coalition with two fervently nationalistic, left-wing, but non-Marxist groups, the *Acción Nacionalista Vasca* (ANV—Basque Nationalist Action) and *Euskal Sozialista Batzordea* (ESB—Basque Socialist Coalition), known as *Herri Batasuna* (HB—People's Unity).[22]

PNV's electoral dominance

It would be quite wrong to think of EE and HB as consisting only of young hotheads, although it is true that both organisations attracted the votes of young people. A doyen of Basque political exiles, Telesforo Monzón (74), one-time Interior Minister of the brief Basque Government before the Civil War (1936–39) stood as a parliamentary candidate and was elected, although he subsequently refused to sit in the Cortes. A militant political dinosaur, Monzón engaged in "direct action" politics throughout the Basque country, only stopping short of terrorism. "Causes are advanced" he maintained "only through tears, blood and persecution."[23]

He linked himself and the young militarists of the late 1970s to a historic line of brave but fruitless struggle:

> I have lived amongst refugees since the age of eight. I have known those from the Carlist War, I was amongst those of 1936. Today there are those belonging to ETA. The present struggle started in 1837 but its roots go back to 1500. Do you imagine that the refugees do nothing but recite the rosary? My uncle Olazábal ran arms for the Carlists, aided by a priest. My grandfather Ortiz de Urruela, who lived near Ascain, used to meet the priest of Santa Cruz, who did exactly what the young people of ETA are today engaged upon. And I myself in 1936 ran arms . . .

It is of such heady stuff that ETA is made.

In the elections of March 1979 *Herri Batasuna* won three seats in the lower house and one in the Senate, with something like 15 per cent of the vote (172,000).[24] These voters did not all actually support terrorism, but they understood the motives and presumably excused the actions of those who did practise terrorism. The majority of Basques voted for the PNV, which returned seven deputies to the lower house. In the municipal elections which followed in April the PNV won 1,084 places to HB's 260, leaving ETA-PM in EE to pick up 85. The great cities of Bilbao, San Sebastián and Vitoria all had PNV mayors. In Pamplona a socialist (PSOE) was elected.

From these figures there can be no doubt that the population as a whole rejected the violence and rejected too the political programme put forth by ETA in any of its guises. Yet it must be admitted that when, in co-operation with the democratic Spanish authorities, the French government revoked the status of political refugees for Basques, banished 13 from the frontier and handed seven over to the Spanish police in January 1979, HB and KAS could call for a general strike which was pretty well observed on the Guipúzcan coast (Pasajes, Lezo, Rentería) between San Sebastián and the border.

In March 1979 HB, in collaboration with EE, called for a "day of struggle" to support the demand for a general amnesty—a pardon one should note for terrorist actions committed under a democratic government and condemned by the whole political spectrum from the right-wing Popular Alliance (AP) to the Communist Party (PCE). Crowds demonstrated in Bilbao, barricades went up in Durango and Basauri and serious incidents took place elsewhere.[25]

The HB parliamentarians believed nothing could be achieved through dialogue and were not prepared to put their point of view in a democratic forum. They opposed the consultative procedures set up by the government to consider how best to channel demands for autonomy into viable political institutions, and when the elected representatives of the Basque people had agreed upon the text of a Statute of Autonomy HB determined to draw up its own.[26]

Statute of Autonomy

All Basque parties with the exception of the socialists had contributed to the Bill for Basque autonomy. It gave to Basque the status of a "national language", identical to Spanish, and set up a General Council for the Basque country, although each province would function autonomously within the Basque community. To the General Council was given the responsibility for maintaining law and order, the state intervening and withdrawing only at the request of the Basque government in any of the three available degrees—a state of alarm, a state of exception or a state of siege. There would be fiscal autonomy with each province responsible for the collection and for the spending of taxes, part of which would be returned by the province to the state and part put into a fund for the poorest regions of Spain.[27]

Already, before the Autonomy Statute was debated in the Cortes— indeed before it was drawn up—Madrid had established (Feb 1978) a Basque General Council for consultative purposes. It took issue with ETA's openly expressed intention to promote a coup and on 9 January 1979 delivered a stern rebuke: "The present practices have much in common with the totalitarian systems it claims to fight, but which in fact it strengthens." At the same time the Communist Party of Euskadi (in essence the PCE in the Basque country) backed the Council in any political initiative which might serve to deprive ETA of support for terrorism.

That year the celebration in April of *Aberri Eguna*, the Basque national day, was marked by large turnouts in rallies organised by the PNV in support of the Statute of Autonomy. HB also marched, despite its opposition to what it considered a half measure: but a measure nonetheless drawn up and discussed by Basques in the historic centre of Guernika, the seat of the ancient Basque parliament. Those that pressed close to the HB banners in Bilbao, which had the largest crowds, shouted puerile insults[28] at the Spanish and French governments and called for more guns for ETA before they finally burnt the Spanish flag in the Plaza de España.

The point to grasp about such an event is that to survive the PNV, as the mother of Basque national politics, must, and will always be prepared to welcome back into its fold ETA supporters. To disinherit a nationalist is not possible for the PNV, within whose ranks there will always be those who cherish "autonomy today, independence tomorrow", as some PNV banners read on that very march. Indeed one PNV senator alluded to Adolfo Suárez's UCD government in Madrid as an enemy of Euskadi.

There was in April 1979 a strong feeling in the PNV that ETA was benefiting from a new wave of support because Madrid was dragging its heels on regional autonomy. In the opinion of its leader, Carlos Garaikoechea, the Basque country's

> need for self-government has been trivialised by those in power, who for the past two years have been playing with the Basque General Council, to which they handed over substantial power ... Such action could cost the government dearly, for many people feel frustrated and sceptical towards the whole political process, thanks to the political stalemate. People have become more radical in the streets, support ETA and shout that a statute will not do because, amongst other things, they are convinced that it will be trimmed to a half measure.[29]

But the PNV's fears proved groundless. In July the Prime Minister announced that he had reached agreement with the Basques, and the Statute of Autonomy passed into law. They were granted their own police force, powers to raise and spend taxes, powers over industrial and economic policy, town and country planning, energy resources, public works, agriculture and fisheries, social services, culture, the state savings banks and local nationalised industries. When this package was put to the Basque people in a referendum in October 1979 ETA-PM interrupted a TV transmission to campaign in its favour. ETA-M opposed. In the event 59 per cent turned out to vote on 25 October and 90 per cent of this figure supported the proposals.

The seal of approval to this agreement was given on 15 December when the Lendakari, Jesús María de Leizaola (83), President of the Basque government-in-exile, officially returned from France to surrender his powers to the President of the Basque General Council. The long exile had ended: the democrat had outlived the dictator.

Although in theory Madrid had understood the need to grant autonomy to the Basque country, it did not for a number of reasons hand over the powers of government to the regional authorities. In protest at the delay the majority PNV withdrew from the Cortes in January 1980, leaving for a while many Basques without parliamentary representation. Yet such a move did not stop the process of devolution. Once the Basque country had become in law an autonomous region a provisional government met to decide upon elections for March 1980.[30] By April Euskadi had a government headed by Carlos Garaikoetxea (41) leader of the conservative and

Catholic PNV. It is to this body that Madrid looked to provide the political leadership in the fight against terrorism. Yet the government fatefully delayed final transference of power in the summer of 1980, allowing thereby a new head of steam to gather behind the extremists.

THE ETA MILITARY CAMPAIGN

The first ETA slogans appeared in 1960 in San Sebastián, Bilbao and Tolosa. Daring youngsters sprayed the mathematics of the Basque country's provincial divisions $(4 + 3 = 7 = 1)$ on walls and buildings. As the graffiti was hard to wash off, the security forces rendered it illegible by applying additional strokes of paint to the original message. Soon enough certain bars and restaurants became "post boxes", used by ETA for its communications. Sometimes the local priest, especially if he were young, lent his services: but those that were sympathetic to the cause were soon suspect and fell under close surveillance. It became dangerous for militants to frequent their homes.

The organisation had to find funds, and turned in the first instance to bank robbery. The sums were never exceptionally high, but they sufficed to purchase arms abroad from dealers who had previously supplied the Algerian FLN. It was easy enough to run them across the border hidden in vehicles or using methods traditional to the Basque shepherds for centuries. By sea the task was no harder, for small fishing craft and pleasure boats crowded the coast, especially in the tourist season when it was impossible to maintain a check. Few weapons were required anyhow to arm an amateur coterie of militants, although it was later affirmed that a handful had received training in Cuba in Spring 1964.[31] Such a suggestion implied that ETA had more body to it than was in fact the case, for by the end of the 1960s the police had uprooted the network. It had achieved little more than the occasional sabotage attack on régime monuments, government offices and radio and television installations.

ETA in the 1960s had depended upon the enthusiasm of one man, Francisco Javier Echevarrieta Ortiz, who, as recorded above, was killed on 7 June 1968. The official reaction to ETA's reprisal killing of Melitón Manzanas, the man responsible in San Sebastián for police interrogation, was the imposition of a six-month "state of exception". This gave the security forces sufficient latitude to uncover the organisation and put the leaders on trial at Burgos. They found that ETA lacked leadership, ideological cohesion and structure. The very fact that it used French territory caused divisions within it between the exiles, open to outside influences, and those who were active in Spain, where the brunt was felt.

A second military phase began with the emergence of Eustakio Mendizábal, who attempted to influence the outcome of the 1970 Burgos trial by kidnapping the honorary German consul in San Sebastián, Eugenio Beihl, and holding him hostage in France for 23 days. In the event his release was negotiated by Telesforo Monzón, who had founded a French organisation for Spanish Basque refugees known as *Anai Artea* (Amongst

157

Brothers) and which ETA used as a mouthpiece. But such were the divisions in ETA that those on trial in Burgos were horrified by the thought of such a deal—kidnapping was an action which did not involve the masses, even although those on trial did not reject armed action.

Yet kidnapping had its attractions from several points of view. Criminal cases aside, the practice was not in the early 1970s customary in Europe, so it attracted immediate publicity. Secondly, Mendizábal was concerned to help better the workers' condition in the Basque country, not least to establish support for his own militancy. The man selected in 1972 was a very typical local industrialist—Lorenzo Zabala, the hard-working owner of a small concern, *Precicontrol*, which he ran personally. The conditions for his release had to do with industrial matters for which the workers were on strike and which were granted at once. Within five days Zabala was a free man and the ETA team had crossed the border into France.[32]

A third kidnapping was organised by Mendizábal before his death, that of Felipe Huarte Beaumont of Pamplona in January 1973. Huarte was in a different league, for he was responsible for a very large financial concern with wide national interests: on this occasion ETA demanded and received a ransom of 50 million pesetas in addition to the settlement of strikers' demands in a particular factory—*Torfinasa*. Seized by four men[33] on his return home to his detached and somewhat isolated villa on the outskirts of Pamplona, Huarte was held for a while near Isasondo in a cave, which as a child Mendizábal knew well. Later he was taken to a garage in Lasarte and held by a second team until the ransom had been paid in two halves in Paris and Brussels over a period of a week. He had imagined he was in the French countryside; in fact he had been hidden, blindfolded for most of the time, in a tent, around which bales of hay and chicken coops had been stacked inside the garage.

Despite Mendizábal's concern to intervene in specific labour disputes, ETA had not achieved any degree of influence over Basque workers by the time he died in the Algorta shoot-out with police on 19 April 1973. On the contrary, Basque workers interested in trade union matters found their political activities hampered by police reacting to ETA's armed actions, as a result of which ETA undoubtedly lost much general public sympathy, although it is true militancy produced recruits.[34] But the newcomers were young and inexperienced and were quickly picked up by the police. They had been involved in minor actions of theft and explosives attacks on buildings, which were planned spontaneously and independently, unlike the direction given to Carrero Blanco's assassination in December 1973 by the veterans.

For a second time, in 1974 and 1975, ETA suffered enormous deprivations as a result of police work. When ETA revived, it did so in a new and ugly phase, displaying audacity, technical brilliance, and imagination. But the extension of the terrorist campaign into murder and cruelty as never before proved psychologically difficult to accept for many ETA members, so that the tactic was lengthily debated within ETA ranks.

In 1975 there were plans to kidnap Prince Juan Carlos at an international yachting regatta. A chalet had been hired near Monaco and a "peoples' prison" prepared for a royal guest. Bold enough to sport the *ikurrina* (Basque flag) at sea, the terrorists gave their game away. However, the Prince's father, Don Juan, Count of Barcelona, nearly succumbed later on to the pirate Basque yacht, moored not 200 yards away. This, and the thought of kidnapping Franco's daughter, came to nothing. Sometimes the police successfully infiltrated the command, sometimes amateur inefficiency intervened. When a yacht was prepared to kidnap Prince Juan Carlos' brother-in-law in Zarauz the intrepid militants moored it so unskilfully that it floated out to sea. Fishermen returned it and the police discovered the arms and false papers.

Death and intimidation

At home on land ETA had greater success. In January 1976 José Luis Arrasate (26) was ransomed for 30 million pesetas after 40 days' captivity. The organisation was intent purely on raising funds. Two months later ETA-PM kidnapped and murdered after 21 days Angel Berazadi (58). It was the first occasion that a kidnap victim in the Basque country had lost his life. It provoked killings within ETA and bitter quarrels between ETA-M and ETA-PM. For the first time the PNV denounced the separatists, whose support was already affected by the government's reform programme. Money was also raised by making demands ranging from 3 to 10 million pesetas upon local industrialists and businessmen.

Within a couple of years more than 40 people had paid up, some were murdered for not doing so, others were shot in the legs. The demands continue and run into hundreds, but a stand was made in April 1980 by Juan Alcorta Maíz (58). A father of seven children, one of whom used to belong to ETA and is in Mexico, and president of the Banco Industrial de Guipúzcoa, he publicly rejected ETA's threat. "I rebel against the idea of having to pay to save my life, and against the absolute fear of dying. I am

ETA TERRORIST ACTIONS AND THE DEATH TOLL
1968 to mid-1980

	1968	1969	1970	1971	1972	1973	1974	1975	1976	1977	1978	1979	1980	Total
Terrorist actions	30	27	17	19	77	43	113	262	87	146	270	1471	250	2812
Police deaths	2	—	—	—	—	4	5	11	8	8	33	32	9	112
Civilian deaths	—	1	—	—	1	1	14	6	8	5	28	33	9	106
Military deaths	—	—	—	—	—	1	—	—	—	—	4	10	3	18

After the above statistics for 1980 were issued in March a further 39 people died up to 4 July 1980. Of the total of 275, 38 died in San Sebastián, 32 in Madrid, 28 in Bilbao and 22 in Vitoria. Other towns where up to 10 people died are Lemóniz, Oñate, Tolosa, Irún, Galdacano, Pamplona, Azcoitia and Mondragón.

not a hero, nor do I wish to be. I know that by such a decision I place in jeopardy those years that remain to me. But there is something in my conscience, in the way I am, that leads me to prefer anything rather than to give in to blackmail, which is destroying my land, my people and my family." His stand could have an extraordinary effect upon the population, bolstering determination to withstand intimidation.

Once the step embracing murder had been taken, targets were selected in the region. In October 1976 Juan María Araluce Villar was shot dead in San Sebastián. A Counsellor of the Realm, a member of the Cortes and President of the Diputación of Guipúzcoa, he represented everything ETA rejected. The military, too, became a target in 1977. The following year ETA proved its capacity to operate outside the Basque country by mounting two important assassinations in Madrid. On 21 July 1978 General Juan Manuel Ramos Sánchez Izquierdo died in a gun attack and in November the Supreme Court Judge, José Francisco Mateu Cánoves, fell victim. The following year ETA selected Madrid's military governor, Lt. General Ortin Gil, on 3 January and on 25 May Lt. General Gómez Hostiguela.

At home on their own ground ETA-M disciplined its own ranks by murdering suspected informers. Politically motivated deaths jumped fourfold between 1977 and 1978 and have since climbed higher still. Democratic parliamentarians were attacked in 1979, when Democratic Centre (UCD) deputy Cisneros Laborda was seriously wounded on 3 July, and then on 11 November ETA-PM kidnapped Javier Rupérez, another UCD deputy and party secretary for international affairs.

The cost of terrorism to the Spanish economy rose astronomically in 1979 and 1980 thanks to a limited campaign of beach bombings in tourist resorts along the Mediterranean coast. The months of June and July were chosen in 1978 to explode ten devices in Fuengirola, Torremolinos, Marbella, Málaga, Castellón, Peñíscola, Benidorm and Santa Cristina de Aro (Gerona). ETA-PM mounted a similar campaign in 1980, when tourist receipts were reported to be 30 per cent down, some, although not all, being due to cancellations. Clearly the opportunities to hurt the economy, especially where the tourist industry is highly developed, are wide open for exploitation by terrorists and could be put into immediate effect in other countries, notably Italy and France. The cost to the terrorist organisation is minimal: indeed the threat alone may make itself felt economically.

Autonomous commandos

The development of terrorism from Basques in Spain has been seen not only in the ruthlessness of ETA-M, the most dangerous group, but also in ETA-PM. In addition a breakaway faction known as the "autonomous commandos" were active. They broke away publicly in November 1979, when they announced their intention to create "nuclei of armed popular insurrection". For these militants the "armed struggle, was an indispensable means of developing the class struggle, not elaborated in an élitist manner, but endeavouring to extend it so that the Basque working people undertake it in practice and adopt it theoretically". It occurred to Madrid that the autonomous commandos had been infiltrated by another revolutionary group in Spain: the *1st October Anti-Fascist Resistance Group* (GRAPO), which had emerged in 1976 as the violent wing of the Reconstituted Spanish Communist Party (PCE-R). Whatever the truth, armed violence had developed in Spain into a complex constellation of planets and satellites.

The autonomous commandos had existed in fact since 1977 but first came to the fore in April 1978. They engaged in a number of minor bombing incidents. Ideologically they were far to the left of the Spanish Communist Party, using such key words to describe themselves as "assemblyism" (*asamblearismo*) and "self-acting" (*autogestión*). Their target was the orthodox left, both socialists and communists. With the death in October 1979 of a socialist party (PSOE) worker, Germán González, the left organised the first large demonstration (10,000) against ETA at the funeral in Zumaya. Even the ETA-PM front leaders from EIA, Bandrés and Onaindía, attended. The Basque socialist leader, Enrique Múgica, took the murder as "a declaration of war", which required the "mobilisation" of a political response. *Herri Batasuna* (HB) considered the assassination "a grave political error".

ETA-M still had not in 1980 employed the indiscriminate terrorism displayed by the Irish Republican Army. No bombs had caused the deaths in public places of bystanders, although it is true that innocent people, other than the selected victims, had died in assassinations. On the contrary, ETA displayed an awareness of popular political issues—it attempted by promoting sabotage actions against the development of nuclear power at Lemóniz to harness the popular protest on this issue to its own campaign.

Furthermore it took steps in 1980 to eradicate the growth of pornography in Basque cities by threatening publicly cinemas which screened sex films. The establishments concerned all changed their programmes. Fashionable bars in which drugs were pushed also became a target in May. ETA saw the drug racket as a deliberate attempt to debilitate the population, and above all the Basque workers. Not only would it attack the premises, but "physically eliminate" those responsible.

The new and latest violent phase is the worst that the region has faced, but it has galvanised a united response across the political spectrum. A new sophistication is apparent in the terrorist structure of hides, safe houses and "people's prisons". This applies equally to ETA-M and ETA-PM. In June 1980 two ETA-PM "people's prisons" were discovered in Vigo, Galicia. The entrance to one was through a grid in a shower leading to a coal bunker. Others had carefully engineered mechanisms for entry involving pulleys and weights, which worked perfectly.

Foreign links

Such developments were not achieved without help from abroad. It can be found in Europe, particularly amongst Latin American exiles from Uruguay and Argentina, whose terrorist cadres fled the security force reaction of the early and mid-1970s in their own countries and found havens in Rome and Paris. There can be no doubt that terrorists learn from one another. A recent firmly documented link was revealed by the Dutch authorities in May between ETA and the Red Resistance Front in Holland. Training, it is known, has taken place over a number of years in Algeria, but also in the Middle East.

The Dutch police discovered four Basques[35] returning from South Yemen (PDRY), where the dissident rejectionist front of the Palestinians (PFLP) have training facilities. Earlier all four had been active in political violence in the Basque country and as members of the autonomous commandos had undergone urban guerrilla training in the PDRY, a Marxist–Leninist state allied to the Soviet Union. Spain formally protested to the South Yemeni government and found support for its cause publicly in Iraq. At the same time Madrid also approached Libya, Algeria and the Lebanon, where it was known training had been given. In Algeria the Spanish authorities considered that at least 160 had received training in 1977 and 1978. It amounted to powerful outside support at a moment critical to the welfare of Spanish democracy.

More generally, there had for a decade been contacts between Basque exiles and other minority European groups, including the Bretons, the Flemish and the Northern Ireland Catholics. For the most part the relationship had been one of mutual political support, which did not extend to jointly organised political violence. It operated for the PNV as it did for the Basque Trotskyists (LKI), who in the 1980 Basque elections had the support of Bernadette Devlin from Ulster as well as Hugo Blanco from Peru and the father-figure of the Trotskyist movement, Ernest Mandel, from Brussels. Yet recently there has been growing concern that ETA links with the IRA amount to more than fraternisation.

France of course, for ethnic and geographical reasons, has been the greatest comfort to ETA. Franco's government had always complained of the harbouring of exiles, but these were given refugee status. ETA took advantage of the position until the status was withdrawn in January 1979. But recriminations still flow from Madrid, which believes that France could do more. It is a complaint with a long history attached to it, so that only limited satisfaction is likely to result. However, the fact remains that today ETA's directives come from France, principally from an executive committee headed by Iturbe Abasolo (36) who works through two liaison men, Francisco Múgica Garmendía (26) and Juan Angel Ochoantesana Badiola (25). Clearly as much international co-operation as possible is urgently required to counter the threat.

THE WAY AHEAD

Police action in the Basque country had had considerable success since ETA began its military campaign in the mid-1960s. Time and again the organisation suffered severe depletions, but under Franco security force success on the ground was never accompanied by political reform or by devolution, which by cutting off ETA's potential support might have isolated the terrorists. That is no longer the case, and provided Madrid has sufficient courage, coupled with political imagination, there is hope that peace can be returned to the provinces.

The difficulty lies in the peculiar context of contemporary Spain: the bulk of the Spanish military swore allegiance to General Franco as Head of State, who fought not only against Godless communism but to maintain the unity of Spain. The threat of disintegration loomed large in the Nationalist mind in 1936, and after Franco's victory in 1939 the military were taught to think of themselves as the guardian of historic Spain. Franco's successor therefore has to exercise care that reform does not undo the unity which 36 years of authoritarian rule maintained.

Although the likelihood of military intervention in politics diminishes day by day, it still cannot be discounted entirely, for it rests upon a lengthy nineteenth-century tradition, which in Central and South America has still not been eradicated. It must therefore concern the government, whose task is to convince the military, and indeed the country, that the best means of restoring peace lies in providing the Basques with responsibility for their own affairs and above all in policing themselves. Having their own liberty and welfare to defend, there can be no doubt that in the long term such an industrious and principled people, if given the right structures, will put them to good use.

The problem of providing law and order is aggravated as we have seen by the proximity of the French border and the fact that terrorists can find sanctuary on the other side of it and can plan there in relative safety. Yet, unlike in Northern Ireland, patriotic sentiment is not following two loyalties, for a Basque is a Basque. Fortunately the PNV very much provides the Basque people with a political vehicle for their nationalism: its historic task must be to embrace the militants, whose principal motivation is patriotic fervour.

It is true there is the problem of ideology, which provides the terrorists with a potential, as well as an actual measure of support from other revolutionary groups in Spain and even overseas. Yet in the past this very element has been the cause of grievous splits and virulent factionalism, resulting on occasions in murder. It is therefore, equally, a debilitating factor.

It should not be beyond the bounds of government, even working in an unfavourable climate of rising unemployment[36] and inflation, to provide the wherewithal for peace. What is required is an understanding that the campaign must be patient and long-term, although not tardy in application. Political measures must go hand in hand with steadfast police action. Advice and help should be sought abroad, as indeed it is, so that foreign experience, unhappy though it may be in certain instances, can enlighten the Spanish course. Self-help is the principal ingredient of success, and the very stuff of which determination is made—and to be found wanting in will is tantamount to failure.

Should the irritant of terrorism persist, despite the minuscule nature of its resources, the fabric of Spanish democracy could tear, to the detriment not only of Spain, but of Europe. For the grand design of the future Europe, if it is to play its part, must be whole. Without Spain it lacks a principal component.

Sadly, under Franco's military illegitimacy, intellectually, artistically and diplomatically Spain slept, and was consequently ignored. But a renascence has come about. As it is the intention of France and West Germany, so too is Britain set upon encouraging Europe as a whole to play a global role: democratic Spain has much to contribute, and of a unique nature. No other country could so effectually influence Central and South America, which is surely a neglected area and one where the civilising voice of democracy requires encouragement. Indeed, Spain provides an example to the Latin world of economic development almost as startling as its political transformation.

Furthermore, belonging itself to a militant tradition in religious matters, Spain is a country which is likely to appeal to the fervour of revolutionary Islam, an area where Europe requires advocates. Her historical interaction with the Arab world too, and her present stance in the Arab–Israeli dispute, make her ideally suited to become Europe's spokesman in Arabia. If these and many other advantages are to accrue to Europe, Spain needs Europe's attention in her struggle with political violence.

NOTES

[1] It was first written in the sixteenth century.

[2] Six men were accused by the Spanish state of this atrocity: José María Beñaran Ordenana, José Ignacio Abaitua Gomeza, José Antonio Urruticoechea Bengoechea, Javier María Larreategui Cuadra, Pedro Ignacio Pérez Beolégui and Juan Bautista Santisteban.

[3] Ignacio Arregui Liciaga, a relative of Pagoaga Gallástegui.

[4] The ETA members killed were: Echevarrieta, Goicoechea, Múgica Zumeta, Martínez de Murguía, Aranguren Múgica, Arteche Ayesta, Echeverria Sagastume, Eustakio Mendizábal, Pagazaurtundua.

[5] The PNV was founded in 1894 to establish the autonomous region of Euskadi.

[6] At that time those most prominent in the Basque movement were Julián de Madariaga Aguirre, José María Benito del Valle, José Manuel Aguirre Bilbao, Sabino Uribe Cuadra, Francisco Javier Berreno Echevarria and Manuel Gallástegui.

[7] Significantly the date is that of Saint Ignatius of Lóyola, patron saint of the region.

[8] *Zutik* (1962).

[9] Julián de Madariaga, José María Benito del Valle, Barreño Omaechevarría, José Luis Alvarez Emparanza and Ignacio Irigaray.

[10] The word was coined in 1886 by Sabino de Arana y Goiri, founder of modern Basque nationalism, to describe the Basque country. Originally spelt with a "z" now usually with an "s".

[11] *Hitz*, March 1975.

[12] *A los Revolucionarios, Demócratas, Antifascistas de Euskadi y del Mundo Entero* (August 1973).

[13] Joaquín Gorostidi Artola, Francisco Javier Izko de la Iglesia, Eduardo Uriarte Romero, Mario Onaindía Nachiondo, Francisco Javier Larena Martínez and José María Dorronsoro Ceberio.

[14] Particularly important in its eyes were fishermen, farmers, administrative workers, small property owners, businessmen, industrialists, students and intellectuals.

[15] The only reliable figures, made available by the French authorities in November 1972, cite a total of 1,300 Basque refugees in France. Possibly some 200 crossed between then and the end of 1973.

[16] *Ponencia Otsagabia*, 7 July 1976.

[17] *ETA and the Armed Struggle*, 4 August 1976.

[18] Forty-three mayors met in Vergara in March 1977 and threatened resignation if no amnesty were forthcoming; others joined them as the months passed.

[19] *Euskal Herriko Alderi Sozialista* (EHAS—Basque People's Socialist Party), *Langile Abertzale Iraultzalen Alderdi* (LAIA—Patriotic Basque Workers Revolutionary Party), *Langile Abertzale Batzordea* (LAB—Patriotic Basque Workers Unity), *Langile Aberzale Komiteak* (LAK—Patriotic Basque Workers Committee).

[20] They included *Euskadiko Gasteria Gorria* (EGG—Young Basque Reds), *Euskadiko Gasteria Kommunistak* (EGK—Young Basque Communists) and *Iraultzo Taldea* (IT—Revolutionary Group).

[21] The *Guardia Civil* and the old *Policia Armada* were very largely recruited from the south of Spain, and in policing the north they found themselves working in a very different society.

[22] HB also grouped within it HASI (Popular Revolutionary Socialist Party) and *Langile Abertzale Iraultzaleen Alderdia* (LAIA).

[23] *Le Monde*, 2 February 1979.

[24] Telesforo Monzón (75), Francisco Letamendia (35), Pedro Solabarría (50), and Senator Miguel Castells (48).

[25] In Pasajes, Rentería, Oyarzun, Hernani, Andoain, Tolosa, Villabona, Elgoibar, Eibar, Mondragón and Vergara.

[26] *La Vanguardia*, 15 March 1979.

[27] The Basque country has the highest per capita income in Spain.

[28] "Suárez, Giscard, gobiernos terroristas" and "Giscard fascista, te tenemos en la lista" were among the identifiable slogans.

[29] *La Vanguardia*, 25 April 1979.

[30] The parliament had 60 seats, 20 for each of the three provinces, Alava, Vizcaya and Guipúzcoa. On a cold wet day 59 per cent of the electorate voted for 25 PNV, 11 HB, 9 PSOE (Socialists), 6 UCD, 6 EE, 2 AP (Popular Alliance) and one PCE.

[31] Jaime Caldevilla, one-time information attaché at the Spanish Embassy in Cuba, April 1973.

[32] Police considered those responsible were Domingo Iturbe Abasolo, José Ramón Arizcorreta, José María Beñaran Ordenana and Tomás Pérez Revilla, then 29, 27, 23 and 35 years respectively.

[33] Pérez Revilla, Joaquín Villar Gurruchaga, Jesús María Zabarte and Juan Goiburu.

[34] In the 1973 general strike in Pamplona ETA played no part. It was organised by the *Organización Revolucionaria de Trabajadores* (ORT—Workers' Revolutionary Organisation).

[35] Juan Carlos Yurrebaso, 25, Juan Ignacio Urrutibeasco, 29, José Manuel Arzullus, 23, and José Antonio Aguirrebarrena.

[36] In 1979 unemployment in the Basque country ran at 16 per cent, higher than the national average; traditionally it has run lower.

SELECT READING LIST

Agire, Julen. *Operación Ogro. Como y por qué ejecutamos a Carrero Blanco* (Hendaye, 1974). Recounts the murder of Carrero Blanco.

Amigo, Angel. *Pertur, ETA 71–76* (San Sebastián, 1978). Essential reading for the development of ETA-PM and the writings of Moreno Bergareche.

Boussard, Leon. *Jeiki, Jeiki, Etxenkoak ou le défi des Basques* (Paris, 1975). A general historical introduction to the Basque problem from a sympathetic viewpoint.

Clark, Robert P. *Basque Insurgence* (Madison, Wisconsin, 1984). A fundamental work.

Garmendia, José María. *Historia de ETA* (San Sebastián, 1983). A fundamental work.

Halimi, Gisèle. *Le Procès de Burgos* (Paris, 1971). A factual and documentary account of the Burgos trial.

Hills, George. "ETA and Basque Nationalism" (*Iberian Studies* Vol. 1, No. 2, 1972).

Medhurst, Kenneth. *The Basques and Catalans* (Minority Rights Group pamphlet, 1977).

Ortzi. *Historia de Euskadi: el nacionalismo vasco, ETA* (Paris, 1975). An excellent and detailed account of ETA in the 1960s and early 1970s by a principal spokesman for Basque nationalism (Francisco Letamendia).

Payne, Stanley. *El nacionalismo vasco* (Barcelona, 1974). A scholarly historical account.

Portell, José María. *Los Hombres de ETA* (Barcelona, 1974). A popular account by a journalist subsequently murdered by ETA.

Portell, José María. *Euskadi: Amnistla Arrancada* (Barcelona, 1977). A more useful book with documentary appendices.

The *Annual of Power and Conflict* 1979–80 (ISC) details ETA activities, with a full chronology of incidents.

First published 1980. Minor amendments 1985.

The Red Brigades:
A Challenge to Italian Democracy

Vittorfranco S. Pisano

Years of mounting violence and terrorism in Italy reached a new level of ruthlessness and precision with the abduction and murder in 1978 of the highly respected Aldo Moro, Christian Democratic leader and prospective President. The callous crime, which produced shock waves around the world, underlined the seriousness of the leftist threat to the stability of a country weakened by years of inefficient government and notoriously prone to political crises. This study traces the escalation of violence over the period January 1968 to 31 March 1980. It describes the rise of the notorious Red Brigades and other leading groups among the scores of terrorist organisations; analyses the methods used in the systematic execution of intimidatory and retaliatory murders, woundings and raids; and the terrorists' international ramifications.

I. THE SETTING, INCIDENCE AND BACKGROUND

On 16 March 1978, at approximately 9 a.m. former Premier and incumbent Christian Democratic Party president Aldo Moro was abducted in Rome on his way to the Parliament to participate in the vote of confidence for Italy's thirty-first government under the Republican Constitution of 1948. In a terrorist attack on the Moro cars four escort members were murdered in a matter of seconds, and a fifth died later.

This urban guerrilla operation, for which the Red Brigades (*Brigate Rosse*—BR) claimed responsibility, was conducted with such precision and attention to detail that even the telephone lines in the immediate vicinity were cut in advance by the security-minded terrorist commando. Moreover, the night before, a florist's pick-up-truck, usually parked during business hours by the Via Fani intersection where the abduction took place, had all four tyres slashed in its habitual night parking space, elsewhere in the city, in order to eliminate this encumbrance from the abduction site.

Moro himself was held in captivity for 54 days and was finally "executed" on 9 May 1978, following the Government's refusal to release 13 terrorists on trial, including Renato Curcio, the reputed historic leader of the Red Brigades.

The reaction of the governing class, the population, and the media was one of shock. Yet this terrorist action, notwithstanding the significance of the target and the sophistication of the operation, was but one in a long series of acts of terrorist intimidation perpetrated in a climate of social strife and political violence that has characterised the Italian scene since

1968. In fact, 173 terrorist incidents were recorded that year, 573 were recorded in 1974, 702 in 1975, 1,353 in 1976, 1,926 in 1977, 2,238 in 1978 and 2,514 in 1979. Compared to the sporadic political violence present in Italian society since time immemorial, these statistics are indicative of unprecedented escalation and intensity.

While minor acts such as simple arson and other forms of damage to public and private property make up the core of these statistics more serious crimes, including political abductions, leg shootings and assassinations, are disquietingly frequent. It has been estimated that from 12 December 1969 to 6 January 1980, 116 killings and 355 woundings have resulted from terrorist violence.

Operationally, Italian domestic terrorism is kept alive by four components corresponding to the anarchist, separatist, neo-Fascist, and Marxist–Leninist ideologies. The anarchist component, albeit the oldest, is at present the least menacing. It was responsible, alone or in conjunction with neo-Fascist groups, for bombing attempts in the late 1960s, but currently maintains a minority presence in some of the smaller Marxist–Leninist terrorist bands. Separatist terrorism has affected the island of Sardinia and the ethnically Germanic South Tyrol (Trentino–Alto Adige) region. Notwithstanding the exploitation of Sardinian separatist groups by Marxist–Leninist terrorists and the recent recrudescence of violence as a means towards South Tyrolean political aspirations, the separatist component of Italian terrorism is not at present as highly operational as in the 1950s and 1960s.

Neo-Fascist or rightist terrorist violence was most in evidence in the late 1960s and early 1970s, largely through indiscriminate and unclaimed bombing attacks. It should therefore be distinguished from other forms of political violence, still persisting to date, such as bodily clashes in the streets between groups of the neo-Fascist and Marxist–Leninist persuasions. Terrorism of the Right has drawn manpower from extremist fringes of the conservative Italian Social Movement (MSI), from neo-Fascist clandestine

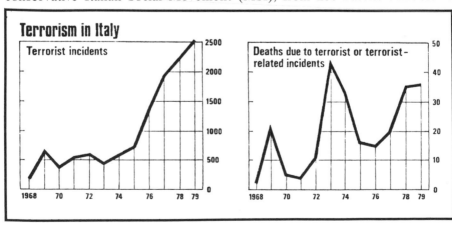

Terrorism in Italy

Terrorist incidents

Deaths due to terrorist or terrorist-related incidents

bands with no apparent ties to the MSI, and from groups whose aim is the reconstitution of Benito Mussolini's outlawed National Fascist Party.

In 1973, after some bombing incidents, the MSI began with some success to remove from party facilities and activities the extreme fringes of the Right that had worked their way into the party at the beginning of the decade. The following year, Member of Parliament and MSI Secretary-General Giorgio Almirante also proposed the adoption of the death sentence for terrorist killings. Responsibility for the more serious incidents of rightist extremism in the late 1970s—mainly bombing attacks on property with occasional casualties—has been claimed by the Armed Revolutionary Nuclei (NAR) and the Popular Revolutionary Movement (MRP). Both are considered to be small groups, technically unrefined, with rather hazy ideology.

Menace from the Left

The terrorist component of the Left, imbued with Marxist–Leninist thought, is manifestly the most menacing and has officially been treated as such by the Ministry of the Interior since October of 1978, when the Minister's report to Parliament indicated that out of 147 separate groups that had claimed responsibility for terrorist violence 135 belonged to the extra-parliamentary Left. These elements are indeed materially responsible not only for the escalation and intensity of Italy's contemporary terrorist wave, but also for the unprecedented sophistication of its dynamics.

There is a question mark over the size and extent of the terrorist ranks. According to a study prepared in 1978 by the Italian Communist Party there are approximately 700 to 800 terrorists living clandestinely, and approximately 10,000 others who are often armed and given to arson, pillage, and other violent actions. At about the same time an anonymous source from within the terrorist ranks reportedly disclosed to the weekly *Panorama* the existence of 3,000 "combatants". Subsequent press reports have carried figures that range from a low of 150–180 to a high of 100,000, but the latter includes both terrorists and supporting elements.

In April of 1979 an intelligence source unofficially stated that the hardcore terrorist operatives are "no less than 50, no more than 500". But in a March 1980 interview with the periodical *La Discussione*, Under Secretary Francesco Mazzola, who chairs the Intelligence and Security Services Executive Committee (CESIS), said that any attempt to assess the numerical composition of the terrorist bands of the Left was "haphazard" because "the destructive array of the Left is vast, uneven, and composite". As for the rightist terrorist formations, the Under Secretary stated that they "do not have at their disposal an actual organisation. They are spontaneous aggregations of small extremist groups that frequently operate extemporaneously and suddenly".

Somewhat easier to identify, in spite of their complexity, are the factors behind the upsurge of Italian terrorist violence. **It basically stems from the** social inadequacies, political contradictions, and governmental weakness and permissiveness pertinent to contemporary Italy.

During the comparatively stable years of political "centrism"—characterised by the homogeneous governmental coalitions supported by a comfortable parliamentary majority consisting of Christian Democrats, Liberals, Social Democrats, and Republicans—Italy quickly passed from post-war reconstruction to the so-called economic miracle of the late 1950s and early 1960s. This process has entailed mass migration from southern to northern Italy, as well as from the rural provinces to the industrial cities, which were not equipped in the long run to absorb and to provide for the new population, especially with respect to housing, schools, and hospitals.

The centrist coalitions which governed Italy from 1948 to 1962 stressed industrial expansion and foreign trade over the social structures and facilities in which deficiency was eventually felt. These centrist choices were in response to the mandates of an electoral majority anxious to bury the antiquated economic doctrine of autarky organic to the deposed Fascist régime, to preclude the adoption of the Soviet collectivist model of economy, and to pursue political and economic democracy on the example of American society, including her consumer traits. During these years the Christian Democratic relative-majority partner in the centrist alliance also set up a system of patronage, corruption, and bureaucratic inefficiency that has persisted.

The "opening to the Left"

In a fruitless effort to improve the deficient social structures a new political formula called the "opening to the Left" was devised in 1962–63. It entailed the withdrawal of the rigidly centrist Liberals from the majority coalition and the inclusion therein of the Italian Socialist Party (PSI). The ensuing years, contrary to expectations, were marked by governmental immobility and the extension of the spoils system to the PSI.

The "centre–left" governmental coalitions were first awakened from their torpor in 1968, when Italy experienced her "cultural revolution", initially among university students and later among high school students. Although targeted against the establishment as a whole, its first victims were the academic structure and traditional family discipline. Student demands included "group exams", choice of texts and examination questions, and the establishment of political collectives in the schools, as well as guaranteed passing grades, diplomas and degrees. In several cases students were joined by young assistant professors who took advantage of this disorderly atmosphere to undermine the authority of the ruling full professors. In the process universities and schools were seized by politicised students—occasionally with extraneous help—and acts of violence and vandalism ensued.

The 1968 "cultural revolution" had its spill-over effect on the workers the following year. The "hot autumn" of 1969 gave way to labour union unrest ranging from demonstrations to unbridled strikes, from the seizure

170

of factories to industrial sabotage, from roadblocks to intimidation and violence against executive personnel and non-striking labourers. The renewal of the collective bargaining agreements did not placate the unions, notwithstanding an improvement in workers' conditions. In their thirst for short-term benefits the unions lost sight of the limited long-term possibilities of the Italian economy, which must depend on industrial know-how and internationally competitive labour costs to offset the lack of natural resources.

Labour union abuses were often aided by judges who, instead of applying the rule of law to labour disputes, rendered their decisions on the basis of a Marxist-oriented "sociological jurisprudence". The loss of productivity since the "hot autumn" not only started trends that have persisted but also aggravated the effects of the oil crisis of 1973, which inflicted a particularly hard blow on Italy because of her reliance on imports for 80 per cent of her needs.

In response to what has been termed an unending state of siege against the institutions the centre–left alliance adopted policies and social legislation that resulted in the downgrading of the educational system, the slanting of labour relations too heavily in favour of employees and the unions to the detriment of the national economy, the weakening of criminal laws and procedures in favour of politicised and non-politicised social deviants, the reduction of military and police efficiency, and the virtual emasculation in the mid-1970s of the intelligence services. The lowering of academic standards has been particularly harmful, because it has produced a substantially larger number of graduates whose increased post-graduation expectations cannot find a receptive job market.

The fragility of Italian society under the centre–left formula further manifested itself in the political relationship between the two principal coalition partners. Even when part of both the parliamentary and governmental majority coalition the Socialists repeatedly assumed positions adverse to the Government and frequently coalesced at the local level (regions, provinces, and municipalities) with the Italian Communist Party (PCI), the major opposition party, in cases where it was numerically possible to govern with the Christian Democrats, still the relative majority party at the parliamentary level.

The malaise apparent under the Christian Democratic–Socialist coalitions has increased with the "second opening to the Left", a political development entailing the matter and extent of PCI participation in the national decision-making process. By projecting a democratic, moderate, honest, efficient, and West-oriented image the PCI was able to make unprecedented gains in the local and national elections of 1975 and 1976, as a result of which it gradually entered the parliamentary majority coalition (but not the cabinet) for the first time, under the Republican Constitution of 1948, on the same day as the Moro abduction.

Although the PCI is no longer a part of that coalition, following a rapid reversal in electoral trends, it still seeks cabinet posts and participation in the national decision-making process. To accomplish this aim the PCI—

and, indeed, the PCI-affiliated Italian General Confederation of Labour (CGIL), the country's major labour union—has had to tone down its traditional Marxist–Leninist line, much to the dismay of those elements influenced by Communist orthodoxy. The formal, if not substantial, softening of the PCI's approach toward Western ideals and solidarity has conversely intensified the tactics of the extra-parliamentary Left and its extremist fringes. At the same time, the uncertain outcome of further accommodation between the Christian Democratic Party and the PCI, who continue to be ideological adversaries despite the latter's efforts to reach West-oriented voters, is adding to the disorientation of the population, especially the youth.

II. THE LEFTIST COMPONENT: STRUCTURE AND DYNAMICS

The socio-political climate largely responsible for turning Italy into a fertile breeding ground for civil strife, political violence, and terrorism continues to be particularly well suited to the aspirations of the extreme Left, which draws its operational inspiration from the South American urban-guerrilla warfare model and its ideological influence from the traditional teachings of the PCI.

Five basic operational patterns reflect the structure and dynamics of Italian terrorism of the Left: 1, rigid clandestinity and systematic violence; 2, simultaneous political action and "armed struggle"; 3, spontaneous and sporadic terrorist actions; 4, auxiliary support; and 5, combined actions.

The **first pattern**—rigid clandestinity and systematic violence—which exercises substantial influence over the others, is usually associated with the Red Brigades (*Brigate Rosse*—BR) and, to a lesser degree, with the Armed Proletarian Nuclei (*Nuclei Armati Proletari*—NAP). The actual militants—to be distinguished from the supporting elements—of the terrorist groups that abide by this pattern have adopted total clandestinity and stress the "determinant and exclusive role of the armed vanguards". Operations are directed at those objectives that represent either the "heart of the State" or those organs of the State, "imperialism", and capitalist society perceived to be particularly "repressive".

Typical human targets include executives, managers, and association representatives in the fields of industry, commerce, and finance, members of the judiciary and law enforcement agencies, professors, journalists, conservative activists, and, not least, politicians associated with the relative majority party.

Standard material targets are obviously the facilities and equipment belonging to the State and to private enterprise. All attacks against persons or property are aimed not only at destroying such targets, but also at the accomplishment of demonstrative actions. It therefore frequently suffices that a target be symbolic. Within this pattern the BR are particularly strict in the application of the rules of clandestinity and compartmentation. When arrested BR operatives, as opposed to mere supporters, have generally proclaimed themselves to be "political prisoners" and have usually refused to make statements other than for propaganda purposes or other tactical considerations.

The **second pattern**—simultaneous political action and "armed struggle"—derives from the conviction that the "armed struggle" cannot be successful if not accompanied by political action. Front Line (*Prima Linea*—PL) and the minor users of this pattern further perceive the "armed struggle" as an intermediate step towards the organisation of a full-fledged revolutionary army. Consequently they oppose full clandestinity on the part of their militants, since it would prevent the necessary fostering of contacts with the masses. Their selection of targets does not deviate from the first pattern.

The spontaneous and sporadic terrorist actions that make up the **third pattern** are frequently perpetrated by previously unknown extra-parliamentary groups which, after making a brief appearance on the scene, are not heard from again. Their operations generally correspond to the less sophisticated acts of terrorist violence such as arson and bombings of property. Some actions that appear to be part of this pattern actually serve purposes pertinent to the previous two, including security (e.g. when a new unit of an already existing terrorist organisation is being instituted in a different area of the country, but is not yet fully organised or sufficiently supported by extra-parliamentary fringes); propaganda (e.g. the spreading of the "armed struggle"); and training and testing of new recruits. Increased organisational and operational capabilities on the part of certain minor groups, as reflected in claims for carrying out woundings, murders, and kidnapping, can be a sign of their graduation to either of the first two patterns.

The more systematically established terrorist organisations (BR, NAP, PL) have regularly drawn support from the rather sizeable fringes of the extra-parliamentary Left—the "Movement" and, more so, the "Autonomy"—that share or sympathise with their violent ideology. Although this support is primarily logistical, it includes operational aspects and therefore constitutes a **fourth pattern**, that of auxiliary support. The cluster of extremist groupings that make up the Autonomy are particularly useful to the terrorist organisations insofar as they provide them with a variety of services ranging from logistics to cover and intelligence, and from medical to legal assistance. As privileged interlocutors of the major terrorist bands, the members of the Autonomy not only furnish an easily accessible recruitment pool but also abet the work of the terrorists through their own agitation and violence.

The **fifth pattern** entails actions planned and/or executed jointly by two or more terrorist organisations maintaining permanent or occasional liaison. Simultaneous claims of responsibility by more than one band following a single terrorist attempt have been interpreted on the basis of this pattern. The liaison existing between terrorist groups of the Left also explains how the remnants of the less successful ones have been absorbed by the more viable.

These five patterns constitute the basic guidelines within which the

Italian terrorists of the Left operate. But, in their effort to generate a climate of terror and destabilise society and the institutions, the various groups also rely on more detailed and increasingly sophisticated methodologies. Such specific techniques undergo a constant process of development, sharing, or imitation on the part of these ubiquitous terrorist bands.

Development of Red Brigades

Because of their long-standing record of terrorist efficiency and pervasive influence on sister groups, the BR provide a primary insight into the terrorist phenomenon of the Left. Born in Italy's student and labour unrest of the late 1960s, they were initially composed of a "historic nucleus" comprising former Catholic students from the sociology department of the University of Trent (e.g. Renato Curcio, Margherita Cagol, and Giorgio Semeria), former activists of the PCI and its youth organisation from the heavily Communist Emilia region (e.g. Alberto Franceschini, Prospero Gallinari, Tonino Loris Paroli, and Lauro Azzolini). There were also former militants of the extra-parliamentary parties and groups of the Left (e.g. Mario Moretti, Pietro Bertolozzi, and Corrado Alunni), most of whom had found employment in the Milan area with such major industrial concerns as Pirelli and Sit-Siemens.

In the mid-1970s, the "historic nucleus" gave way to a "second generation" of brigadists made up of technically more proficient individuals, but less intellectual and more violent. Although, as a result of extensive recruitment, limited information is available on the "second generation", there is evidence that several of its members are former activists of the now dissolved Worker Power (*Potere Operaio*). Some of these had also been PCI members.

Beginning in April 1979 the judiciary ordered a number of arrests and has proceeded with a series of indictments of professors, intellectuals, writers, and activists within the ranks of the extra-parliamentary Autonomy, the most notorious being Professors Toni Negri and Franco Piperno of the universities of Padua and Cosenza respectively. The prosecution argues that the dissolution of Worker Power in 1973 was merely tactical since its members secretly agreed to form two parallel branches of the dissolved organisation: the first consisting of clandestine elements that became part of the BR; the second consisting of a supporting "legal organisation" that came to be known as Worker Autonomy (*Autonomia Operaia*), the best organised and most militant component of the broader Autonomy.

According to the prosecution the leadership of both branches remained vested, however, in a unitary directorate that was to provide both ideological and operational guidance. Whereas at this early stage of the judicial proceedings the specific contentions of the prosecution still require examination, the support and complicity afforded by Worker Autonomy is not a

174

recent discovery. Its activism runs parallel to the operations of the BR and sister groups.

It initially pursued the politics of confrontation primarily in the factories, but progressively strayed away from mere dissent vis-à-vis the system, instigating disorders and violence, especially during labour union unrest and public demonstrations. Its tactics have included public instigation to commit crimes, and urban guerrilla actions entailing the use of firearms and Molotov cocktails, the most serious incidents of this nature occurring in Bologna and Rome in 1977. Worker Autonomy has generally organised itself into "counterpower" units within the plants and has fought the establishment both autonomously and by infiltrating the existing labour organisations.

Indicative of its ideology is the slogan "Work is not a manner of living, but the obligation to sell oneself in order to live". From the struggles within the factories for "guaranteed wages", the "autonomists" expanded their campaign to include illegal actions to obtain or promote the reduction of rent and public-utility rates, seizure of unrented apartments, resistance against eviction, and "political shopping prices in the supermarkets". Worker Autonomy also gives much attention to convicts, primarily through the action of Red Aid (*Soccorso Rosso*), which renders gratuitous assistance to "political detainees stricken by the bourgeois repression". Another target is the school system, defined by the "autonomists" as the "school of unemployment, selectivity, and repression".

Their outlook and activism render the "autonomists" natural allies of the BR, whose ideology perceives Italy—or more specifically Italy's Communists in a broad sense, her proletarians, workers and the "exploited" in general—as being dominated by the "imperialist state of the multinationals". To the BR the Christian Democratic Party constitutes the "foremost representative" of the imperialist State, the force behind a "corrupt régime", and a merely *pro forma* democracy".

The BR also accuse the PCI of collaboration, but do not usually refer to it by its official name or at least not unqualifiedly so. They generally use such terms as "Berlinguer's party" or the "Berlinguerians". Apart from repeating much of the Marxist–Leninist rhetoric the BR claim that the "counter-revolution" is not generated by them but by the State itself, since "counter-revolution" is the "substance" of the State. In their analysis of the international situation they point to reactionary exploitation as being the objective and practice of the United States of America and of the Federal Republic of Germany. Within Italy, they see the presence of the "American Party".

Escalation of violence: four phases

The avowed objective of the BR is "to mobilise, to extend, and to deepen the armed initiative against the political, economic, and military centres of the imperialist state of the multinationals". This aim is reaffirmed in all of their writings through a variety of synonymous expressions. To accomplish the goal the BR indicate that it is necessary to "develop and unify the Offensive Proletarian Resistance Movement". They often refer to it simply as the MPRO, and distinguish between the MPRO and the "Combatant Communist Party". According to the BR, a "dialectical relationship" exists between them, but the two are not "identical". Allegedly, the MPRO provides the "impulse" and the "Party" acts as the "vanguard". It is the practice of the BR to capitalise those words to which they attribute ideological meaning, even if such words do not represent an existing organised body or movement.

Actual BR operations may be divided into four principal phases. The first, essentially confined to the city of Milan, lasted from 1969 through 1972. It served to a large extent as a training period for the "historic nucleus". Operations entailed almost exclusively the clandestine distribution of Marxist–Leninist revolutionary propaganda in the factories and relatively light damage, primarily through fire bombings, to the automobiles and other private property of industrial executives, well-known conservatives, and rightist activists. Some rudimentary sabotage operations were also undertaken against industrial machinery and commercial vehicles. Isolated attacks of an exploratory nature on party offices of the MSI and other rightist targets in Rome in 1971 demonstrated that the BR had no stable support outside of the Milan area at that early stage.

The second phase, which ended in mid-1974, marked the expansion of BR operations from Milan to the industrial triangle of Milan–Turin–Genoa. During this period, as their tactics graduated from the sporadic to the systematic, the BR perfected political kidnapping techniques and learned how to exploit the attendant media coverage. Six such abductions were perpetrated from March 1972 through April 1974 in Milan, Turin, and Genoa. The BR murder of two MSI activists in a party office in Padua on 17 June 1974 was termed by the supportive ultra-leftist publication *Controinformazione* "a work accident".

The third phase—September 1974 through January 1976—is characterised by the decline of the "historic nucleus" and the gradual emergence of the "second generation".

Some resounding law enforcement successes such as the capture, and recapture after his escape, of historic leader Renato Curcio, the killing of his wife Margherita "Mara" Cagol during a fire engagement with the *Carabinieri*, and the liberation of liquor producer Vittorio Vallerino Gancia, who had been abducted for ransom, led some hasty observers to conclude that the days of the BR were numbered. A more accurate indication as to what was yet to come should have been afforded by the seemingly isolated leg shooting of Christian Democratic councilman (now Member of Parliament) Massimo de Carolis in Milan on 15 May 1975. The fourth and current phase is indeed the bloodiest. Under "second generation" dominance, BR activities have expanded to the rest of the country, murders have become deliberate, and leg shootings are nearly a daily occurrence.

The sheer number of BR actions, which is *per se* sufficient to achieve the

176

terror effect, is further aggravated not only by the highly selective and sophisticated nature of certain operations, but also by a clearly discernible link between the operations themselves, many of which represent menacing clusters. The full impact of BR terror can thus be analysed more effectively through the examination of specific techniques rather than through the doleful recital of the chronological record.

The first concrete demonstration that the terrorist campaign of the BR was intended to strike beyond mere political adversaries or the capitalist system took place on 18 April 1974, when the authority of the State was directly challenged by the kidnapping of Genoa's Assistant Attorney General Mario Sossi, who had prosecuted some members of the October XXII Circle, a now defunct terrorist organisation. Sossi was abducted in the evening while returning to his residence and was held in political captivity for the then unprecedented duration of 35 days.

Intimidation of the courts

Not only was he "tried" by the "people's court", as opposed to the mere "interrogation" of previous political kidnap victims—rightist labour leaders and industrial managers—but the release of eight convicted members of the October XXII Circle was demanded in exchange for Sossi's freedom. In the course of the "trial", the "people's court" issued eight communiques and two pictures of the "defendant". By resorting to procedural technicalities, Genoa's Attorney General Francesco Coco was able to block the provisional release of the convicts granted under duress by the Court of Appeals. Notwithstanding the State's ultimate refusal to bend to their demand, the BR did release Sossi in the apparent belief that the State's authority had been sufficiently undermined. Moreover, those were the days when BR violence tended to be more demonstrative than lethal.

However, on 8 June 1976 a BR commando consisting of two teams shot down Genoa's Attorney General Coco and his two escorts. One team ambushed Coco and his bodyguard, while the second simultaneously hit his driver. This operation was meaningful on two accounts. In the first place, Coco had prevented the release of the October XXII Circle convicts demanded by the BR in exchange for Sossi; hence the retaliatory aspect. Secondly, as the result of the Coco murder and the concomitant threats on the lay jurors, the ongoing Turin trial against the notorious Renato Curcio and other historic BR operatives had to be postponed; hence the intimidatory aspect.

Intimidation was to prevail again one year later when the adjudicating panel, consisting of magistrates and lay jurors, was finally reconstituted. In fact, on 25 April 1977 Fulvio Croce, president of the Turin Bar Association, was murdered by three brigadists as he entered his office building. Thereafter, 36 out of 42 potential jurors preliminarily selected for the Curcio trial asked to be excused for "medical reasons". The trial had to be postponed once again. Although it was finally concluded with 29 convictions on 23 June 1978, even the Moro operation was *in part* motivated by the BR's intent to interfere with this trial and indeed with the entire administration of justice.

BR attacks on human targets generally reflect a rather rigid typology that capitalises upon the element of surprise. There is usually a single victim, but sometimes there are two or three victims, as in the case of attacks against people travelling by car. The victim's habits are carefully surveyed before the ambush, conducted by a commando unit varying from three to five members, usually masked. Frequently the unit includes a woman. Once the victim has been killed or wounded responsibility is claimed by means of a leaflet and/or telephone call usually directed to a newspaper or news agency, providing the BR with extensive media coverage. Varying degrees of sophistication are lent to the basic ambush technique by the adoption of several complementary measures.

In some cases a specific category of individuals is singled out and attacked in a surprisingly brief time span either in the same area or in cities comparatively far apart in relation to Italy's territorial surface of 300,000 sq. km. In mid-February of 1977, an executive, a supervisor, and a medical employee of FIAT were wounded in Milan within 48 hours. Between 1 and 3 June of the same year, three journalists were shot in the legs at the rate of one a day: Socialist-learning Vittorio Bruno of *Secolo XIX*, a Genoa paper; conservative Indro Montanelli, founder and editor of Milan's *Il Giornale Nuovo*; and Christian Democrat Emilio Rossi, head of TGI of Rome (one of the television news services).

All three were accused by the BR of subservience to the "imperialist design". On 5 May 1978 the BR shot in the legs a Sit-Siemens executive and an Italsider labour-relations employee in Milan and Genoa. Between 5 and 7 July of the same year three other representatives of the industrial establishment were wounded in the legs by the BR at the rate of one a day: a Pirelli executive in Milan; the president of the Small Industry Association in Turin; and the deputy-manager of Intersind in Genoa. In this instance, all three cities of the industrial triangle were represented.

Political victims

On other occasions the BR have resorted to a stepped-up rhythm of violence against specific categories of individuals. A typical target-class is the intermediary cadre of the Christian Democratic Party. As opposed to the isolated leg-shooting of then councilman Massimo de Carolis in 1975, seven Christian Democratic regional, provincial, or municipal councilmen or activists were wounded with firearms in 1977, four in 1978, and three in 1979. Two more were stabbed to death in 1979. Another was killed in January 1980. These casualties were recorded in the industrial triangle, in Rome, and in Palermo.

Even though all BR actions are demonstrative, regardless of the target or degree of violence, the selection of certain targets is particularly significant and lends an added dimension to the sinister character of the standard ambush technique.

Major classes of victims of terrorism and related violence
(16 May 1972–6 January 1980)

Class	No. killed	No. wounded
Policemen/escorts	51	28
Christian Democratic leaders	4	12
Judges/prosecutors	6	3
FIAT staff	3	19
Other enterprises (industry–commerce–finance)	—	23
Academics	—	13
Medical personnel	—	7
Journalists	1	6

In several cases a single victim represents more than one institution that the BR plan to destroy. Fausto Gasparino, victim of a wounding attack in Genoa on 7 July 1978, was both a former Christian Democratic regional deputy-secretary and the deputy-manager of Intersind. Provincial councilman Italo Schettini, murdered in Rome on 30 March 1979, was a Christian Democratic politician and the owner of property rented to low-income families. Fausto Cuocolo, wounded in Genoa on 31 May 1979, was both a Christian Democratic regional councilman and Dean of the Political Science Department of the University.

Although there are many more examples the most significant target in this cluster is represented by *Carabinieri* Lieutenant-Colonel Antonio Varisco, who commanded the unit in support of the Rome Court House. He was ambushed and killed instantly by sawn-off shotgun fire early on 13 July 1979 as he was driving to his duty station. Within the *Carabinieri* structure Varisco's position was not exceptionally important, but was highly visible. Since his duties included the maintenance of order in the courtrooms he was perceived by the BR as a link between the police, the judiciary, and the prison system. Moreover, since his name often appeared in the media in conjunction with important trials the BR also knew that in choosing this target they could count on broad media coverage.

The significance of target selection also lies in the time context within which the attack takes place. The murder of Supreme Court judge Girolamo Tartaglione on his doorstep on 1 October 1978 was presumably in response to a series of successful *Carabinieri* operations that led to arrests within the terrorist ranks and to the uncovering of terrorist archives, stores, and operational bases. The ambushing of a Public Security vehicle and the consequential wounding of a patrolman on 24 October 1978 was the BR's answer to the Interior Minister's report on terrorism to the Parliament that same morning.

Attacks conducted against Christian Democratic targets—both human and material—throughout the country in the weeks preceding the 3 June 1979 parliamentary elections were part of the BR's counter-electoral campaign. The ambush wounding of a supervisor and other acts of intimidation against FIAT in Turin on 14 December 1979 coincided with the opening of the judicial proceedings following FIAT's dismissal of 51 employees accused of political violence and abetting terrorism. Finally, the ambush murder in Milan of three Public Security agents on 8 January, and of two *Carabinieri* in Genoa on 25 March 1980 need no interpretation. The BR themselves called these actions a "welcome message" to retired *Carabinieri* General Palumbi, who was appointed Prefect of Genoa, and to *Carabinieri* General Dalla Chiesa, who assumed command of the First *Carabinieri* Division headquartered in Milan.

Retaliatory murders

Other targets have been selected on account of retaliatory considerations. Apart from the Coco operation a particularly important case is the one involving Italsider worker, CGIL labour union activist, and PCI member Guido Rossa, who was murdered in Genoa on 24 January 1979 because his testimony had led to the conviction of Francesco Berardi, a "courier" entrusted with the distribution of BR literature in the plant. Also within this cluster falls the 12 March 1977 murder of Public Security NCO Giuseppe Ciotta, responsible for the arrest of brigadist Anna Garizio.

Ambush tactics have also been applied by the BR to targets of opportunity, such as the random killing by a BR "patrol unit" of two *Carabinieri* in Genoa on 21 November 1979 as they were drinking coffee prior to their duty shift.

These ambush-type operations have further been combined with forcible and non-forcible entries into dwellings and offices. In such cases, the victims have been subjected to varying degrees of violence. On 23 May 1979, while pursuing a technique reminiscent of the style of the "historic nucleus" of the first half of the decade, a BR commando chained Christian Democratic councilwoman Rossella Sborghi to the staircase of her apartment-building in Genoa and photographed her with a BR poster hanging from her neck. The wounding two days later of Professor Cuocolo of the University of Genoa mentioned above, took place in the University itself—an exception to the more frequent technique of hitting a victim on his way to or from work. This technique was resorted to again on 12 February 1980 in the University of Rome, where Professor Vittorio Bachelet, who was also the Vice President of the Superior Council of the Judiciary, was shot dead.

BR operations against material targets, on the other hand, generally serve a complementary purpose insofar as they often produce less reaction than attacks on individuals. The BR have frequently broken into industrial, commercial, and professional offices for the purpose of acquiring files on individuals active in those areas. On other occasions such break-ins have served to damage or merely demonstrate against these targets.

Within this general tactic one operation deserves particular attention. On 3 May 1979, as the parliamentary electoral campaign was underway, the BR conducted a morning assault on the Christian Democratic Committee in Rome's Piazza Nicosia. Approximately 15 brigadists entered the premises, overpowered, and handcuffed two guards and a dozen party workers and members. Other brigadists were left behind to cover the rear of the raiding party.

As a Public Security motor patrol reached the scene in response to a telephone call it was ambushed by the covering party. Two patrolmen were killed and the third was wounded. While the supporting elements were holding off the police, the raiding party detonated three explosive devices which damaged part of the building. The raiding party was able to leave the building, together with the hostages, undisturbed. The only flaw in the planning and execution of this operation is reflected in the fact that some of the brigadists had to steal a car at the last minute in order to get away with the rest of the commando group.

This operation was repeated on a smaller scale on 29 May 1979 when the Christian Democratic regional offices in Ancona were raided by a BR commando unit that exploded three firebombs. As for material targets, it is worth noting that the BR have in their inventory some devastating weapons. On 16 November 1979, for example, the BR fired upon a *Carabinieri* barracks in Turin with a grenade launcher.

Moro propaganda tactics

As the foregoing indicates, elements present in one cluster of operations frequently recur in other clusters, thus lending cohesion and depth to BR actions. The Moro case is particularly instructive in this regard. Besides the obvious planning, logistical, and operational elements involved additional details deserve consideration.

During Moro's 54 days of captivity the BR used techniques they had already developed during previous political kidnappings, particularly the Sossi abduction. As the BR "tried" Moro they issued nine communiqués (an additional one purportedly issuing from the BR was subsequently repudiated) and, on two separate occasions, furnished the media with a photograph of the elder statesman, who was "allowed", moreover, to write to a number of political figures, friends, and family members. In addition to handling the delivery of these missives, the BR kept up telephone contacts with the victim's family and representatives of the family to spur negotiations with the State.

When it became evident that the authorities would not negotiate Moro's release against that of 13 terrorists on trial (fellow brigadists, members of sister bands, and even one politicised common criminal), the BR finally "executed" Moro and returned his body on 9 May 1978, in the trunk of a stolen Renault which they parked half way between the headquarters of the Christian Democratic Party and of the PCI. The symbolism was clear since Moro was Communist Secretary—General Berlinguer's primary counterpart in the "historic compromise" politics of the two parties.

Throughout Moro's captivity the BR did not limit themselves to managing the affair and eluding the unprecedently massive police search, but carried out a series of complementary operations, including two murders and six leg shootings in Milan, Turin, Genoa, and Rome. This is indicative of their flexibility and resources.

BR "columns" and "cells"

Some knowledge of the BR structure has been acquired from the documentation seized by the police in their operational bases and refuges and from the statements—albeit debatable—made by captured brigadist Cristoforo Piancone and by anonymous informers to the media. Apparently the organisation follows "a pyramidal structure with closed compartments, each headed by a person who acts as a filter and ensures access to the higher compartment". The historical unit of the BR is the "column", which coordinates subordinate units within its own pyramidal structure. The basic units are the "cells", consisting of three to five members each. Columns have been established in the cities of the industrial triangle, in Rome, and possibly elsewhere, as operations in north-eastern and southern Italy, as well as in the islands of Sicily and Sardinia, might indicate.

In the course of an impromptu press conference with various journalists during the recess of judicial proceedings, Renato Curcio stated that the BR are active in 60 cities. According to Piancone, each column consists of 1,500 members and enjoys operational autonomy. In their documents the BR also refer to a "strategic directorate" and to a number of logistical and administrative services called "fronts".

The BR's security norms, as they call them, appear to be in conformity with those of all clandestine organisations. There has been much speculation in the media about its intelligence channels. According to a recurring rumour they have a particularly effective source in the Ministry of Justice. Although such a source has not been uncovered, eleven magistrates are under investigation at the time of writing because of suspected links with the terrorists. Material discovered in BR bases seized by the police includes long lists of detailed information on public and private figures. Part of this information has ostensibly been acquired from open sources. The organisation of these data reflects the attention devoted by the BR to intelligence gathering and processing.

Not only do the BR derive support from the extra-parliamentary Left and politicised common criminals but they finance and resupply themselves by means of abductions for ransom (to be distinguished from political or demonstrative kidnappings), bank robberies, gunshop holdups, vehicle thefts, and various other "proletarian expropriations". No claim is generally issued for these logistical operations. Premises for BR bases are frequently purchased by cash payment under assumed identity. Documentation is either stolen or falsified. The BR have also resupplied themselves with manpower and facilities by absorbing the remaining human and material assets of less successful sister groups such as Giangiacomo Feltrinelli's Partisan Action Groups, the October XXII Circle, and the NAP.

The current threat posed by the BR to Italian society is perhaps best depicted by the major operations conducted by them early in 1980:

- Murder of the President of the Region of Sicily, Christian Democrat Pier Santi Mattarella, in Palermo on 6 January;
- Murder of three Public Security patrolmen in Milan two days later;
- Murder of a *Carabinieri* officer, a soldier and an army officer in Genoa on the 25th of the same month;
- Murder of Silvano Gori, deputy manager of Petrolchimico—"the death factory"—in Mestre four days thereafter;
- The already mentioned murder of Prof. Bachelet, Vice-President of the Superior Council of the Judiciary, in Rome on 12 February;
- The wounding of Alfa Romeo manager Pietro Dell'Era in Arese and of Italsider executive Roberto Della Rocca in Genoa, on the 21st and 29th respectively.

On 16 and 18 March there followed the murders of Salerno Attorney General Nicola Giacumbi and of Supreme Court Judge Girolamo Minervini (barely designated to supervise the prison system) in Rome, the wounding of Giancarlo Moretti, a Christian Democratic professor of tax law, in Genoa on the 19th; and a raid on an army barracks in Padua with the consequential wounding of an NCO on the 30th. (To these operations can be added a Rome bank robbery of Lir. 500 million which, in the words of the BR—who did claim responsibility for it—"will be used for the purposes of the revolution".)

Without detracting from the present danger some law enforcement officials have privately observed, however, that for the first time in ten years the BR are also displaying a plurality of *coexistent* weaknesses.

These reportedly include an over-extension of recruitment, which makes selection, control, discipline, and training more difficult; an unprecedented carelessness in safeguarding documents and other materials, as reflected by personal effects forgotten in public places and compromising items unwisely kept so as to link captured brigadists and uncovered hideouts with other members or facilities of the organisation; an incipient fear of the special prisons, where living conditions are particularly poor; a partial loss of security resulting from co-operation with other terrorist organisations lacking the same degree of ideological commitment; and varying degrees of internal dissent on policies and operations. Should the BR be unable—as opposed to their past record—to cure these shortcomings, future counter-terrorist operations could obviously be facilitated.

"Feltrinelli group" merges

In conjunction with the pattern of rigid clandestinity and systematic violence, which is primarily applicable to the BR, two other terrorist organisations should be briefly examined: the Partisan Action Groups (*Gruppi di Azione Partigiana*—GAP) and the NAP.

The GAP were reportedly founded in Milan in 1969–70 at approximately the same time as BR came into being. It is uncertain whether they were directly organised by millionaire publisher Giangiacomo Feltrinelli—their primary source of financial support—assisted by former Communist partisans, or whether Feltrinelli became associated with the GAP after they had come into existence. In either case, additional members were later recruited by Feltrinelli among Sardinian bandits and Italian immigrants in Germany. Feltrinelli was convinced to the point of obsession that a rightist coup was forthcoming and could be pre-empted only by resorting to a clandestine form of resistance modelled on partisan warfare. This fundamental difference from BR urban guerrilla tactics apparently prevented an early merger between the two organisations, notwithstanding the existing and continued liaison between their representatives.

GAP propaganda tactics included interference with television broadcasting by suddenly interjecting revolutionary and anti-Fascist announcements. The first GAP units operated in both the Milan and Genoa areas, where they conducted arson attacks against warehouses, oil refineries, and shipyards. Other targets were the offices of the Unified Socialist Party (a brief merger between Socialists and Social Democrats) and the US Consulate in Genoa, where they conducted joint actions with the October XXII Circle, which imitated the GAP's broadcasting-interference techniques.

Terrorist attacks elsewhere in northern Italy were perpetrated under different names, an early attempt to propagandise the "armed struggle". The GAP practically ceased to exist as an independent organisation on 14 March 1972, when Feltrinelli accidentally blew himself up in the Segrate area as he was applying an explosive charge to an electric power pylon. The remaining human and organisational assets were taken over by the BR, in one of whose bases documentation relative to both Feltrinelli and the GAP was later discovered.

NAP takes conflict to prisons

Whereas the operations of the GAP and the BR ran virtually parallel to each other the NAP (Armed Proletarian Nuclei) have been influenced by the latter and, in at least one area, have exercised their own influence on the BR, which have absorbed their remnants too. Not unlike the BR, the NAP drew their inspiration from the social unrest that has affected Italy since the late 1960s. The wave of demands generated by the students and the workers spread to the prisons as well. As early as April of 1969 two major uprisings erupted in the Turin and Milan prisons.

Thereafter, until the mid-1970s, other penitentiaries throughout Italy, including those in Genoa, Rome, and Naples, experienced uprisings, protests, and strikes. On 10 May 1974, for example, hostages were taken during an uprising in the prison of Alessandria and a number of the policemen and inmates were either killed or seriously wounded before order could be restored. During this period the Movement of Proletarian Prisoners, which was particularly active in promoting unrest in the prisons, unsuccessfully sought a merger with the leftist extra-parliamentary party Ongoing Struggle (*Lotta Continua*).

The NAP, born in the spring of 1974, are the natural offspring of the

Movement. Original members were former Ongoing Struggle militants and former convicts with internal contacts in the prisons. The NAP became immediately concerned with organising the "armed struggle" inside and outside the prison system. Initial operations, which were rather rudimentary and generally confined to the Naples area, are reminiscent of the early BR actions. By way of contrast, the NAP resorted from the very start to the use of explosives, usually targeted against prisons and asylums for the criminally insane.

Unclaimed bank robberies and kidnappings for ransom were adopted as self-financing measures. With the initial proceeds from these criminal activities the NAP strengthened their Naples structures, while subsequent proceeds were used to expand their sphere of action primarily to Rome, but also to other areas of the country. The BR practice of ambushing victims and firing upon them with hand-guns was imitated by the NAP from October 1976. They wounded a prison guard, a judge, a Public Security patrolman (a retaliatory action) and a FIAT executive, but killed the FIAT security director of the Cassino plant.

Only on one occasion, however, did they acquire national notoriety. In this case, too, they imitated the BR by kidnapping in Rome, on 6 May 1975, Supreme Court Judge Guiseppe Di Gennaro, detailed to the Ministry of Justice. His release was made contingent upon the transfer to prisons of their choice three jailed NAP members, who had unsuccessfully attempted to escape from the Viterbo prison. The prisoners were transferred within 48 hours and the judge was released.

Throughout their history the NAP suffered many arrests and casualties in fire engagements with the police and through the carelessly self-destructive use of explosives. Starting in late 1975, they conducted a series of joint actions with the BR against police barracks and vehicles in Pisa, Rho, Genoa, Turin, Rome, Naples, and Florence, but this collaboration did not revitalise the NAP. Their inability to renew themselves is attributable to various factors. Most obvious are their lesser degree of discipline and security consciousness, as exemplified by the failure to recycle a conspicuous ransom, which was instead haphazardly distributed among various NAP units; their lack of tight controls over explosives; and their indiscriminate recruitment among common criminals, prison inmates, and poor southern workers, which inhibited the establishment of a solid, ideologically-motivated cadre base and of a tight operational compartmentation that could prevent cumulative identification by the police.

As long as the NAP were operational the BR paid comparatively little attention to the prisons. Following the virtual disappearance of the NAP the BR have taken over where the former left off. (By early 1978, the remaining members and safe houses of the NAP had been absorbed by the BR.) The BR's new commitment to the prison system is not only reflected in the number of prison guard victims of the ambush technique, but also by their "literature", which now includes such exhortations as "Fight for the liberation of all imprisoned Communists".

In this sense, the NAP have affected the BR. Moreover, the politicised common criminal formerly absent from the ranks of the BR—as opposed to the GAP and the NAP—is now part of the BR recruitment pool. Finally both BR and NAP share behind-the-bars techniques. Captured militants of both organisations continue the struggle against the system even from their trial benches. As BR defendants hailed from the courts the BR operation against Moro and his escort as "the highest act of humanity", the NAP defendants have saluted the BR raid on the Piazza Nicosia Christian Democratic offices and the murder of *Carabinieri* Lieutenant Colonel Varisco.

"Front Line" terrorism

PL, which follows the operational pattern of simultaneous political action and "armed struggle", officially entered the Italian terrorist arena on 29 November 1976, the same year that a number of minor groups began to emulate the already well-established BR. PL has gradually come to be as well known as the BR. On 29 November five terrorists broke into a FIAT office in Turin, tied up all the employees, "expropriated" all the cash on hand, removed corporate documents, and before leaving sprayed the name "Front Line" all over the walls. Three days later another PL commando set fire to the Monza offices of the Industrialists' Association, and two days later still another PL commando exploded a bomb in the offices of the Milan daily *Corriere della Sera*.

For the next five months, PL apparently remained dormant; however, some observers believe that it was in fact operating under the names of Armed Proletarian Squads, Proletarian Patrols, Armed Proletarian Groups, Armed Patrol, and Combatant Territorial Nuclei. In May and June 1977, PL resurfaced by name and claimed a number of attacks in Milan, including the blowing up of subway tracks and the burning down of Sit-Siemens and Magneti Marelli warehouses.

On 6 June six Front Liners, all students between 18 and 20 years of age, were caught by the police in the act of attempting to blow up the Turin trolley system. Of the six, Marco Fagiano escaped, while the rest were apprehended, including one Cesare Rambaudi, who turned out to be particularly talkative and recited the entire chronicle of his association with PL. On the basis of Rambaudi's account it would appear that recruits had to prove themselves "in the field". In Rambaudi's case, his test of "worthiness" entailed setting fire to the offices of a firm that makes worker-overalls. He also described the rather primitive facilities—an attic—used by the organisation for training and storage, and revealed laxness in security and haphazard operational planning.

On 20 June PL overcame the problem of careless use of explosives by adding firearms to its inventory. On that day a commando in Milan shot a Sit-Siemens loading supervisor in the legs. Two days later in Pistoia, PL wounded a Christian Democratic activist employed by Breda. Again 48 hours later, Roberto Anzalone, president of a Milan medicare organisation, was shot. The following day the same fate befell an Alfa Sud executive in charge of labour relations in Naples. From this point on, PL actions appear to run parallel to those of the BR with respect to both their technical execution and their violent escalation. Moreover, in a communiqué taking credit for a series of bombings and leg-shootings perpetrated in May of 1978, PL expressed its unity of intent with the BR.

A tangible indication of co-operation between the two organisations came to light on 13 September 1978, when Corrado Alunni was captured in a Milan hideout on the Via Negroli. Alunni, a leading brigadist of the "historic nucleus", had become active in PL and carried out liaison between the two organisations, as evidenced by his own notes seized by the police. Terrorist material found in the Via Negroli base included records and documentation regarding both the BR and PL.

Mass leg-shooting

On 11 October, the day following the BR murder of Judge Tartaglione, PL claimed responsibility for the killing of one of Tartaglione's assistants, criminology professor Alfredo Paolella. Next month, a PL commando ambushed and killed Frosinone's Attorney General Fedele Calvosa, together with both his escorts.

Terrorists of the Left imprisoned, indicted, or identified
(as at 19 December 1979)

Red Brigades (BR)	357
Armed Proletarian Nuclei (NAP)	182
Front Line (PL)	131
Revolutionary Action (AR)	36
Communist Combat Units (UCC)	26
Other	10
	742

The more selective actions carried out by PL in 1979 include the 19 January murder of Milan Assistant Attorney General Emilio Alessandrini, who was preparing a data bank and other measures relating to the control of terrorism; the attack in Turin on 9 March on a Public Security patrol (enticed into a bar by a fake "emergency call") in retaliation for the killing of two Front Liners by the police during a fire engagement a week earlier; and the murder on 21 September in Turin of Carlo Ghiglieno, the highest ranking FIAT executive so far attacked. But the most amazing PL operation, which rivals the BR's most daring, also took place in Turin on 11 December. About 15 Front Liners penetrated into the School of Industrial Management, seized some 130 members of the faculty and student body, and selected ten individuals (five professors and five students) for the first mass leg-shooting. The entire operation, including the escape of the raiding party, was accomplished in 20 minutes.

As opposed to the BR preference for total clandestinity, PL operates semi-clandestinely. Its militants lead a double life. The first is that of seemingly ordinary citizens who hold regular jobs and have a clean police record, while the second entails terrorist acts and other clandestine operations. Their overt activity enables them to stay in contact with the masses and to exercise political influence. Structurally, PL is reportedly made up of "fire groups", rather than "columns", as in the case of the BR.

The functions of the fire groups—the best organised are said to operate out of Milan, Turin, Florence, Naples, and Cosenza—are nonetheless the same as those of the columns. At the lower echelons leadership is not reportedly vested in any individual on a permanent basis, but is exercised in the course of each operation by whoever is capable of doing so. According to the revelations made by an alleged Front Liner to the weekly *Panorama*, this organisation is not constrained by the rigid territorial boundaries peculiar to the BR structure. A commentator has recently referred to PL as a "federation of connected groupings lacking the rigid military organisation of the BR".

Indicative of the current threat posed by PL are major operations it conducted in the first quarter of 1980. Between 5 and 7 February PL claimed a murder a day perpetrated in Monza, Rome, and Milan. The first victim was Paolo Paolella, an Icmesa executive; the second Maurizio Arnesano, a Public Security patrolman; the third William Waccher, "a spy" because of his testimony's leading to the indictment of two fellow "autonomists" for the murder of a goldsmith. On 19 March, moreover, PL killed Judge Guido Galli. On the previous day the BR had murdered Judge Minervini. The threat posed by PL is further aggravated by the consideration that it does not always operate under its own name and by the fact that its organisation—contrary to that of the BR where police arrests and seizures may have made some deep inroads—appears to be virtually intact.

Among the minor groups that presumably originated from the spontaneous and sporadic actions pattern, three stand out. The first, Revolutionary Action (*Azione Rivoluzionaria*), apparently active since 1977, has been characterised as a band of anarchists, leftist terrorists, and common criminals. One of its jailed members, Gianfranco Faina, a former political science professor, is the author of a book dedicated to Ulrike Meinhof. Various transnational elements have appeared in its ranks.

The second, Communist Combat Units (*Unità Combattenti Comuniste*), "an armed appendix of Worker Power", attracted much publicity when they unprecedently demanded the distribution of large quantities of meat at "political" (below-market) prices in June of 1976 for the release of a kidnapped meat dealer. They acquired national notoriety once again in July of 1979 when the *Carabinieri* discovered in a Vescovio (Rieti) base soundproof facilities suspected of having been used in the course of the Mòro captivity. The third group, *Barbagia Rossa*, active since 1978, appears to include elements of Sardinian separatist and of BR-linked ideological aspirations.

The Communist influence

What has been the attitude of Italy's Communist Party towards the leftist terrorist phenomenon? As noted earlier, the PCI, in pursuance of its electoral image, adopted a softer Marxist–Leninist line, but several observers have attributed varying degrees of responsibility to the ideological influence of the party's traditional doctrine. The language of the BR, for example, is recognised as reflecting the hardline Communist parlance: Rossana Rossanda, formerly of the PCI and now of the Manifesto, has commented that it is that of the PCI of the 1950s. She went on to say that "it's like leafing through a family album".

There are those, moreover, who recall the instructive precedents of the 1940s and 1950s. In those days, Communist partisans who had expected the war of liberation to bring about the "Italian Soviet Republic" gave birth to paramilitary formations such as Red Star (*Stella Rossa*) in 1944 in Turin and the Red Strike Force (*Volante Rossa*) in 1945 that remained active in various areas of northern Italy at least well into 1949. Other PCI card-carrying members were likewise responsible for uprisings and violence in Ragusa and Schio (53 murders in Schio alone) in 1945, in other towns of the north in 1946, and also through much of the rest of Italy after the abortive attempt on the life of PCI leader Palmiro Togliatti on 14 July 1948, by one Antonio Pallante acting spontaneously.

On the evening following the attempt, Luigi Longo, Togliatti's successor in 1964 as secretary-general and current party president, was reported as saying: "Let's see how things go. If the protest wave increases, we will allow it to increase. If it decreases, we will block it". The following day, both Longo and Secchia, another PCI hard-liner, reportedly made this statement before the central committee:

> The insurgent forces are concentrated in the large cities of the north, but even in the north the campaign is not certain; communications among the cities would be uncertain. The rank-and-file are saying: "We have the factories in our hands: we have the cities in our hands". Let the comrades reflect: for the time being neither the police nor the army have intervened: if they will do so, they will have cannon and tanks against which it is impossible to resist.

Notwithstanding the documented party membership of such "militants"—and the PCI's use of the Red Strike Force in 1948 to "keep order" during the VI Party Congress and to escort the Soviet delegates and French Communist Party leader Maurice Thorez—the PCI branded them as Trotskyites, provocateurs, and reactionaries if they were arrested or otherwise in difficulty with the authorities. This policy of subsequent excommunication is reminiscent of contemporary PCI policy vis-à-vis today's terrorists of the Left.

Apart from such historical-precedent considerations, notice has been taken of direct PCI influence over the terrorists of the 1970s, who predominantly trace their political indoctrination to the PCI, its youth organisation (FGCI), and/or extra-parliamentary offshoots. It has been observed that while between 1968 and 1970 the strength of the FGCI dropped from

135,000 to approximately 66,000 members, the drop-outs have reportedly streamed toward the violent "groupuscules" of the extra-parliamentary Left.

"Stalinist wing"

Students of the Italian terrorist phenomenon, including Giorgio Bocca, a former partisan and a Socialist, have stressed the existence of "a Stalinist wing in the PCI". Bocca further stated ". . . when I wrote that in Genoa there are links between old leaders of the PCI and the BR, Pecchioli (the PCI's expert on police matters) said that I am a provocateur. But in the Communist circles in Genoa they know that this is true and they speak about it frequently". According to a poll conducted by Doxa, 12 per cent of the card-carrying members of the PCI would like closer contacts between the party and the extra-parliamentary Autonomy. Another commentator, Massimo Tosti of the weekly *Il Settimanale*, has drawn attention to the fact that BR leaflets critical of the PCI refer to it as "Berlinguer's party".

Also relevant is a statement by BR member Piancone after his capture: "In the event of a violent governmental repression against terrorism, the PCI will guarantee our physical survival. The legalitarian attitude adopted by the PCI will never allow the State to adopt measures against us that are too strong". Various commentators, including the American columnist George F. Will, have remarked on the comparatively negligible number of physical attacks by terrorists of the Left on the PCI. In fact, there have been two leg-shootings and one murder, none of which has been claimed by the terrorists as anti-Communist in nature.

As to the political beneficiary of Italian terrorism, philosopher Sergio Cotta has concisely stated that *"every wave of terrorism has accelerated the leftward drift of actual power and the decomposition of constitutional democracy in favour of the disorderly mass organs manoeuvred by the PCI and the labour unions"*. At the same time, journalist Livio Caputo has suggested that if the PCI were really interested in putting a stop to terrorism all it would have to do is "denounce all those individuals that were part of the PCI and its affiliated labour union before taking up clandestinity".

For its part, the PCI—despite Senator Pecchioli's belated concession in late 1977 and early 1978 that there is terrorism of the Left—has continued to refer to the "forces of reaction", a theory dear to the Soviets. In the course of an October 1978 visit to Moscow the PCI delegation called terrorism "the adventurous activity of criminal groups with whose assistance the forces of reaction attempt, through the organisation of terrorist acts, to block the development of the democratic achievements of the workers and of the Italian people".

The Italian and Soviet Communist parties therefore jointly condemned terrorist activity as "absolutely contrary to the workers' movement and to the democratic movement". The PCI's basically unchanged attitude is best reflected by one detail in its periodic reports on terrorism. These address both terrorism of the Right and of the Left, but only the word Left appears between quotation marks. Moreover, PCI foreign bureau chief Giancarlo Pajetta categorically ruled out in March of 1978 the existence of links between Italian terrorism and East European states.

III. INTERNATIONAL CONNECTIONS

In February of 1978 the BR issued a "strategic resolution" whose contents also espoused "the necessity to develop to the fullest extent historically possible operational co-operation, reciprocal support, and solidarity" with the elements that constitute proletarian internationalism. The resolution names the German Red Army Fraction, the French *Noyau Armé pour l'Autonomie Populaire* (Armed Nucleus for Popular Autonomy—NAPAP), and the "autonomous movements possessing a Socialist nature". The last is a reference to the Irish Republican Army/IRA and to the Basque ETA. The resolution further defines guerrilla as "the organisational form of proletarian internationalism in the metropolitan centres" and associates it with the "war for world liberation against imperialism". Linkage between Italian and foreign terrorism elements has been a matter of record, however, before and after release of the resolution.

Between 1970 and 1972 Andreas Baader visited Italy twice to discuss with the BR, represented by Curcio and Moretti, the "anti-imperialist struggle" on the Continent and reportedly advised them not to limit their sphere of action to the factories and industrial executives, but to carry the attack to the political structures of the State. In subsequent years, members of the Baader–Meinhof gang pursued by the German police found refuge in Italy and apparently planned their operations from Italian territory. Known or suspected German terrorists arrested or reported in Italy include Ludwig Herman Bicknease, Christian Klar, Adelheid Schulz, and Willy Peter Stoll.

In the Moro abduction circumstantial evidence has been introduced of further collaboration between the two groups: an agenda listing expenses in conjunction with air travel to West Germany by one Fritz was seized in the BR Via Gradoli base in Rome, together with two German licence plates; witnesses to the abduction heard German spoken by one of the terrorists; among the items left behind by the assault party, a German-manufactured imitation-leather handbag was recovered; and some of the weapons used by the commando were reportedly part of a stock stolen in Switzerland (part of the same stock had previously been used in Germany for the Schleyer kidnapping, whose dynamics inspired the Moro operation).

In August of 1978 "retired" German terrorist Hans Joachim Klein sent a letter to the weekly *Der Spiegel* stating that on one occasion he had personally carried weapons through Rome's international airport in diplomatic luggage with the complicity of an unnamed ambassador. On 20 February 1979 the Italian police arrested in Pisa two Italians (Rocco Martino and Carmela Pane) and two Germans (Rudolf Piroch and Johanna Hartwig), who were travelling in a vehicle loaded with explosives similar to those used by Revolutionary Action.

The connections of the Italian terrorists and extremists with their foreign counterparts extend well beyond Germany. Excerpts from prosecution documents quoted by the media in December 1979 and January 1980 refer to logistical and training arrangements with elements of the IRA dating back to the early 1970s and to the subsequent participation of a BR representative in a secret meeting held in Yugoslavia by European, Latin American, and Palestinian elements to discuss "the international strategy and planning of the revolution".

South American base in Rome

In July of 1977 the police uncovered in Rome a Montonero base containing weapons, stolen passports, and subversive documents. Later four Argentinians—Fernando Vaca Narvaja, Maria Josefa Fleming, and Eduardo and Teresa Sling Gerl—were convicted *in absentia*, since they had become fugitives.

Four months after the initial discovery of the base and issuing of arrest warrants, one of the four (Narvaja) held a conference at the "Cultural Club 'Levi' " of Rome outlining Montonero aims and activities. Participants reportedly included the late Senator Lelio Basso (Independent Left), Communist Members of Parliament Vetrano and Bottarelli, and Socialists Avolio and Maggi. Following the Autonomy-inspired riots in Bologna on 11 March 1977 out of 32 students arrested by the police six were foreigners (five Greeks and one Libyan). Two days later, among 47 arrested there were three Greeks, an American, and a German. Three more foreigners (two Greeks and one Haitian) were arrested during the subsequent spring riots in Rome. The Haitian was looting an arms shop.

One of the unexploded devices used by the BR in Rome during the May 1977 commando raid on the Piazza Nicosia Christian Democratic offices was held together by subversive posters written in French. In July, two Austrian terrorists were arrested in Foggia. Also in July two French nationals, who had spent long periods in Italy, were arrested in France on charges of supplying weapons to Italian terrorists. But of particular interest are the documented and hypothesised links of the Italian terrorist bands with the Middle East, Cuba, and East European states.

According to press sources a small number of unidentified Italians was trained in Lebanon between 1973 and 1976 in camps other than those reserved for Al Fatah and the PLO. Other sources—including a jailed criminal, one Berardino Andreola—have reported that Giangiacomo Feltrinelli's financing and friendship with Baader had also opened the door for training in an Al Fatah camp. References to negotiations for such training also appear in the above-cited prosecution documents. Moreover, Enrico Paghera, an Italian terrorist associated with Revolutionary Action, was arrested while in possession of a Palestinian training camp map.

In April of 1978 three Swiss nationals suspected of contacts with the BR through a post office box were arrested in Cairo. According to the Egyptian Attorney General, one of them confessed to having conveyed to

Palestinian elements in Cairo the BR's desire to establish co-operation with them. On 8 November 1979, three Italian extremists of the extra-parliamentary Autonomy were arrested in Ortona (Chieti) for possession of two Soviet Strela (SAM-7) missile launchers acquired through Palestinian sources.

The Cuban connection

Initial contacts with Cuba were reportedly established by Feltrinelli—himself a former PCI member—who spent time there as Fidel Castro's guest in the mid and late 1960s. In 1967 Feltrinelli went to Bolivia specifically to witness the trial of Régis Debray, a Frenchman who had followed Che Guevara on his last expedition. Bolivian Consul Quintanilla, considered responsible for Guevara's capture and death, was subsequently murdered in West Germany with Feltrinelli's pistol. Feltrinelli also became the Italian editor of Cuba's revolutionary publication *Tricontinental*. Brigadists Curcio and his late wife "Mara" interrupted their honeymoon to follow Feltrinelli's trail and stayed there, as later reported in a book published by Feltrinelli's company.

Subsequent contacts with Cuba appear to have taken place on two different levels. On one hand, several militants of the extra-parliamentary Workers' Vanguard (*Avanguardia Operaia*) and of the Autonomy movement in Rome repeatedly undertook "political trips" to Angola in 1977 and 1978 to confer with the Cuba-linked MPLA. Moreover, in early 1979, a former activist of the defunct Worker Power, Achille Lollo, had become a sergeant in the Angolan militia. On the other hand, the Cuban presence in Italian terrorist bands has apparently been achieved through Chilean "refugees". One Aldo Marín Piñones, who had spent one year and a half in Cuba before arriving in Italy as a political exile, accidentally blew himself up in Turin in 1977 while campaigning in the ranks of Revolutionary Action.

Piñones's room mate, Juan Teófilo Paillacar Soto, another Chilean "refugee" wanted by the Italian police on charges of subversion, was at long last overpowered in Rome on 9 April 1979 while resisting, gun in hand. This time "refugee" Soto proclaimed himself a "political prisoner". Still another Chilean, Ernesto Reyes Castro, had been arrested in Lucca on 19 April 1978 in the company of one Spanish and three Italian terrorists, including the above-mentioned Enrico Paghera with his Palestinian map.

Other Chileans apprehended under compromising circumstances include Juan Carlos Araneda de Cerra, Jaime Ramírez Ibarra, and Julio Jaime Opazo. A final incident involving the Chilean connection, but not Chilean nationals, took place on 16 July 1979, when four activists associated with the Socialist Party and the Communist-oriented CGIL labour union were arrested following an abortive attempt against the Bristol Hotel in Abano Terme. The four were reportedly involved in extortion to finance the Chilean resistance movement.

Czech training centres

Frequently cited indicators of linkage between Italian terrorists of the Left and East European "patron" states include the former's extensive use of such weaponry as Nagant pistols, Skorpion sub-machine-guns, and Kalashnikov rifles; the discovery of Czech keys in a BR base seized by the police in Ostia (Rome); and the travels and sojourn of terrorists Giangiacomo Feltrinelli, Renato Curcio, Alberto Franceschini, Fabrizio Pelli, and Augusto Viel in Czechoslovakia. These circumstances acquire greater significance if Czechoslovakia has indeed established in Karlovy Vary and Doupov centres for training foreign agents in destabilisation operations. The existence of such centres has been corroborated in an interview given to the American journalist Michael Ledeen by the defector General Jan Sejna, former Secretary General of the Defence Committee of the Czech Central Committee, and published in *Il Giornale* of Milan. He said some 13 Italians were trained there before his defection in 1968.

Czech clandestine connections with Italy—apart from Sejna's revelations—were already operating in the late 1940s and the early 1950s, when those PCI members who had participated in the unlawful activities of the Red Strike Force and analogous paramilitary formations escaped arrest by finding asylum in Czechoslovakia, where some are still living today. In those Cold War years PCI clearance was a requirement for the acceptance of such "refugees" by their East European host. Even Francesco Moranino, a notorious Communist partisan who had committed political and common crimes, lived in Czechoslovakia and worked there for Radio Prague until pardoned by the President of the Republic. (Moranino was later elected to the Senate on the PCI slate.)

Radio Prague has consistently transmitted broadcasts in the Italian language. Political scientist Giorgio Galli has observed that throughout the Cold War years it was commonplace to hear Italian Communists from the Emilia region refer to it as "our radio". Those were also the days when the PCI kept its files in Prague, a practice that lasted at least until Stalin's death.

The asylum granted between 1970 and 1974 to brigadists Franceschini and Pelli and to Viel of the October XXII Circle—all three wanted by the Italian police, a fact that could hardly have escaped the Czech consular authorities who issued the visas—does not therefore constitute a new practice for the Czechs. Nor does Pelli's employment with Radio Prague constitute a precedent. Moreover, according to Sejna, Feltrinelli (who later accompanied fugitive Viel to Prague), Franceschini, and Pelli received training in Karlovy Vary and/or Doupov. Press accounts have also reported that Alvaro Lojacono, a member of the extra-parliamentary "Via dei Volsci collective", and Roberto Mander, another extra-parliamentary activist in contact with anarchists and the NAP, passed through Prague.

Subversives' KGB contacts

Of significance also are the statements made on 19 May 1978 during a parliamentary debate by Member of Parliament Vito Miceli, who had previously served with the rank of General as the head of Italian intelligence (SID). He stated that on 9 May 1972 SID had reported to the Minister of Defence proof of links existing between Feltrinelli, subversive groups of Italy's extreme Left, and KGB agents working under diplomatic cover in the Soviet Embassy in Rome. At that time SID had also recommended the expulsion of 22 Soviet agents from Italy. (Great Britain had previously expelled 105 Soviet agents on similar grounds.)

According to General Miceli SID wanted to strike at the Soviets while they were still in the initial stages of setting up espionage rings and subversive groups. Although both the Minister of Defence (Restivo) and the Minister of Foreign Affairs (Moro) were in agreement with the proposed measure it was vetoed by the then Prime Minister (Andreotti).

A second report was forwarded the following year. It stated that the Soviet Union had prepared a ten-year plan for the purpose of dominating Western Europe. Measures outlined included the employment of subversive activities by the extreme Left. Yet, according to the General, he was personally summoned in January 1974 by the Minister of the Interior (Taviani), who tried to persuade him that the threat to Italy did not come from the Warsaw Pact countries but from another West European nation, which the General did not specify in his account of the conversation. Finally, Miceli confirmed press reports to the effect that Italian youths had participated in training courses held in Prague, Moscow, and Cuba.

On 3 October 1978 Renzo Rossellini, a journalist of the extra-parliamentary Left associated with a private radio station called *Città Futura*, was interviewed by the Paris daily *Le Matin*. In the course of the interview he reiterated information received from Palestinian friends who maintain that ever since 1945 the Soviet Red Army had taken over a portion of the PCI's partisan organisation. Moreover, at the end of the 1960s this paramilitary organisation had been allegedly restructured by the Soviets, who also reinforced it with terrorists trained in an East European country. General Miceli is reported to have confirmed the accuracy of these allegations.

IV. COUNTER-MEASURES AND OUTLOOK

At the dawn of the 1980s the terrorist threat to Italian society and institutions remains menacing. According to preliminary statistical findings attacks on property during the first quarter of 1980 declined in comparison with previous years, but attacks against persons are on the increase: 27 killings (19 of them resulting from ambush tactics) and 94 woundings (9 of them resulting from ambush tactics). Clearly the containment and ultimate elimination of the terrorist phenomenon should be based upon repressive and preventive measures, supported by accurate and timely intelligence.

Well before terrorism in general and of the Left in particular became a daily menace the police authorities had issued documented warnings. On 22 December 1970 the Prefect of Milan reported to the Ministry of the

Interior that there were 20,000 potential terrorists in his area of jurisdiction. A subsequent report drawn up by Milan's police superintendent on 15 July 1972 detailed violent extra-parliamentary organisations, their numerical composition, sources of support and subversive aims. The groupings indicated in both reports belonged predominantly to the Left. As for the BR in particular, a report had already been prepared on 15 March 1972 by the now defunct Confidential Matters Office of the Ministry of the Interior, reflecting extensive knowledge of their origin, characteristics, and goals.

These early warnings were apparently unheeded and the authors of the reports—somehow acquired and published by the press in 1971, 1972 and 1974—became the object of verbal abuse on the part of the PCI, the Socialists, and the Left-oriented media, which through most of the 1970s tendentiously debated whether terrorist organisations such as the BR were actually leftist or a cover for neo-Fascist subversive designs. The Communist and Socialist attitude reflected in the parliamentary debates and in the respective party dailies, *L'Unità* and *Avanti*, was quickly adopted by such widely circulated non-party press as *La Stampa, Corriere della Sera, Panorama*, and *L'Espresso* and by the self-styled independent *Paese Sera*.

Moreover, the endemically unstable governments which are dependent upon heterogeneous and faction-ridden multiparty coalitions, brought about a vacillating official attitude on terrorism at the Cabinet level that has been blamed for making police investigations and operations more arduous. In the words of senior journalist Domenico Bartoli, "at one time there was only one violent extremism (of the Left), then two opposing extremisms (of the Left and of the Right), then only one (of the Right), finally one full extremism (of the Right) plus one-half (of the Left). Byzantine variations can continue until the victory or the defeat of one or the other".

At the same time, actual or alleged abuses of institutional functions by the former intelligence service (SID) led to the intelligence reform of 1977. The reform law has been criticised, *inter alia*, for vagueness in delineating the responsibilities of the two new services it created—SISMI for military intelligence and security and SISDE for internal intelligence and security—and for blocking the services' access to the following traditional sources of information: members of Parliament; regional, provincial, and municipal councilmen; magistrates; clergymen; professional journalists; and individuals whose record does not guarantee fidelity to democratic and institutional principles.

Furthermore, the members of the parliamentary committee overseeing intelligence and security, which was also created by the reform law, have issued ambiguous statements regarding the legitimacy of infiltration techniques that could discourage their employment by intelligence agencies. Again, as of December 1979, Undersecretary Mazzola indicated that both services were undermanned, with SISMI operating at 70 per cent and SISDE at only 50 per cent authorised strength.

The foregoing would lead to the conclusion that the anti-terrorist burden rests primarily on the police forces, which are not subject to the rigid constraints imposed upon the intelligence and security services by the reform law. At the same time the police lack the capability to conduct typical intelligence operations and to delve into such matters as international terrorist links and possible "patron state" support.

Tougher counter-measures

In mid-December 1979 the Government adopted by law-decree a series of anti-terrorist measures which, after much debate and minor amendments, were made law two months later by Parliament. These measures include mandatory arrest warrants and longer prison terms for crimes connected to terrorism; relaxation of rigid wiretapping laws; extension of pre-trial confinement limitations; special treatment for repentant terrorists who aid police investigations; provisional apprehension of terrorism suspects; house searches in areas where someone wanted for terrorist crimes is believed to be hiding; and mandatory depositor identification for bank deposits in excess of Lir. 20 million. At this writing, the clemency measure *vis-à-vis* repentant terrorists is reportedly producing beneficial results and is expected by some observers to facilitate anti-terrorist operations and investigations.

Another measure that has been favourably commented upon is the institution of a commitee within the Ministry of the Interior for the coordination of the police forces. Statutory members of the committee are the chief of police (Interior), the commander of the *Carabinieri*, and the commander of the Finance Guard. Moreover, the recent appointment of experienced personnel such as Enzo Vicari, Emanuele De Francesco, and retired *Carabinieri* General Edoardo Palombi as prefects of Milan, Turin, and Genoa, respectively, and of *Carabinieri* General Carlo Alberto Dalla Chiesa—who has proved efficient in counter-terrorist operations—as commander of the First *Carabinieri* Division jurisdictionally responsible for northern Italy, might also reap operational benefits.

The major technical problem in combating the current Italian terrorism—and, indeed, the Armenian and Arab transnational elements that have extended their sphere of action to Italy—appears to be the lack of sufficient intelligence information. The other problems seem to be political, since the full success of repressive measures and of preventive social measures is ultimately predicated upon a minimum of governmental homogeneity and cohesion. Whether these attributes can be part of contemporary Italian cabinets remains an open question.

SELECT READING LIST

Bartoli, Domenico. *Gli italiani nella terra di nessuno.* Milano, Mondadori, 1976.
Bocca, Giorgio. *Il terrorismo italiano 1970/1978.* Milano, Rizzoli, 1978.
Cantore, Romano, *et al. Dall'interno della guerriglia.* Milano, Mondadori, 1978.
Mazzetti, Roberto. *Genesi e sviluppo del terrorismo in Italia.* Milano, Armando, 1979.
Ronchey, Alberto. *Libro bianco sull'ultima generazione.* Milano, Garzanti, 1978.
Soccorso Rosso. *Brigate Rosse.* Milano, Feltrinelli, 1976.
Tessandori, Vincenzo. *Br: imputazione banda armata.* Milano, Garzanti, 1977.

First published 1980.

West Germany's Red Army Anarchists

Hans Josef Horchem

The anarchist movement belongs to the nineteenth century. Its prerequisite was the age of reason, its inducement the industrial age. The German philosophical anarchist Max Stirner remained without any political influence. Political anarchism has no tradition in Germany where—unlike the Latin countries—it did not influence either the socialist movement or the trade unions.

The activists of the Red Army Group (RAG) were called anarchists but they did not see themselves as such. There was no anarchist—and still less nationalist—motivation in their acts of terrorism. They looked on their actions as forms of intervention in the revolutionary struggle, as applied by a "faction" of the world revolutionary movement. Yet anarchist elements soon asserted themselves, which in turn were reflected in their statements. The utopia of the student protest movement culminated in the old demand repeated and formulated by Rudi Dutschke, the revolutionary student leader known as "Red Rudi", to abolish the "power of people over people". It is this formula that forms a link between anarchists and Communists. From this anti-authoritarian movement there arose the *Baader–Meinhof* group, who called themselves the Red Army Group (*Rote Armee Fraktion*), in an attempt to transform the theoretical dream into reality.

The justification for acts of violence by suppressed minorities proclaimed by Herbert Marcuse held the attention of the students for only a short time, but it did create a sense of international solidarity with the world's revolutionary movements. Those who joined the movement used Marcuse's theory of refusal to justify their adherence.

The Easter attacks in Western Germany in 1968 concentrated mainly on the Springer publishing house after the attempt on the life of Rudi Dutschke.[1] Discussions arising from this act produced a theoretical difference between violence against things and violence against persons. The first was justified as a means in the fight of minorities against repression and institutions which cause this repression. Already at this stage, however, the dialectical nature of such theories of justification became evident and it did not exclude acts of violence against people in the future.

When the 1968 revolt spread from Berlin to universities in West Germany even representatives of the "establishment" justified the movement by arguing that without the student revolt the College Reform Act (*Hochschulreform*) would never have been passed. The student revolt mirrored the revolutionary groups in the Third World. Revolutionary violence against dictatorship and "terror from above" in the Third World served as an example for dissident youth and as a justification of their own violence against a democratic society.

The first politically motivated act of violence, which made use of the feeling of outrage at the Vietnam war, was to act as a rallying beacon and could not be explained without this transfer of emotion—made possible only by the efficiency of modern communications. Arson at a department store in Frankfurt on 2 April 1968, several days before the attempt on Dutschke, brought the most important members of the Baader–Meinhof gang into contact with one another. Andreas Baader and Gudrun Ensslin were among the activists; Horst Mahler was Baader's defence lawyer; Ulrike Meinhof defended the deed as a columnist in the magazine *Konkret*. In the next two years the student protest campaign against the resulting emergency legislation failed. The movement then fell apart into "basic groups" (*Basisgruppen*) which turned to the task of Marxist indoctrination and Marxist analysis of the Federal Republic and the planned revolutionary organisation. By the spring of 1971 the Red Army Group emerged from this transitional phase with its concept of armed conflict.

Although the burning of the department store in Frankfurt brought the central members of the RAG together, circumstances in Berlin played an important part in the early phase. In the summer of 1969 anarchists from the student movement had joined the central committee, consisting of roaming, "hash"-smoking rebels. The students wanted to gain refuges where they could freely enjoy their drugs. Above all they were to be held responsible for a series of bomb attacks and arson in the winter of 1969–70. Their targets were judges and other officers of justice, American institutions, the office of the Israeli airline El Al, a warehouse and a lawyers' ball. "Molotov cocktail" attacks on schools, administration and office buildings followed in March 1970.

An increasing trend towards violence became apparent before and after demonstrations culminating in that of 18 March 1970 when the demonstrators took violent action in support of Horst Mahler, whose legal credentials were to be withdrawn. These anarchists were not strongly organised, but consisted of small, loosely knit groups which linked up on occasions. This activity changed the climate of political debate.

The arsonists of the Frankfurt department store had been sentenced to three years' imprisonment, but after nine months' detention during investigation they were released until the sentence was due to begin. They then refused to deliver themselves up to justice. Two subsequently did so in 1970, and Baader was arrested in Berlin on 4 April that year during a car check. His liberation on 14 May 1970, only a few weeks later, was the signal for the RAG to take action. Both Mahler and Ulrike Meinhof took part in the escape plot when they opened fire, wounding an outsider. All participants went underground and began to set up an organisation with far-reaching aims.

It was necessary to secure funds, flats, garages, equipment to change the colour of cars, to forge identification cards and papers, to intercept the security forces' radios and to set up their own radio communications. A supply line for weapons and explosives, as well as incendiary devices, was also required. Most of the money was secured by armed bank robberies. In the early stage of setting up the organisation, three bank robberies of 29 September 1970, all committed simultaneously in Berlin provided a spectacular event in which about DM 220,000 was stolen. At least 12 people were involved, using six cars, five of which bore false Berlin licence plates and registrations.

The RAG extracted more than DM 1.7 million by robbery and blackmail. Identification cards, passports and car licences were forged by using the genuine form secured by robbery or by reprinting with the aid of film. Flats were acquired by fellow-travellers who presented false identification papers. Garages were procured by the same means. Cars were rented and equipped with false registration plates or were stolen and then prepared to serve as a duplicate by preparing registration and papers exactly corresponding to other cars of the same type, year of construction and colour.

Armed revolution

Weapons were bought through go-betweens and connections with foreign countries were used. Explosives were made from easily-acquired ingredients. Bombs were mainly of the pipe variety, some being for liquid gas. Clocks served as detonators, but a remote control radio system was also planned. In a statement in the spring of 1972 the RAG replied to the reproach that it was only pursuing logistics—meaning bank robbery—and not popular actions. It said that only the "solution of logistics problems" could secure the continuity of the revolutionary organisation; the technical means could be acquired only in a collective process of working and learning together. Nothing was to be left to chance.

The concept of the RAG was based on the principle that *the revolutionary is armed*. The weapon keeps him company, not only in his actions but permanently. It is for use in such actions as bank robbery or whenever needed to deter the police during checks and especially to resist arrest. It is laid down that in the event of a sudden attack police will be shot. (This happened in Kaiserslautern on 22 December 1971 when a policeman was gunned down during a raid on the Bayerische Hypotheken-und Wechselbank.) Earlier, a few weeks after the release of Baader, Ulrike Meinhof explained in an interview (published in *Der Spiegel*, 15 June 1970): "We say the person in uniform is a pig, that is, not a human being, and thus we have to settle the matter with him. It is wrong to talk to these people at all, and shooting is taken for granted . . ."

In the opening paragraphs of the first RAG paper, *The Urban Guerrilla Concept*, a self-critical position is adopted. This self-criticism is intended mainly to counter impressions within the movement of the "New Left" that the RAG consists of uneducated anarchists. At the same time it is claimed that at every encounter the police were the first to shoot. In 1972 the RAG turned from the preparatory stage of amassing supplies to offensive actions, even though many members had already been arrested, including Mahler,

Grusdat, Ruhland, Jansen, Bäcker, Proll, Herzog, Pohle, Roll, Grashof and Grundman.

A series of 15 bomb explosions on six targets started on 11 May with an attack on a United States corps headquarters in Frankfurt. An American officer was killed. Four days later the State Criminal Office and the police headquarters at Augsburg were attacked. Thirty-eight people were seriously hurt when two bombs exploded in the Springer publishing house in Hamburg. Other bombs smuggled into the building failed to explode. A further attack upon the headquarters of the American Army in Europe followed on 24 May.

In messages to press agencies, newspapers, radio stations and magazines, the RAG claimed responsibility for the attacks. The commando groups were the "Petra Schelm" (Schelm was shot on 15 July 1971 during a police search), "Thomas Weisbecker" (shot on 2 March 1972 in Augsburg) and "2 June" (Benno Ohnesor died on 2 June 1967 in Berlin from a bullet wound).

The attacks were deliberately planned to bring other revolutionary groups (New Left) to co-operate with the RAG. This was made clear by the active RAG member Ulrike Meinhof during a teach-in of the "Red Help Frankfurt" on 31 March 1972:

> Our actions against the exterminating strategists of Vietnam are already understood today by everybody. Our actions for the protection of life and health of the arrested and for followers of the RAG can already be understood by everybody.

The bomb attack upon the Federal Judge Wolfgang Buddenberg in Karlsruhe on 15 May 1972, in which his wife was injured, was admitted by the commando group "Manfred Grashoff" in a letter of 20 June which was circulated in the publications put out by "Red Help" in Hamburg and Berlin. It was directed at Judge Buddenberg as being responsible for investigating the case and further actions against public prosecutors and judges were threatened. This example of individual terror, which was to be followed by other group actions, indicated a new stage in planned actions. Meinhof defined it on 31 May 1972. But one year before Horst Mahler, in his paper *An Armed Struggle in Western Europe*, had advocated this individual terror which he justified by detailed reference to Lenin. Mahler explained that the revolutionary forces held officials personally responsible for actions which in their opinion were hostile to the people. These individuals were selected for their "crimes", which were classified according to their gravity, and were then brought to trial. He named social workers, teachers, judges and lawyers.

Nation-wide network

RAG activists worked first in Berlin, where members of the basic group had come together and had taken their first steps. From there they left for the Near East in June 1970. Already in the autumn of 1970 they had started to extend their field of operations to West Germany. Cars were rented under false names or stolen, mainly in Hesse, Lower Saxony and North Rhine Westphalia. In Lower Saxony and North Rhine Westphalia offices were entered to steal forms of identification and stamps. Conspiratorial flats were rented. These activities were intensified in 1971. The 1972 series of bomb attacks was confined to West Germany.

The RAG could rely on a large number of members—at least 60—holding flats at their disposal, renting cars and acting as accommodation addresses. The circle of sympathisers was spread over the whole Federal Republic, the intellectual sympathisers extending far beyond that of active supporters. Up to the spring of 1972 more than 60 cars had been stolen and more than 30 conspiratorial flats throughout the Federal Republic, including Berlin, had been traced. Furthermore, there were links with foreign countries, mainly France and the Netherlands, but also including Italy, Switzerland, Belgium and Denmark.

In addition to this RAG core six regional groups with similar aims, but of a different nature, were formed. Members of these groups made contact with members of the RAG and worked with them. Thus rivalry could not be avoided as the hard-core members of the RAG claimed the leading role in the revolutionary battle, having already developed and published their theory of armed conflict. It should also be borne in mind that discipline was strictly enforced in the RAG group.

In Munich, Heidelberg and Berlin other groups arising from the local students' movement had come into existence, and their political actions included acts of violence. In Berlin and Munich it was anarchists, among whom a Berlin group took the name "2 June Movement". In Heidelberg a group which attributed individual illness to repressive social relations, and which justified violence as an act of liberation and a means to overthrow society, was called the Heidelberg Patients' Collective (SPK). This organisation worked independently, but after 10 members had been arrested in July 1970 other members who went underground co-operated with the RAG. Already in the 1960s there were close links between the anarchists of Berlin and Munich. Each group acts on its own, but both represented a "reservoir" from which activists changed over to the RAG.

The RAG activists come, with a few exceptions, from bourgeois families normally associated with the professions. The 17 hard-core members in 1970 included a lawyer, a junior barrister, a medical assistant and two journalists. The majority were students, one of them from a welfare home background and there were two women—a hairdresser and a photographer. An identical background is found among members of the larger circle of activists of 1971 and 1972, who had either joined the RAG or changed over to it. Most of the sympathisers and helpers also came from the professions. Although the revolutionary activists maintain that the leadership should come from the working class, it has not, and they have scarcely commented on this fact publicly.

Only Mahler, the most determined of them, has drawn the consequences theoretically in "*Close the loopholes of revolutionary theory*", which attempts to bring theory into line with practice. He contended that a contemporary revolutionary theory should be developed by those who, because they are not members of the working class, are able to stand aside and view both past and present struggles objectively; a capacity for abstract thought allows them to appreciate modern class struggle within its historical context. This attitude of mind was characteristic of the young, together with the fact that their own class was increasingly menaced today.

The generation gap

There is a school of thought which also ascribes collective ways of behaviour mainly to psychological factors. This is problematical. Yet some psychological aspects are worth mentioning. The student protest movement was supported by a generation that had grown up during a period marked by a rapid growth of materialism as the affluent society was developing. From this, as well as from the contemporary conditions, the following was deduced: an increasing conflict between generations; the inability of young people to understand the attitude of the generation born before 1945; the primarily materialistic interests of parents since then; and neglect of the intellectual and spiritual education of children.

The father of the leader of the Gudrun Ensslin group, a clergyman, in an open letter in February 1972 addressed "all those parents who were seriously concerned about the mutual conflicts between parents and children during the last 10 to 15 years". He said that an increasing number of young people, critical of the injustices and dishonesty in society, were unable to adjust to the social environment of the Federal Republic. Before 1967, this failure produced conditions of neurosis, depression and psychosis.

The tendency towards anarchistic revolutionary action cannot be solely attributed to upbringing. Several hard-core activists have grown up without parents. At least two of them failed to meet the requirements for further education. What is more, this is not unusual. Whoever takes an objective view of the activists will not find clear psychological causes that would account for their behaviour.

In a letter of 24 January 1972, sealed with his right thumb print, Andreas Baader said: "Successful announcements concerning us can only be: arrested or dead. The strength of the guerrilla is the determination of each one of us." Ulrike Meinhof refers to this in the RAG paper *Urban Guerrilla and Class Conflict* (April 1972): "We think that the guerrilla is going to spread and gain a footing, that the development of the class struggle will carry through the idea ... that the idea of the guerrilla developed by Mao, Fidel, Che, Giap, Marighella is a good idea, that no one will ever be able to do away with it. . . ." Horst Mahler says in *Der Spiegel* of 14 February 1968, referring to the idea of "Sacrificing of Comrades":

> This idea adopts bourgeois error, according to which there are only leaders and led, as if not every comrade who is fed up with the bourgeois disorder, who cannot continue what he has done before, cannot decide by himself how he is going to lead his life when he finally succeeds in escaping from the ghetto and pulls down the walls, irrespective of the fact that his lifetime might be shortened.

The statement indicates a subjective feeling of almost incomprehensible repression. It is a fiction, but an effective one. The subject comprehends it vicariously, and therefore, as it were, theatrically, in the fate of the Vietnamese, Blacks in the US, Indians, Palestinians, and other oppressed groups. Is it the sensibility of the individual which reacts in such a way to the repressive basic conditions of life in a surrounding world of wealth? Herbert Marcuse has explained this fatalism in a logical and effective way in his essay on "Repressive Tolerance". During the department store fire trial Baader referred explicitly to the last sentences of this essay in which Marcuse said that the "suppressed and overpowered minorities" have the "natural right" to apply extra-legal means.

Women in the RAG and other groups not only act as helpers, advisers and spies, but also as fighters who hide under their coats or in their bags pistols up to a calibre of 9mm which they use if faced with arrest. A few of them act not only as fighters but as organisers (Ulrike Meinhof in her own writings and Gudrun Ensslin in her instructions written in prison). While the influence of women accounts for the lack of realism in the overall revolutionary concept, yet they are responsible for day-to-day actions of a practical nature, such as renting a flat under an assumed name and gathering and analysing information. There are 12 women among the 22 activists of the RAG core. Among the 20 activists who changed over to the RAG there are eight women. Indeed the fervour with which the feminine activists adopted women's liberation played an important part in the RAG's concept and activities.

The revolutionary movement in the Third World has given an incentive to the theoreticians of the New Left and student movement. The first actions in Berlin were aimed at Tshombe of the ex-Belgian Congo and the Shah of Persia. In 1970 Dutschke called for a combined action by Third World revolutionaries and those in the "imperialist" countries' capitals, but he still thought in terms of specific forms of struggle "which correspond to the state of historical development achieved in metropolises". One such form of struggle for Dutschke is "organised refusal". Without the revolutionary organisation of the Tupamaros in Uruguay there would have been no example for the RAG to follow.

The German revolutionaries used the Mini-manual of the Brazilian urban guerrilla Carlos Marighella. In edition No. 63 of the Berlin anarchist publication *Agit–833*, 18 June 1970, the first serialised reprint of a translation of this handbook appeared. In 1970 at least two different editions appeared, translated and published by groups of the New Left and sold in the newly established revolutionary bookstores. More than a year later the text appeared in pocketbook form, published by a large company under the title *Destroy the Islands of Wealth in the Third World*.

On 14 May 1970 Andreas Baader was freed. Next day a bank robbery took place in Berlin. In June the core members travelled via Damascus to Jordan for military training in a camp used by the Al Fatah Palestinian guerrillas. It was during this period that Jordanian troops attacked the thousands of armed Palestinians of the fedayeen organisation and drove them from the country. The RAG visit was a failure, and the group only held discussions. Horst Mahler, who after their return in August 1970 was free for just two months, wrote in his work on armed conflict: "A fighting group can only come into being through conflict. All attempts to organise, educate and train a group without the existence of such conflict lead to the most ludicrous results—often with a tragic outcome."

In the New Left group, which carried on indoctrination and basic training after the collapse of the student protest movement in the autumn of 1968, the "correct" analysis of the system and the organisation for a revolutionary struggle were not decided even by the spring of 1970. The phase of organisation and party initiatives still continued. Most of the groups worked in the factories and attempted to convey a revolutionary consciousness to the working class, primarily among apprentices and other young workers. The cadres reckoned on a long-term struggle. The orthodox German Communist Party (DKP) was newly established and its organisation was complete. Several groups and activists from the New Left, primarily in Hesse and Hamburg, joined the DKP, convinced of its "realistic" approach.

Urban guerrilla strategy

During this phase in May 1970, one month after the freeing of Baader, the cry was raised: "Build up the Red Army!" In the first public declaration on 22 May 1970 in the anarchist paper *Agit–833* it was asked: "Does any pig truly believe we would talk about the development of class conflicts, or reorganisation of the proletariat, without simultaneously arming ourselves?" The term Red Army was familiar in guerrilla circles at that time only through the small Japanese extremist group who hijacked a plane to North Korea on 31 March 1970.[2] This name was adopted by the Baader–Mahler–Meinhof gang when they started calling themselves the Red Army Group. In a letter of 17 November 1971 to the Workers Party of North Korea, probably written by Ulrike Meinhof, the name is explained: "The group did not split off from a previously unified movement but was forced to work illegally because of reigning repression—it is not itself a party, but is organisationally, practically, conceptually a necessary component of a Communist party worthy of the name."

The RAG revealed its goals in three campaign publications which appeared between April 1971 and November 1972. Two of these were written by Ulrike Meinhof; the author of the main work was Horst Mahler. *The Urban Guerrilla Concept* appeared in the first publication in April 1971. With it the self-chosen name of the Red Army Group was publicly announced for the first time. The structure of this publication by Ulrike Meinhof resembles that of the "position papers" of other groups, which wanted to develop from a preparatory phase of doctrinal clarification to one of action. It attempts an analysis of the Federal Republic; weighs up the student movement and recognises that its own origins stem from the movement; emphasises, as in all other groups, the precepts of Marxism–Leninism; and explains its own concept of the urban guerrilla and the campaign that this implies. A closing section on "Legality and Illegality" is further supposed to justify this concept.

The publication is unbalanced and the argument for its own concept is not even dialectically conclusive. Its language is rhetorical and uncertain. An introductory section on "Concrete Answers to Concrete Questions" is designed to clarify "untruths" and to justify the use of weapons. "Each time the cops were aiming. To date we have not fired at all, and if we did we were not aiming: in Berlin, in Nuremberg, in Frankfurt. This can be proved, because it is true." "We maintain that the organisation of armed resistance groups at this time in the Federal Republic and West Berlin is correct, is possible, is justified; that it is correct, possible, and justifiable here and now to create urban guerrillas."

In the section "The Primacy of Practice" it is argued that action is correct ideology. The argument proceeds by paradox and not by dialectic. It is doubted whether, under the provisions in the Federal Republic and West Berlin, it is possible to develop a strategy to unite the working class, to create an organisation capable of initiating and expressing the unifying process. But: "We maintain that without revolutionary initiative, without practical revolutionary intervention (this is our own concept) of the *avant-garde*, without the concrete anti-imperialistic campaign, there can be no unifying process. . . ." The paradox is supposed to make the concept convincing: "The class analysis, which we need, cannot be made without revolutionary practice, without revolutionary initiative." The section closes with the sentence: "Whether it is correct to organise the armed opposition now depends on whether it is possible; whether it is possible can only be ascertained by practice."

Several statements are made in the section dealing with the concept of the "Urban Guerrilla". Its supposed origin in Latin America is quoted. Prerequisites are given: the organisation of an illegal apparatus with "residences, weapons, munitions, cars, papers". Experiences are recounted. The role of the urban guerrilla should be played out within the framework of an ordinary career or job, according to the original concept. The RAG found "that that does not work. . . . That the individual cannot combine legal work with illegal". There is a failure to recognise that an armed campaign of small illegal groups without the protection of a legal organisation, or without bases in secure territories, can be sustained only if the fighters swim like fish among the people. Already the name *Fraktion* shows self-deception. The RAG was no faction of a unified movement.

In June 1971 the first copies of the main RAG publication were circulated in Berlin under the title *Close the loopholes of the revolutionary theory—Build up the Red Army*. In October a Berlin publishing house issued the text as Red Book 29 with a title more appropriate to its contents: *RAG Collective—On the armed campaign in Western Europe*. The publisher was Horst Mahler, who wrote it in prison. Mahler's approach is practical; he speaks directly. He wants to propagate armed conflict and win comrades-in-arms. To this end he develops a theory which in itself is logical but undiscriminating. In its plea for one thing and one thing only—armed conflict—it is unrealistic. Mahler accepts that a revolution without a scientific revolutionary theory cannot be victorious. For him "armed campaign as the highest form of class struggle" follows from the fact that the "possessing classes" have secured for themselves the "determining influence on the power levers of the State".

He considers the armed phase of the class struggle unavoidable under existing social conditions. The unlimited acceptance of the primacy of politics means for him only that the military form of the campaign is subordinate to the political goals of the revolution. In the second section he discounts the theory that a general strike leads to general insurrection. For him general insurrection is the "last stage of a long armed conflict against the State apparatus of suppression". All other forms of the class conflict and political actions can, according to Mahler, "only have an auxiliary meaning for the armed conflict". The third section assigns the "*avant-garde* function" to revolutionary intelligence. "It is not the organisations of the industrial working class, but the revolutionary sections of the student bodies that are today the bearers of the contemporary conscience."

Youth versus the State

In the fourth section on the relationship of the *avant-garde* and the proletarian class Mahler comes to the conclusion that class analysis is an instrument in the hands of the revolutionaries who, by concrete examination, are to determine which classes "at present or in the foreseeable future can be won for the revolutionary campaign". The revolutionary must seize every opportunity for collective resistance among the masses, further develop, organise and lead them "even without prospect of victory". There follows a discussion on the role of the urban guerrilla and terror directed against the ruling apparatus. This includes "appropriate actions" against "all institutions of the class enemy, all governing bodies and police posts, against the operational centres, and also against all the functionaries of these institutions, against leading officials, judges, directors, etc.".

Mahler thoroughly endorses the individual terror inherent in such actions, quoting Lenin in support. However, the sections in which he deals with young people in society comprise the most important part of the work. He wants to win over to armed action young people who consider themselves revolutionaries. Since the true situation is neither "repressive" nor "revolutionary", the individual can be solidly won for the armed conflict only if he acts outside society against the law and is thus forced into a continuation of his criminal actions.

He believes young people are willing and determined to unite their personal fate with that of the proletarian revolution, taking upon themselves the risks of armed conflict: "Having once overcome fear of the State apparatus, even the clamour of the revolutionary penmen and braggarts will not prevent them from continuing along this path." Essential to the revolutionary process is rejection of the capitalist system. The "obedience reflex" instilled into the bourgeoisie must be overcome by repeated, conscious and practical violation of the norm. He wants to use for the revolutionary campaign the unique social self-consciousness created by the new cult of youth which no longer reflects the world of adults. The ideology of non-conformity, the characteristic readiness of youth for large-scale aggressive demonstration, are for him the first requisites for the revolutionary use of force.

Ten months later *Der Spiegel*, in No. 18 of 24 April 1972, published excerpts from the third RAG publication, *Urban Guerrillas and Class Conflict*. The style identifies Ulrike Meinhof as author. The work is a compilation of unrealistic journalistic commentaries on political questions and contemporary events. Wishes and possibilities are linked by means of the dialectic, as well as by aesthetic paradox. She is resigned to the fact that: "With the realisation that the opposition of the West German masses against the reign of capital will not be kindled by the problems of the Third World, but can only develop on problems here, they themselves have ceased to make the problems of the Third World a political objective here".

Passages directed at the readers' sentiment give some clues to the thinking behind the text. At one point there is a reference to Mao Tse-tung's dreadful interpretation of an old Chinese proverb on death—"weightier than the Tai mountain is the death of a socialist fighter; the death of a capitalist weighs less than swan's down." There are further reflections on death by group members: "Petra, George and Thomas died in the battle waged against death in the service of the exploiters. They were murdered so that capital may, undisturbed, murder further and that the people may continue to think nothing can be done about it." The work ends with reminiscences on solidarity: "We must avoid unnecessary sacrifices when possible. All men in the ranks of the revolution must care for each other, must lovingly hold together, must help each other."

In the fourth section problems arising from the group's activities—treachery, bank robbery, logistics, and continuity—are dealt with. There are explanations, new interpretations, attacks. *On treachery:* "Traitors must be barred from the ranks of the revolution. Tolerance of traitors produces new treason. . . . One should not be able to be blackmailed by the fact that they are poor pigs. Capital will make mankind into pigs until we do away with its reign. We are not responsible for the crimes of capital."

On bank robbery: "No one claims that bank robbery of itself changes anything. . . . For the revolutionary organisation it means first of all a solution of its financial problems. It is logistically correct, since otherwise the financial problem could not be solved at all. It is politically correct because it is an act of dispossession. It is tactically correct because it is a proletarian action. It is strategically correct because it serves the financing of the guerrilla."

In November 1972 the fourth printing of *Black September in Munich: The Strategy of the Anti-Imperialist Fight* appeared. The first copies turned up in Cologne and Frankfurt. This document is quoted here because parts of the New Left pretend that it was written by the RAG. The title page carried the RAG emblem: the star, sub-machine gun and the initials of the RAG. However, it was not written by Horst Mahler or Ulrike Meinhof. It is also uncertain whether it was written by any other member of the RAG. Several things tend to disprove it. The document is vague, theoretical and clumsy in its argument. The action taken during the Olympic Games in 1972 in Munich by *Black September* is praised, for "at one blow it made clear the essential nature of imperialist domination and the anti-imperialist struggle as no other revolutionary action before had done in West Germany or West Berlin." For an understanding of the RAG, for the theoretical background of the actions of this group, the document is valueless.

The groups of the New Left emerging from the protest movement of 1967–68 have from the start commented on the actions of the RAG, questioning the theory behind them. Above all, they formed a wide circle of sympathisers, some of whom supported the RAG full-heartedly, others only half-heartedly and some unwittingly. An example of aid is the supply of passes and identification documents, which are expertly forged by the activists and have been proved more secure than stolen documents, the numbers of which are recorded. New Left groups reacted to individual actions with teach-ins at the universities, as when Petra Schelm was shot in Hamburg on 15 July 1971 or after Manfred Grashof was shot on 2 March 1972. They were unanimous in condemning the behaviour of the police, whose actions, in their opinion, were directed against the entire Left. All groups feel the need for solidarity. Only after the bomb attack of May 1972 did a wider split follow; it was shown thereafter that the activists of the RAG were indeed isolated.

The assessment by groups with which the RAG was and is close, is shown by two quotations from a book published by "Association" that appeared in the late summer of 1973 under the title *CSSR—Five Years of "Normalisation"*. A partner in the publishing company is a defender of the RAG activists. "The open attempt to show up class relationships in the Federal Republic was physically liquidated by the State apparatus amid the infamous and shabby applause of the majority of the Left; those comrades of the RAG who survived are slowly being tortured to the point of insanity without any noteworthy protest from the rest of the Left"; and: "Where was the sworn 'socialist' solidarity when the comrades of the RAG were shot by the FRG police apparatus?" The orthodox Communists of the DKP have left no doubt that this sort of revolutionary struggle is adventurist; at the same time they have criticised the work of the security forces.

Activists of the RAG continue their campaign even after imprisonment. They categorically refuse to make any statement, in many cases even to state their identity. They use trials, whether they appear as witnesses or defendants, for revolutionary purposes, for sharp, even personal attacks on the judges and attorneys. Completion of the proceedings is methodically hampered. Horst Mahler, for example, was especially effective when he opened a statement at his trial on 9 October 1972 before the First Criminal Senate of the West Berlin Supreme Court of Justice with the words:

They accuse me of having, with other comrades, "formed a closely-knit group, united to fight with all means and especially violence the social conditions in the Federal Republic following the model of the South American urban guerrilla, and thus to create favourable revolutionary conditions which promise victory". The accusation rebounds on its authors. They themselves, this gang formed by General Motors, Ford, ARAMCO, General Electric, ITT, Siemens, AEG, Flick, Ouandt, BASF, Springer, Unilever, United Fruit, and others—the transnational capital partnerships, the imperialistic monopoly as a whole—are the most monstrous criminal union in history. To destroy this with all necessary and attainable means is a necessity of life for more than three thousand million men.

Mahler, who has been in prison since October 1970, wrote the main work of the RAG there: *On Armed Conflict in Western Europe*. He was also able to publish further "analyses" and views in *Der Spiegel*. In January 1972 in a commentary quoted under the title of *The Revolutionary left is criminal* by the editorial staff he called the five decades of parliamentarianism "the darkest period of all history to date" and explained the concept of the revolutionary campaign of the RAG. A month later the magazine published Mahler's "ideological observations" on questions put by the editorial staff. In them he distinguished a first and second phase of the RAG campaign. The powers of the RAG were indeed still small, but they sufficed, for the first phase. The second phase he called the "phase of exemplary attacks on the suppressive apparatus". It would develop out of the first phase.

Another example of effective continuation of the struggle from prison is a "Guide" to precautions and other actions which the leading activist Gudrun Ensslin had smuggled out of prison. It was found in Ulrike Meinhof's purse when she was arrested on 15 June 1973. Gudrun Ensslin was arrested on 7 June 1972. The instructions dealt with the cancellation of safe houses, further explosive attacks and the taking of hostages.

Leftist lawyers' "collective"

Ensslin's secret work throws a strong light on the role of the lawyers. The lawyer Otto Schily visited Gudrun Ensslin in prison on 12 June 1972 and talked with her for more than two hours. It was claimed by the authorities that only he could have taken her "Guide" out of the institution. The Supreme Court ruled for the exclusion of Schily from the defence on the ground that the function of the defence is incompatible with the role of suspect accomplice. The Federal Court repealed this exclusion since there is neither a legal nor a common law precedent for the exclusion of a defence counsel.

Mahler, himself a barrister, together with other barristers in Berlin, founded the first "Socialist Barristers Collective". Since 1967 he had played a leading role in the protest movement in Berlin and in March 1970 was sentenced to imprisonment for disturbing the public order, but received an amnesty. Like Mahler, there were other lawyers who were members or sympathisers of the revolutionary movement, several of whom at least supported the activists' political goals. A letter by the lawyer Stroebele of 16 June 1973, retrieved three days later in Berlin, is evidence of activity extending well beyond the defence of the accused. Stroebele apparently wrote it after visits to several prisoners. The letter reports a "new project", to bring work for months and years: a plan to establish an Information Centre. Necessary papers had not yet appeared: first they had to be written. In this context, there is no doubt that they *were* to have been written by gaoled activists. The aim was to produce analyses and stimulate group indoctrination. This letter provided grounds for the federal authorities to issue a search warrant of the cells of several activists. Initial inquiries were started against various lawyers.

In the task of finding financial assistance for the prisoners and launching "solidarity actions" the Red Help groups proved effective. The name "Red Help" first appeared in the spring of 1970 in Berlin, where the organisation was created. It moved its headquarters into the "Socialist Centre", a communications headquarters of the protest movement. In Munich Red Help was organised in June 1970. In Frankfurt it was the successor organisation of a *Board of Republican Help*. In Hamburg the Red Help did not materialise until early in 1972; there lawyers were the initiating force. At a function early in February to win help for the establishment of a Red Help organisation one of the lawyers said: "This State has not produced any justice. Stands made in favour of resisting the State had to be defended." In this instance he was referring to the RAG. The four cities named were the main centres of Red Help.

In December 1971 the first edition of the magazine *Red Help* appeared, run in turn by the four organisations. It was in a Hamburg edition of the magazine in the summer of 1972 that the letter in which the RAG admitted the bombing attack of May was published. The Red Help of Frankfurt organised the teach-in at which on 31 May 1972 the tape-recorded statement of Ulrike Meinhof was played. Partly alongside the Red Help groups and partly in contact with them, groups of *Black Help* were formed by anarchists who wanted not only to help the prisoners from the RAG but also turn it into *Gaol Help*. Criminals in prison, too, were to be won over to the revolutionary struggle. These initiatives, however, came to nothing. In 1973 the concept of "isolation torture" became the catchword for a new campaign for the benefit of gaoled activists. The isolation of the prisoners was defined as "objective" torture, independently of the question to what extent this was *subjectively* desired. The charge of torture was made against *the penal system* of the Federal Republic.

In the summer of 1972 all members of the core of the RAG were arrested, with one exception. Several opposition activists were also arrested. Since then further individual arrests have followed. Nonetheless, activists remained in hiding, while others returned to the underground after their release from prison. Above all, members of groups that had accepted the concept of the RAG remained active and wanted to improve it: activists from the "Movement of 2 June" and from "Information Centre of the Red People's University" (IZRU), a successor group to the "Heidelberger Patienten-Kollektiv" (SPK), had contact with the RAG.

Several incidents in 1973 with explosives and incendiaries, as well as bank robberies, showed that terrorist activities were continuing, although to a lesser degree. Noteworthy were attacks in Hamburg shortly before the opening of the trial of a youthful anarchist, who started fires in Hamburg stores on the anniversary of the death of Petra Schelm (15 July 1971) and bomb attacks against the residence of a judge of the Kaiserslautern Court, who was responsible for dealing with some RAG activists. Successor groups have started organising but they lack such effective propagandists of armed revolutionary conflict as Horst Mahler and Ulrike Meinhof.

The ideologically motivated concern about political problems came to the fore again in the student protest movement, which to a considerable extent developed into a new dogmatism. With it a way of thought soon emerged which defined most problems concerning Man and his institutions as political problems. Such simplification of thought creates confusion; the desirable is declared already attainable tomorrow—the only prerequisite is that the change should be desired.

Where such concepts begin to mould thought, opinions vacillate as to which means should be used to effect the desired change and which should be excluded, and the viability of the normal democratic processes is tested. In this atmosphere of provocation and uncertainty the task of searching out RAG members became more difficult. Activists exploited their sympathisers' "solidarity" ruthlessly, often concealing their real intentions and identity. Many sympathisers, in turn, showed uncertainty, clearly fearful of committing themselves to a cause whose criminal actions were masked in ideological language. The young teacher in whose home Ulrike Meinhof and her partner sought refuge shortly before their arrest was in this situation "Uninvited, and often anonymous, they stand before the door."

This ideological sympathy increased the problems for the security services. Identifying sympathisers with the activists diverted attention to those who for the most part knew little about the organisation. On the other hand, those who justified the sympathisers' conduct drew absurd parallels with the Gestapo, portraying a situation in which support for the hunted endangered one's own life. Press commentaries during the months of intensive investigation reflected this confusion of thought.

Self-defeating violence

The West German security services are subject to the normal legal limitations. They faced an uncommonly difficult task in the search for a criminal group of normally intelligent people who worked conspiratorially, could enlist the support of intellectual sympathisers, operated freely in an open society, made use of modern communications and were determined to thwart every executive move with extremist methods. Modern thinking on police restraint has increased this difficulty for the security services. Yet the apprehension of almost all members of the RAG core proved that even a group of this kind can be uncovered and eliminated by legal means, although these are expensive and can create their own problems. For instance, armed police had to be used in making arrests. The incidents of

213

1972 showed, however, that a majority of West German citizens understand the position. Nevertheless, extreme methods are not in themselves sufficient; what is needed is greater reliance on intelligence work, to ensure selective and purposeful action. Intelligence work in anarchistic groups is often complicated by the risk that sources can turn into *agents provocateurs* or lead to criminal actions.

The police often found that their routine methods were inadequate and led to casualties. For example, for the arrest of hard-core members of the RAG in Frankfurt armoured vehicles were brought in. It has been found by experience that the most expensive method is often the most effective. With few exceptions arrested activists stay silent about their activities and about other members, thus hampering inquiries and the gathering of evidence for the prosecution. In fact the prosecution was forced to rely largely on forensic evidence, helped by clues supplied by the public as a result of the enormous publicity surrounding the movement.

The RAG's armed conflict is anarchistic, no matter how its activists justify it subjectively. It challenges the State institutions responsible for security. They have to respond. A free democratic society openly acknowledges its conflicts, for its strength lies in this openness. The activists did not recognise that their actions, especially their attacks during the second phase, *improved the standing of the security services*, which otherwise were open to criticism. The resort to violence and anarchism was self-defeating; so long as the institutions of the State are supported by the vast majority of citizens, this form of revolutionary conflict has no chance of success. This does not ensure that there will be no activists in the future; Mahler explicitly declared that the battle must be fought *without a view to victory*. Ideological conviction and a romantic feeling of solidarity with other fighters support the hard-core activists. There are few national States in the world that regulate conflict openly. In many parts of the world communities have not yet formed a national identity that is recognised by all members. In the resulting basic conflicts extremist means are justified by the parties.

To this should be added the experience of previous years, which shows that what is valid in a national framework is not necessarily valid in an international one. International terrorism is more likely to succeed within a State than violent anarchism. For example, the terrorism of the Palestinians does not challenge any institution necessary for the survival of a community with a common identity. They tend to use the parties and divergent interests *within* a State. The Israelis recognised this early on and acted decisively, with the result that on the whole terrorism has damaged the *Palestinian* cause. But it has also attracted attention to the plight of the Palestinians and opened up greater possibilities for future success.

There are other reasons, however, which make it unlikely that violent anarchism will die out. The belief in a perfect society based on technology is still widely held. Experience to the contrary has not, as yet, changed this view of the world; dissatisfaction continues to produce a readiness to accept an ideological solution to all conflicts. Generally, practical experience teaches young people the limits of their idealism. Where the commitment to idealism is extreme and where society is highly politicised anarchism is likely to find adherents. It is in the reality of warfare that the anarchist experiences liberation, the supposed goal of his struggle.

APPENDIX 1

Reappearance of terrorists

On 4 February 1974 police in Hamburg and Frankfurt-Main searched four houses that had been rented by members of a group using false names who planned to continue RAG activities. Seven members of this group were arrested, four in Hamburg and three in Frankfurt, and later two more were caught in Amsterdam. Six automatic pistols, two sawn-off shot guns, 13 pistols and revolvers, more than 25 hand grenades, munitions, explosives and mines were found. Additionally, a large number of personal identity documents, passports, drivers' licences, blank registration certificates, German marks and foreign currency totalling more than DM20,000, forgery material, and documents describing the formation, organisation and method of the RAG as well as the planning of bank robberies and other criminal actions were seized.

It took the police several months of careful intelligence work, including the tapping of telephones and code-breaking, before they were able to launch this successful action. The group's behaviour made it clear that they had received training in subversive techniques. Members travelled to Paris and the Lebanon, and besides the bases in Frankfurt and Hamburg the group established a base in Amsterdam.

Of those arrested, one belonged to the old core of the RAG group, and three participated in the "Socialist Patients' Collective" (SPK), the Heidelberg group whose leading members were arrested in July 1971. Two others had left the Trotskyite *International Marxist Group* (IMG) at the beginning of 1973 and had participated in April–May 1973 in a militant house occupation in Hamburg. The seventh, a lawyer, was engaged in the defence of gaoled RAG members. Two members had been sentenced for, among other things, support of the Baader–Meinhof group, but had afterwards ignored orders to report to the authorities.

APPENDIX 2

Group leaders' backgrounds

Andreas Baader. Born 6 May 1943 in Munich. Father an historian who died in World War II. Attended elementary school and several high schools, but did not gain school leaving certificate. At 18 went to Berlin, where he supposedly worked for a newspaper. Has illegitimate daughter by an artist.

Ulrike Meinhof. Born 7 October 1934 in Oldenburg, daughter of art historians who died young. Grew up under the guardianship of the historian Professor Renate Riemeck, co-founder of the Deutsche Friedens-Union

(DFU). Studied philosophy, education, sociology and German at Marburg, Hamburg, Freiburg and Munich. Contributor to the magazine *Konkret*. From 1961–68 married to publisher Klaus-Rainer Roehl. In 1968 moved to Berlin.

Horst Mahler. Born 23 January 1936 in Haynau, Upper Silesia, son of a dentist who died in 1949. After taking school leaving certificate in 1955 he studied at the Free University of West Berlin and joined the student corporation Thuringia. Since 1964 practising lawyer. Defended leading members of the student protest movement.

Gudrun Ensslin. Born 15 August 1940 at Bertholomae, Swabian Alb. Father is minister in Stuttgart-Bad Canstatt. Studied German, English and philosophy in Tübingen and Berlin. Teachers' examinations. Gave birth in 1966 to a child whose father was a German student, Bernhard Vesper, son of the author Will Vesper (former member of the National Socialist Reich's Literary Chamber). 1964 went to Berlin.

Holger Meins. Born 26 October 1941 in Hamburg. Father was business manager. Gained school leaving certificate in 1962. In 1961 recognised as conscientious objector; in 1962–66 attended film division of the Creative Arts School in Hamburg, and then went to the film and television academy in West Berlin. Also worked there for television.

NOTES

[1] Dutschke secured academic asylum in Cambridge after being shot by a young right-wing extremist in Berlin, but was not allowed to extend his stay because he had taken part in political activities—a decision that aroused controversy but was upheld by an immigration appeals tribunal. He obtained a part-time university post in Denmark which he lost in the summer of 1973.

[2] In May 1972 Japan's Red Army hit world headlines when three of its members joined in the Palestinian guerrilla conflict by flinging hand grenades and firing automatic weapons at Israel's Lod Airport. They killed 24 people and wounded 78.

First published 1974.

Index